ALCOHOLISM AND THE LAW

ALCOHOLISM AND THE LAW

by

FRANK P. GRAD,

AUDREY L. GOLDBERG

and

BARBARA A. SHAPIRO

A Study Prepared for the National Institute of Mental Health by the LEGISLATIVE DRAFTING RESEARCH FUND of Columbia University.

1971

OCEANA PUBLICATIONS, INC.
Dobbs Ferry, New York 10522

Library of Congress Catalog Card Number: 72-116057

International Standard Book Number: 0-379-00457-7

The research upon which this publication is based was performed pursuant to Contract No. PH-43-68-89 with the National Institute of Mental Health, Public Health Service, Department of Health, Education, and Welfare.

MANUFACTURED IN THE UNITED STATES OF AMERICA

Table of Contents

ix

Preface

This report on *Alcoholism and the Law* is part of the product of an eighteen-month study conducted by the Legislative Drafting Research Fund of Columbia University under contract with the National Institute of Mental Health. The study also resulted in a model statute, prepared on the basis of policy consultations with N.I.M.H. staff, which drew on the Fund's research and preliminary report. This model *Alcoholism and Intoxication Treatment Act,* presently under review by N.I.M.H., is reproduced in the Appendix.

The work of the Legislative Drafting Research Fund in the area of legal problems of alcoholism carries forward a long-standing interest in matters of public health, broadly conceived. It also reflects a recurring concern of the Fund with matters of social control and treatment within a framework of firm constitutional protection of individual liberties.

While, as indicated, the project staff assumes full responsibility for the content of this report, we wish to express our warm appreciation to Dr. Thomas F. A. Plaut, and to Mrs. Judith P. Wolfson, of the National Center for Prevention and Control of Alcoholism N.I.M.H., for their helpful advice and guidance, and for their splendid cooperation. We also wish to thank the scores of knowledgeable professionals, too numerous to mention, who responded to requests for comments on the Model Act, and to the many state and local officials who answered a detailed questionnaire on alcoholism treatment programs; their answers were used not only in the preparation of Appendix C, but also provided basic information for other parts of the work.
July 31, 1969

FRANK P. GRAD
Director
Legislative Drafting Research Fund
Columbia University

INTRODUCTION

Alcoholism As A Legal Problem: Purposes And Aims Of The Study

The purposes of this study are to examine the present state of the law relating to the problem of alcoholism, to evaluate the effectiveness of present legal mechanisms in the light of current knowledge of the causes and treatment of the disorder, and if possible, to provide a basis for sounder legal approaches to reach desirable social ends. Thus, this is not merely a study of "what the law is." While knowledge of the precise legal situation is important, it is just a beginning of the more significant consideration of the aims of the law in dealing with persons who are problem drinkers or alcoholics, and of the uses of law in contributing to the solution of the alcoholism problem in the light of present knowledge. Broadly stated, it is necessary to consider, knowing what we do about alcoholism and its treatment, whether existing law advances or retards the solution of the problem, and whether a change of legal approaches —to be accomplished by appropriate legislation—would reach these aims more effectively.

It is apparent that knowledge and theories concerning the nature of alcoholism have significant bearing on the direction of the law. To give an example or two, if specialists on alcoholism say that only a properly "motivated" alcoholic can be treated successfully, what does this tell us about the usefulness or effectiveness of laws that provide for the mandatory commitment of alcoholics? Or if the evidence is clear that only a very small percentage of skid row alcoholics can be treated successfully or rehabilitated—what is the implication of such a conclusion for the allocation of scarce treatment resources? Or, for that matter, if it is evident that different treatment modes and facilities are appropriate for different "kinds" of alcoholics—what does this imply in terms of the formulation of legislation that would provide treatment opportunities for alcoholics generally?

Finally, the research for this work has already served to provide the basis for a number of recommendations that were utilized in the development of the model Alcoholism and Intoxication Treatment Act. While clearly much more needs to be learned about the nature of alcoholism, it is evident that the trend of the law is to view alcoholism as a disease, rather than a self-inflicted condition for which criminal sanctions ought to be imposed. A number of jurisdictions have already adopted legislation with a primary treatment emphasis. The Model Act, prepared by the Legislative Drafting Research Fund of Columbia University, carries this emphasis even further. The study should, therefore, be viewed also as a contribution to the development of criteria for effective legislation on alcoholism. Such legislation should utilize the existing momentum toward treatment-oriented laws, reflecting the current insights of the medical and behavioral sciences, leaving room in the process for flexible responses to the needs created by rapid advances of current knowledge.

The dimensions of the national problem of alcoholism have been adequately described in the recent report on *Alcohol Problems* by the Cooperative Commission on the Study of Alcoholism, prepared by Dr. Thomas F. A. Plaut.[1] There are an estimated 4-6 million alcoholics in the nation, and additional hundreds of thousands of "problem drinkers." The number of alcoholics is not entirely certain, and the number of problem drinkers is even less so, because who is a problem drinker is even less well defined than who is an alcoholic. It is clear, however, that alcoholism blights the lives of millions of persons who are afflicted, and of many millions more who are members of families of alcoholics. In addition to interfering with the economic well-being of the alcoholic and his family, alcoholism takes a severe psychic toll of the children and wives or husbands of alcoholics. The cost of alcoholism to industry and national production in terms of absenteeism, industrial accidents and interference with production is staggering, and recent evidence (embodied in a report on *Alcohol and Highway Safety* from the U.S. Department of Transportation to the Congress)[2] has shown that the cost in terms of automobile accidents is also enormous, with alcoholics accounting for a far greater proportion of accidents, even, than drunken drivers generally. Another cost, not nearly as obvious, is the strain imposed under present legal arrangements on the machinery of law enforcement, including both police and the courts. As the President's Commission on Law Enforcement and Administration of Justice has noted, one out of every three arrests in the nation is for an offense in which drunkenness forms a necessary element (*i.e.,* public intoxication, drunk and disorderly, vagrancy involving intoxication, and the like), *not* including arrests for drunken driving.[3] Thus, alcoholics and problem drinkers account for a major diversion of police efforts from more important aspects of public protection, and take up a great deal of the time and effort of the lower criminal judiciary.

The prevalence of alcoholism varies in different groups—economic, social, ethnic or religious. Most alcoholics do not come to the attention of the police, and this large and invisible group of hidden alcoholics certainly causes the far greater part of the social and economic cost of alcoholism. The most visible group of alcoholics are of the "police inebriate" or skid row type. It is to this most visible type that much attention has been devoted, by police, by recent treatment laws, and by many of the studies in the field.

While the special, visible problem of the skid row alcoholic has sometimes been referred to as the "cutting edge" of the alcoholism problem, it is by no means a major part of it. Any attempt to formulate legislative approaches to alcoholism must necessarily begin with a formulation of the outer limits of the problem to be dealt with and of the social ends to be served by the law. If the aim of the law is merely the suppression of the "unsightly" symptom of skid row, then different, more limited measures are called for than if a broad attack on acoholism in all of its aspects is planned. The present study is intended to reflect this broader, more fully encompassing approach.

The question sought to be answered in this work is how the law can best arrange the management of persons whose uncontrolled or compulsive drinking creates major social and economic disruptions for society as well as for themselves. While there has been a growing concern over the problem of alcoholism with the ever-increasing evidence of its prevalence, the urgency of a re-examination of the field became acute when in 1966, the traditional model of dealing with persons apprehended for public intoxication—a category that includes many alcoholics—was suddenly challenged in a number of lower court cases that held that to punish an alcoholic for public intoxication would be to punish him for his illness—and that to do so would violate the constitutional prohibition against cruel and unusual punishment. In view of the fact that the criminal law up to that time had provided the major method of dealing with drunkenness (and, therefore, with a significant portion of the alcoholic population that comes to the attention of public authorities), a search for alternatives became imperative. The case of *Powell* v. *Texas,* decided subsequently by the Supreme Court, gave the states a reprieve, allowing them to continue the use of the procedures of the penal law —arrest, detention, conviction and, finally, release after service of a sentence—but, as will presently appear, this reprieve may be short-lived, and the search for alternatives must continue, for practical reasons as well as for conscientious ones.

Some reference has already been made to the relationship of intoxication and its treatment in the law to the subject of alcoholism. While fortunately not all persons who get intoxicated are alcoholics, a considerable majority of the persons who are arrested for drunkenness offenses are. The evidence is clear that the overwhelming number of arrests for public intoxication, drunk and disorderly conduct and vagrancy involving a charge of habitual drunkenness are in fact arrests of persons who are alcoholics. Hence, any meaningful approach to the legal problems of the treatment of alcoholism must concern itself with the most usual and common point of contact between the alcoholic and the law—the point at which his drunken conduct comes to the attention of the public authorities. Because drunkenness is symptomatic of alcoholism, and also because apprehension for public intoxication may provide the first opportunity to introduce the alcoholic to treatment facilities, considerable space has of necessity been devoted to the legal approaches to public intoxication and other offenses in which drunkenness constitutes one of the elements.

The study is divided into a number of parts. The first part deals with the legal and practical alternatives in dealing with persons found intoxicated in public, particularly persons in need of medical and other help. It analyzes the prevailing method of criminal treatment through arrest, sentencing, detention and release, and examines the law relating to drunkenness offenses. It then proceeds to the more recently enacted laws and proposals that would substitute treatment approaches for correctional ones. The facility for emergency treatment of intoxicated persons, a replacement for the old drunk tank, is thus viewed, in part, as one of the points of intake for alcoholics in need of more extensive treatment.

The second part of the study deals with legal devices currently available to deal with alcoholism and proposes methods for the legal treatment of alcoholics. It examines voluntary and involuntary commitment legislation for alcoholics in the light of current knowledge of treatment methods, and it looks into the legal framework and into the administrative structure necessary to make available a broader range of outpatient treatment on both a voluntary and involuntary basis. Analogies are drawn to other similar commitment and treatment statutes in the field of mental health, narcotics addiction, juvenile offenders and sex offenders.

The third and final part deals with miscellaneous legal problems relating to alcoholism, but emphasizes problems of alcoholism relating to criminal law. The impact of alcoholism on criminal responsibility is considered, as is the question of alternative treatment approaches for the person who is an alcoholic but who is arrested for or convicted of a crime which, at least on its face, is unrelated to his drinking problem. The issue there examined is whether such a person should be held by the state correctional apparatus with appropriate treatment for alcoholism there, or whether he should be handled by the mental health or other public health authorities as a person in need of treatment in lieu of correctional management.

From what has been noted previously it is clear that a discussion of "alcoholism" or of the "alcoholic" as a legal problem will depend to a considerable extent on the definition of these terms. To some extent, recent cases, including the case of *Powell* v. *Texas,* have cast the definitional issue of what is "alcoholism" and who is an "alcoholic" into the rather rigid framework of rules of responsibility under the criminal law. When the defendant's status as an alcoholic is alleged as a defense to a criminal charge of public intoxication, the terms "alcoholic" and "alcoholism" are likely to be given a rather narrow meaning, lest such a defense become too easily available. On the other hand, there may need to be a less cautious or narrow definition of these terms, if the designation "alcoholic" is to serve mainly to define a category for whose benefit certain treatment facilities and services are to be made available. But while a single broad definition of the term "alcoholic" may suffice to provide a basis for an inclusive characterization of the group to be treated, it may then need to be further delimited for such a purpose as the designation of the class of alcoholics subject to civil commitment.

Although the basic orientation that regards alcoholism as a "socio-medical" or behavioral disorder has been accepted as a working hypothesis for this report, the legal and practical consequences of different definitions will be noted.

INTRODUCTION NOTES

[1] T. PLAUT, ALCOHOL PROBLEMS (A Report to the Nation by the Cooperative Comm'n on the Study of Alcoholism, 1967).

[2] U.S. DEPT. OF TRANSPORTATION, ALCOHOL AND HIGHWAY SAFETY (A Report to the Congress, 1968).

[3] PRESIDENT'S COMM'N ON LAW ENFORCEMENT AND ADMINISTRATION OF JUSTICE, TASK FORCE REPORT: DRUNKENNESS 1 (1967).

[4] 392 U.S. 514 (1968).

PART I

LEGAL APPROACHES TO INTOXICATION

CHAPTER 1

Criminal Prosecution For Intoxication And Its Relationship To Alcoholism

Public intoxication is the most obvious and visible aspect of the problem of alcoholism though it is certainly not its most significant aspect. Alcoholics very commonly come to the attention of public authorities, both correctional and care-giving, through arrests for public intoxication. The large majority of persons who are arrested for public drunkenness are in fact alcoholics.[1] Therefore public drunkenness—though it may cause the arrest of some intoxicated persons who are not alcoholics and though it may cause the arrest of only a minority of alcoholics—must still be viewed primarily as part of the larger social problem of alcoholism. It must be kept in mind that the problem of alcoholism is much greater and more significant than the problem of public intoxication. However, public intoxication, being the visible part of the problem, has generally caused the more immediate public concern. Because it is the most frequent point of contact between the alcoholic and the public authorities it provides a convenient initial approach to the broader more important problem.

PUBLIC INTOXICATION AND THE QUESTION OF DANGER TO THE PUBLIC

Public intoxication has itself been regarded as an issue of great magnitude. There are about 2 million arrests[2] annually for public drunkenness, and indeed this number represents more than one third of all criminal arrests each year.[3] Undoubtedly many more publicly intoxicated persons are never arrested. The enormous police effort and the enormous expenditure of time on the part of the lower criminal judiciary involved in arresting and trying that many intoxicated persons implies that society regards public intoxication as a serious danger. In view of the fact that this danger has long

1

been considered of sufficient magnitude to require the criminal law for its control, it may be in order to examine precisely how society is endangered by persons who become drunk in public.

The physiological effects of intoxication are well known and have been adequately described elsewhere.[4] Alcohol on the whole operates as a depressant, but particularly in the initial stages of intoxication there results a lessening of restraints and inhibitions which has sometimes been considered as creating special dangers to the public. Although the lessening of inhibitions by intoxication may lead in some instances to violent or assaultive behavior, when the evidence is weighed in any realistic sense, it appears that intoxicated persons create little danger except to themselves. They mostly cause public annoyance, violate urban esthetics, and outrage the public sense of morals.

There is no firm evidence that intoxication is causally related to crime in general, although studies do show a fairly high coincidence between intoxication in either the victim or the perpetrator in cases of homicide[5] (one study showed that in 64% of the cases studied, either the victim or the perpetrator was intoxicated, and in 55% the perpetrators were)[6] and in cases of assault and aggravated assault.[7] Intoxication and alcohol problems also appear to be more common among felons convicted of crimes against the person than in the total population,[8] or even in the total population of convicted felons.[9] In spite of this statistical correlation, there is no conclusive evidence of a causal connection between intoxication and crime, although the studies clearly suggest that intoxication, by lowering inhibitions, may be a factor in the commission of assaults or other offenses involving violence. However, there are many other hypotheses which can explain the apparent correlation of intoxication and assaultive crime. The socio-economic groups which produce most assaultive or homicidal felons quite independently show a particularly high incidence of intoxication and alcoholism. It has also been suggested that criminals who are habitually or frequently intoxicated may lack the skill necessary to perpetrate crimes other than assaultive crimes, thus resulting in a numerical preponderance of intoxication and alcoholism amongst criminals convicted of crimes against the person. Finally, it has been suggested that intoxication and alcoholism are more likely to be causally related to the criminals' getting caught rather than to the commission of crimes. There is so far no conclusive evidence which would support one of the theories relating intoxication, alcoholism and crime to the exclusion of any other.

Although intoxication may be related to assaultive crimes, intoxication of the type and degree that is likely to result in an arrest for public intoxication is not likely to be such as to cause a likelihood of assaultive behavior. Only one third of chronic drunkenness offenders have records of serious crimes,[10] and the evidence shows that these men tend to abandon criminal careers between the ages of 33 and 40 and that their record of arrests for public intoxication substantially increases thereafter.[11] Thus it would appear that chronic drunkenness offenders are frequently men who were unsuccessful in their criminal careers. Thus in most instances persons who are arrested repeatedly for public drunkenness are likely to have their major record of criminality in their past rather than in their future. As the physical symptoms of intoxication increase, ability to control motor activity decreases progressively so that effective acts of violence become more and more difficult for the inebriate to accomplish.[12] A severely intoxicated or near-comatose individual is probably incapable of violence. There is therefore a question whether enforcement of laws directed at public intoxication will ever reach the intoxicated person at the stage at which he might be most dangerously assaultive. The person who is arrested for public intoxication is far more likely to show such advanced physical symptoms of intoxication as to be in fact past the point of danger to others.[13] While a small minority of experts have noted that violent behavior sometimes accompanies moderate to severe intoxication,[14] and while a substantial number of assaults are committed by persons with as high a blood alcohol concentration as .39,[15] it would seem that most severely intoxicated persons are unlikely to be violent most often because their advanced degree of intoxication renders them incapable of violence.

Therefore, although there is some evidence of a connection between violent crime and intoxication, it is neither sufficiently conclusive nor sufficiently implicative of intoxicated persons likely to be arrested for drunkenness offenses to provide a rationale for criminal laws against public intoxication. On the contrary, it is likely that public intoxication laws generally miss the potentially assaultive inebriate, and tend to be used against persons who are so intoxicated, or so far gone in alcoholism, as to pose a danger to no one except themselves. In fact, the possibility of assaultive behavior does not appear to be a primary rationale for laws against public intoxication. Consideration of the literature on public intoxication—as well as the history of the enactment and repeal of the twenty-first Amendment of the Constitution leads to the conclusion that public drunkenness laws are intended mostly to protect moral and esthetic values rather than to protect the public in any real sense against acute and palpable hazards. Even in its most recent pronouncements on public intoxication in *Powell v. Texas*,[16] the Supreme Court was hard put to find justification for public drunkenness arrests. The only justification for a policy in support of arrests for public drunkenness which appears in the majority opinion is as follows:

> It would be tragic to return large numbers of helpless, sometimes dangerous and frequently unsanitary inebriates to the streets of our cities without even the opportunity to sober up adequately which a brief jail term provides. Presumably no state or city will tolerate such a state of affairs.[17]

Note that the Court was charitably vague with respect to the description of the hazards created by inebriates, relying far more on their helpless and unsanitary condition to provide a rationale for their arrests. Historically laws directed against public intoxication have long been viewed as laws for the protection of morals. As actually used in the past—and still used at present—these laws, similar to the laws on vagrancy, are mostly designed to incarcerate the poor, the unsavory looking, and persons who, for whatever outward reason, arouse the suspicion of the police and of their fellow citizens. The discussion which follows of the various provisions of the criminal law that have been used to control public intoxication should be read in the light of the relative lack of danger which inebriates create to the public. In general the question which ought to be considered with all of the provisions of criminal law that regulate this area is whether the dimension of the real hazard—apart from imaginary hazards—warrants the enormous expenditure of time and effort that is devoted to maintaining the present machinery of control.

CRIMINAL PROSECUTION OF PUBLIC DRUNKENNESS AND DRINKING

There are a number of different approaches which the criminal law has devised to control public intoxication as well as public drinking. On its lowest level, the law prohibits drinking in public outright, regardless of whether such drinking is accompanied by intoxication or by any kind of disturbing, threatening or annoying behavior. The next approach is that of prohibiting public intoxication, with no clear definition of what such intoxication is to consist of and of what evidence is necessary to prove it. On a more stringent level the law prohibits drunk and disorderly conduct. While the offense of public intoxication merely prohibits the act of appearing drunk in public, the commission of the offense of drunk and disorderly conduct would seem to require something more, namely disorderly conduct while the perpetrator is in an intoxicated condition. Understandably what constitutes drunk and disorderly conduct is sometimes difficult to differentiate from what constitutes public intoxication. Nor has it been made very clear whether drunkenness is a necessary element in the offense of disorderly conduct, because disorderly conduct may be prohibited even in its absense. Finally, intoxication-connected offenses include the status crime of vagrancy. In many states the definition of "vagrant" includes "common drunkard." In view of the fact that in order to be guilty of vagrancy a person must be found in public, there is a nice question whether any person picked up as a vagrant on account of drunkenness could not just as easily have been apprehended as being publicly intoxicated. In the review of the specific drunkenness-connected offenses that follow, it should be noted that the actual differences in proof necessary to establish any one of them are very slight indeed. It may be asserted without fear of contradiction that the nature of the charge depends as much on the police officer's designation of the offense in his complaint as it does on the objective circumstances of the perpetration of the offense itself. Moreover, the police do not arrest everyone who might be charged with a drunkenness offense. In some areas police practice is more tolerant than in others, and whether a person is arrested may depend on whether he has a home, rather than on his conduct or condition. In many areas, a person arrested on a drunkenness charge may be released upon posting bail—which he may choose to forfeit, thus ending the matter.

The Offense of Intoxication or Public Intoxication

A majority of states have statutes which prohibit intoxication. A few are generally worded, calling for the criminal conviction of any persons "found intoxicated or becoming intoxicated."[18] The more typical statute limits the prohibition to public intoxication. A representative example is: "whoever is. . .found in any public place or a place of public resort in a state of intoxication. . ."[19] The punishment is usually a fine, imprisonment, or both; no state provides solely for jail terms.[20] Monetary penalities range from a low fine of

$0.67 in Pennsylvania[21] to a high of $1,000.00 for being drunk in specified places in Missouri and Tennessee;[22] the more typical range is from $25.00 to $300.00.[23] Imprisonment is usually for a period of 30 days to 3 months, though Arkansas provides for a minimum of 5 days[24] and a few states provide for up to one year in prison.[25]

The litigation surrounding the statutes predictably focuses on the two facets of the crime: what places are "public" so as to come within the prohibition of the statute, and how drunk must the defendant be to be considered "intoxicated" within the meaning of the law. The more general statutes, as they have been interpreted, seem to prohibit intoxication anywhere, and have occasionally been interpreted, even, as including the prohibition of intoxication in one's home.[26] The statutes that specify that intoxication must be public occasionally contain statutory definitions of what constitutes a public place; for example, a typical statute reads:

> . . . upon any railway engine, railway car, railway train, aircraft, boat, landing wharf, or depot of any common carrier or on any highway or street or in any public place or building. . .[27]

However, most states which have interpreted such lists regard them as illustrative; only Georgia[28] and Kentucky[29] have considered them as exhaustive.

In determining then what is a public place it is generally held that "a public place is a place or area where the public as a whole has a right to be."[30] It is usually a place accessible or visible to any member of the community.[31] "Public place" includes public highways or public roads[32] or even the area adjacent to public roads,[33] and most civic buildings, including local schools.[34] It includes, as well, privately owned places of public accommodation, such as railroad stations,[35] barbershops,[36] pool rooms,[37] general stores, and gasoline stations.[38] But, at least according to one court, it does not include all places where people may happen to congregate; it does not, for example, include a private residence, even when it is used for an assemblage of people for a social gathering or the like.[39] It is apparent that what is public may in an individual situation pose problems, but that general and objective standards are available.

The second issue, namely what constitutes intoxication, stands on a different ground. The problem of defining or determining what constitutes intoxication is really reflective of the purpose of these statutes which, in effect, condemn conduct which is not demonstrably harmful to others. The statutes themselves do not define the term, and the blood level concentration tests relevant to the crime of "drunken driving" or "driving under the influence" are not utilized.[40] Typically the arresting officer makes a preliminary determination and then it is for the judge or jury to decide whether or not the defendant was actually intoxicated.[41] Although some courts state that drunkenness needs no definition or description since it is understood by the jury in its normal sense,[42] the courts do speak in terms of the impairment of the defendant's faculties, using such terms as "judgment impaired," or "passions excited,"[43] and they speak of the degree of public attention which may be attracted, or the degree of offense to others.[44] Some decisions discuss specific evidence of intoxication. They seem to conclude that intoxication is best shown by evidence that the defendant talked incoherently or unusually loudly,[45] was unsteady on his feet or staggered,[46] or smelled strongly of liquor.[47] Other evidence that has been held persuasive has been the testimony of witnesses that the defendant was drunk,[48] or testimony that a half-empty bottle was found on the defendant,[49] or that he was seen taking a drink,[50] or that he had a dishevelled, lipstick-smeared appearance.[51]

The Offense of Public Drinking

Less than half the states have prohibitions against drinking in public—most states that do prohibit public drinking do so in the same law which makes public intoxication a crime,[52] and in a few instances states limit the prohibition of public drinking to specified places such as drinking in a church,[53] on a train[54] or at an interscholastic athletic event.[55] In most states persons convicted of public drinking can be fined or imprisoned, or both types of penalties can be imposed.[56] Monetary fines allowed range from $1.00[57] to $1,000.00[58] and time for which imprisonment can be ordered ranges from 5 days[59] to one year.[60]

The paucity of cases and the infrequent discussion of the crime suggests that drinking in pubic is seldom prosecuted. The lack of prosecution is undoubtedly well advised because the prohibition seems to serve no socially useful purpose. Prohibition of public drinking at certain specified places reflects an effort to legislate what are matters of good taste, and the more general prohibitions of public drinking serve at most to protect against conduct which may be esthetically displeasing, though less annoying than public intoxication. However, if public intoxication is no longer to be made criminal, the prohibition against public drinking may be used to prosecute "skid row" persons who now enter the "revolving door" of criminal prosecution through a public drunkenness charge. Thus, it would seem to be important in any repeal of public intoxication statutes to include a repeal of prohibitions against drinking in public.

The Offense of Drunk and Disorderly Conduct

States which do not prohibit intoxication *per se* but which have criminal laws against intoxication typically concern themselves with something more than mere public drunkenness.[61] While some statutes limit the prohibited conduct to public places,[62] others provide a general prohibition against inebriates who are engaged in "boisterous or indecent conduct or loud and profane discourse"[63] or who cause any disturbance of "public or domestic peace and tranquility."[64] Another type of statute prohibits intoxication which causes a danger to the safety of the intoxicated person himself or to others, or which causes public annoyance.[65] Punishment for this type of disorderly conduct includes fines, imprisonment, or both. The fine ranges from $5.00[66] to $1,000.00[67] and the jail term from 5 days[68] to 12 months.[69] In Vermont a pledge of abstinence for an agreed period is permitted in lieu of either punishment.[70]

Although there are thousands of prosecutions under "drunk and disorderly" statutes each year, again there are very few reported decisions, because these cases are generally disposed of summarily and without appeal. Georgia courts have been alone in their concern with interpretation of the law. The few judicial decisions generally hold that these statutes require proof of more than mere drunkenness, but there has been no clear definition or description of what kind of disorderly conduct will satisfy the statute. They have found that falling prone was sufficient demonstrations of an indecent condition to come within the statute[71] and that a stupor after vomiting comes within the prohibition;[72] however, a stupor in the back seat of a car,[73] mere staggering,[74] and fast and reckless driving have been found not to violate the statute.[75] These distinctions are logically untenable, it would seem, and besides, some of the instances in which convictions were upheld have little to do with disorderly conduct in the usual sense.

The purpose of these statutes seems to move away from merely esthetic considerations to aims of deterrence and removal of those who are more clearly troublesome. Although the application of these laws is subject to the same criticisms as the public intoxication statutes, the "disorderly" requirement gives the appearance of a more acceptable response to the purported need of a criminal sanction for drunkenness. Disorderly conduct—properly defined—undoubtedly should be subject to criminal prohibition, but there is no reason for for introducing "drunkenness" as a special element. It does not appear that a disorderly person who is drunk is significantly more of a threat than other disorderly persons. Moreover, the statutes which use danger to the safety of the intoxicated person himself[76] as grounds for conviction contain a particularly unhealthy mix of good intentions and social condemnation. Jeopardy to a person's own safety may provide a proper ground for state intervention for protective purposes, but it is not an appropriate ground for imposing criminal liability.

The Offense of Vagrancy as a "Common Drunkard"

A minority of states include among those punishable as vagrants "common drunkards"[77] which is the more typical term, or "habitual drunkards."[78] In most states sentences for vagrancy can be either fine or imprisonment[79] but a few states provide for only the latter. Fines allowed range from $10.00[80] to $500.00[81] and sentences may be imposed for periods of 30 days[82] to 3 years.[83]

The most patent problem posed by these vagrancy laws is the lack of definition of the term. In most states the courts have either fashioned a definition[84] or resorted to the definitions used in other provisions of the law[85] or to interpretations of those other definitions.[86] This has not resulted in any clear concept of what comes within the term "common drunkard." For example, in Alabama the courts have determined that a common or habitual drunkard is a person whose general rule of life is drunkenness and not one who merely is drunk practically every weekend but at no other time.[87] Moreover, a California court held that a state's prohibition of "common drunkard" was unconstitutional as "ambiguous, vague, uncertain and incapable of being uniformly enforced."[88] The examples given in the decision of the varying interpretations and standards used by other courts furnish persuasive support for the conclusion.[89]

A clear—though unsatisfactory—solution to the definitional problem is found in the Rhode Island vagrancy law. The law defines "common drunkard" so as to include anyone convicted three times of a drunkenness offense.[90] This has the virtue of clarity and easy application, but it does not really resolve the problem—for the

impact of the law is primarily that of a multiple offender provision—
in effect it provides for the heavier vagrancy penalties after the
defendant has been three times convicted of public intoxication.
Rhode Island's statute is unique in another respect. It not only
provides alternatively (as is typical in most vagrancy statutes) for
imprisonment and fines,[91] but it also provides that any "common
drunkard" be examined by the state's alcoholism division, and, if
found to be an alcoholic, that he be committed for treatment.[92]

It is doubtful whether a meaningful definition of "common drunkard" can be fashioned that would not in actual effect be descriptive
of an alcoholic. To punish someone for being a "common drunkard"
thus punishes him for *being* an alcoholic. Since the Supreme Court
unequivocally held in *Robinson v. California*[93] that a state of illness
cannot be a crime, the conviction of a person as a vagrant because he is
a "common drunkard" would again clearly raise the issue of alcoholism
as a disease. There is little reason for punishing a person for the crime
of vagrancy as a common drunkard. The underlying premise of all
vagrancy laws is the generally unproven assumption that the categories
defined as vagrants are likely to be future criminals.[94] There is little
evidence that a "common drunkard," however defined, will commit
future crimes, except perhaps other drunkenness offenses. Except in
circumstances of demonstrable danger, there has always been a strong
sentiment against anticipatory imprisonment,[95] and consequently,
vagrancy convictions for habitual drunkenness have even less in their
favor than criminal prosecution of drunkenness offenses generally.

EFFECTIVENESS OF CRIMINAL PROSECUTION OF DRUNKENNESS OFFENSES

The traditional response to the problem of public intoxication
has been through the criminal law, through prosecution for the offenses previously discussed. Intoxicated persons were—and still are—
arrested for public drunkenness, taken to the "drunk tank" of the
local jail, there to sleep it off. When more or less sober, they are
arraigned and, except in rare instances, they plead guilty. They are
then sentenced to pay a small fine or to a short jail term. As has
been noted earlier, the primary goals of such criminal sanctions
appear to be esthetic—removal of unsightly persons from public view[96]
—and moral—enforcing society's disapproval of drunkenness. Yet
the criminal sanctions have not proved successful in accomplishing
either of these goals, nor are such criminal sanctions appropriate for

the enforcement of purely esthetic and moral standards.[97] The contention that the intoxicated person, if not locked up, is likely to commit other crimes,[98] has already been referred to. It supplies little support for the criminal prosecution of drunkenness offenses.

From the point of view of the usual purposes of the criminal law—deterrence, incapacitation, punishment or retribution, and rehabilitation—criminal provisions against public drunkenness also seem ineffective, particularly when enforced against alcoholics. There is strong evidence that rather than serving to deter alcoholics from public intoxication, criminal sanctions merely result in a "revolving door" situation in which alcoholics are repeatedly arrested, sentenced to short terms, and then released.[99] Recent cases provide dramatic examples of this—Leroy Powell was convicted of public intoxication approximately 100 times in less than 20 years.[100] Joe B. Driver had been convicted at least 200 times,[101] and Dewitt Easter at least 70 times.[102] More systematic surveys produce broader-based evidence; in the District of Columbia only 23% of those arrested for public intoxication in 1965 were first offenders.[103] Although the deterrent effect of the criminal sanctions on persons not arrested has never been measured, the most one can reasonably assume is that some drinkers who are not alcoholics may avoid appearing in public when drunk because of possible arrest.[104] In general, however, there is no evidence that the criminal prohibitions either prevent intoxication, or that they deter public intoxication. There is additional evidence that suggests that, of all the groups in the population, alcoholics are the least likely to be deterred from drink-related crimes by threatened criminal sanctions.[105]

What has been said about the criminal law's failure to deter in the case of drunkenness offenses is equally applicable to its failure to incapacitate. To be sure, offenders cannot drink while in jail, but they do not remain there long, and the very "revolving door" system evidences the absence of effective incapacitation for the commission of other similar offenses.

The punitive or retributive purpose of the criminal law, now largely in disrepute, is even less appropriate than in the case of other offenders when applied to alcoholics, for whom intoxication is more a symptom of disease than a deliberate criminal act. Retributive punishment as a goal of the laws against public intoxication is difficult to defend.

Resort to the criminal law and the "drunk tank" also has not led to the rehabilitation of alcoholic offenders. This is amply demonstrated by their enormously high recidivism rate. Imprisonment may even lessen an alcoholic's chances for rehabilitation in the future, because it tends to force him into the subculture of "skid row" through frequent enforced association and damage to self-esteem.[106]

Criminal sanctions against public intoxication also fail to meet another important need—that of protecting seriously intoxicated persons from the dangerous effects of intoxication. An intoxicated person in a local jail is rarely given adequate medical care, even if he develops delirium tremens. A significant number of deaths from delirium tremens and from injuries suffered while drunk in the streets occur each year in such "drunk tanks."[107] Although the warmth and food provided in jail may not only be welcome to many alcoholics but may indeed cause many to seek arrest, these minimal provisions do not go nearly far enough to meet the needs for care, shelter, and medical treatment.

There are at least two other significant disadvantages to the use of the criminal law to deal with public intoxication. One drawback, which has also been the subject of considerable concern of the President's Commission on Law Enforcement and Administration of Justice, is the tremendous amount of valuable police and court time which making and processing such arrests requires—at least one third of all arrests are for intoxication offenses.[108] Secondly, the laws against drunkenness are almost exclusively applied against the poorly dressed lower class drinker, or against the "skid row" drinker.[109] Sometimes this bias is overt.[110] Most often it is the result of rather arbitrary police practice. The well-dressed inebriate who has taxi fare in his pocket is rarely arrested by the police, even if he is staggering, talking incoherently, or reeking of liquor.

Yet however inadequate the criminal law may be in dealing with public intoxication, the system cannot be abandoned without another instrumentality to take its place.[111] While society may have little reason to punish public intoxication, it still has a responsibility to protect the intoxicated persons and others from the possible danger that may stem from it. To accomplish this purpose, new, non-punitive systems need to be devised to replace the criminal sanctions. Such a new approach has been recommended by the President's Commission on Law Enforcement and Administration of Justice, and by may other authorities. In fact, a number of jurisdictions and The Model Alcoholism and Intoxication Treatment Act have already moved in that direction.

These new methods of handling public intoxication generally provide for treatment at emergency medical facilities sometimes referred to as "detoxification centers," to which intoxicated persons are taken, treated for a brief time, and then either released or turned over to the courts for prosecution, or, usually with their consent, to treatment authorities. This new approach will form the main subject of the next chapter.

CHAPTER 1 NOTES

[1] PRESIDENT'S COMM'N ON LAW ENFORCEMENT & ADMINISTRATION OF JUSTICE, TASK FORCE REPORT: DRUNKENNESS 7 (1967).

[2] *Id.* at 1.

[3] *Id.*

[4] E. JELLINEK, THE DISEASE CONCEPT OF ALCOHOLISM (1960) ; Greenberg, *Intoxication and Alcoholism: Physiological Factors,* 315 ANNALS 22 (1958) ; Gross, *Management of Acute Alcoholic Withdrawal,* 28 Q.J. STUD. ALCOHOL 655 (1967) ; Hoff, *Comprehensive Rehabilitation Program for Alcoholics,* 7 ARCH. ENVIRON'L HEALTH 460 (1963) ; Nason, *A Safe Method of Detoxicating the Acutely Ill Alcoholic,* 8 Q.J. STUD. ALCOHOL 43 (1947).

[5] GLASER & O'LEARY, THE ALCOHOLIC OFFENDER 11-12 (1966) ; TASK FORCE REPORT: DRUNKENNESS, *supra* note 1, at 40.

[6] TASK FORCE REPORT: DRUNKENNESS, *supra* note 1, at 40.

[7] *Id.* at 14.

[8] *Id.* at 42.

[9] *Id.*

[10] *Id.*

[11] *Id.* at 12.

[12] Greenberg, *supra* note 4.

[13] *Id.*

[14] *See* Hoff, *supra* note 4.

[15] Shupe, *Alcohol and Crime,* 44 J. CRIM. P.S. & P.C. 662 (1954).

[16] 392 U.S. 514 (1968).

[17] *Id.* at 528.

[18] CONN. GEN. STAT. ANN. § 53-246 (1960) ("found intoxicated") ; FLA. STAT. ANN. § 856.01 (1965) ("be or become drunk") ; MINN. STAT. ANN. § 340.96 (1957) ("who becomes intoxicated") ; NEB. REV. STAT. § 53-196 (1968) ("found in a state of intoxication") ; OHIO REV. CODE ANN. § 3773.22 (Baldwin 1967) ("found in a state of intoxication") ; PA. STAT. ANN. tit. 18, § 1523 (1963) ("shall intoxicate himself or herself").

[19] IND. ANN. STAT. § 12-611 (1956). The others in this category are: ALASKA STAT. § 11.45.030 (3) (1962) ; ARK. STAT. ANN. § 48-943 (1964) ; D.C. CODE ANN. § 25-128 (a) (1967) ; HAWAII REV. STAT. § 737-1 (1968) ; IDAHO CODE ANN. § 23-604 (1968) ; IOWA CODE ANN. § 123.42 (1962) ; KAN. GEN. STAT. ANN. § 41-802 (1964) ; KY. REV. STAT. ANN. § 244.020 (2) (1959) ; ME. REV. STAT. ANN. tit. 17, § 2001 (1964) ; MD. ANN. CODE art. 27, § 123 (1957) ; MISS. CODE ANN. § 2291 (1956) (public place in the presence of two or more persons) ; MO. STAT. ANN. § 562.260 (Supp. 1967) ; MONT. REV. CODES ANN. § 4-159 (2) (Supp. 1967) ; NEV. REV. STAT. § 207.160 (1957) ; N.H. REV. STAT. ANN. § 570:14 (1955) ; N.C. GEN. STAT. § 14.335 (Supp. 1967) ; N.D. CENT. CODE § 5-01-05 (Supp. 1967) ; OKLA. STAT. ANN. tit. 37, § 8 (1958) ; ORE. REV. STAT. § 166.160 (1965) ; TEX. PEN. CODE art. 477 (1952) ; UTAH CODE ANN. § 32-7-13 (1966) ; VA. CODE ANN. § 18.1-237 (1964) ; WASH. REV. CODE ANN. § 9.68.040 (1961) ; W. VA. CODE ANN. §§ 60-6-9, 61-8-15 (1966).

[20] *See* Appendix A, Chart I, *Criminal Prohibitions Against Drunkenness, infra.*

[21] PA. STAT. ANN. tit. 18, § 1523 (1963).

[22] MO. ANN. STAT. § 562.260 (Supp. 1967); TENN. CODE ANN. § 39-2518 (1955).

[23] *See* Appendix A, Chart I, *infra.*

[24] ARK. STAT. ANN. § 48-943 (1964).

[25] *See* Appendix A, Chart I, *infra.*

[26] State v. Sabczak, 259 Minn. 518, 108 N.W.2d 310 (1961). *See also* Duluth v. Oberg, 210 Minn. 262, 297 N.W. 712 (1941) (interpreting a city ordinance).

[27] ORE. REV. STAT. § 166.160 (1965). Similar lists may be found in: ALASKA STAT. § 11.95.030 (3) (1962); ARK. STAT. ANN. § 48-943 (1964); D.C. CODE ANN. § 25-128 (a) (1967); GA. CODE ANN. § 58-608 (1965); IDAHO CODE ANN. § 23-604 (1968); KY. REV. STAT. ANN. § 244.020 (2) (1959); ME. REV. STAT. ANN. tit. 17, § 2001 (1964); MD. ANN. CODE art. 27, § 123 (1957); MO. ANN. STAT. § 562.260 (Supp. 1967); OKLA. STAT. ANN. TIT. 37 §8 (1958).

[28] Finch v. State, 101 Ga. App. 73, 112 S.E.2d 824 (1960); Laboon v. State, 84 Ga. App. 784, 67 S.E.2d 149 (1951).

[29] Cawood v. Commonwealth, 229 Ky. 522, 17 S.W.2d 453 (1929); Yarbrough v. Commonwealth, 219 Ky. 319, 292 S.W. 806 (1927); Maynard v. Commonwealth, 202 Ky. 684, 261 S.W. 10 (1924).

[30] *E.g.,* State v. Welch, 88 Ind. 308 (1882); State v. Waggoner, 52 Ind. 481 (1876); State v. Sowers, 52 Ind. 311 (1876); Stateham v. State, 95 Okla. Crim. 232, 243 P.2d 743 (1952); *see* Annot., 8 A.L.R.3d 930, 932 & n.2 (1966).

[31] *See* Berry v. Springdale, 238 Ark. 328, 381 S.W.2d 745 (1964); *In re* Zorn, 59 Cal. 2d 650, 381 P.2d 635, 30 Cal. Rptr. 811 (1963); Lewis v. Commonwealth, 197 Ky. 449, 247 S.W. 749 (1923); People v. Hook, 3 N.Y.2d 485, 146 N.E.2d 689, 168 N.Y.S.2d 958 (1957); People v. Soule, 30 N.Y. Crim. 214, 142 N.Y.S. 876 (Ostego County Ct. 1913); Ellis v. Archer, 38 S.D. 285, 161 N.W. 192 (1917); Murchinson v. State, 24 Tex. Ct. App. R. 8, 5 S.W. 508 (1887); Pugh v. State, 55 Tex. Crim. 462, 117 S.W. 817 (1909); Hackney v. Commonwealth, 186 Va. 888, 45 S.E.2d 241 (1947).

[32] Starnes v. State, 30 Ala. App. 156, 2 So.2d 333 (1941); Frederick v. State, 24 Ala. App. 569, 138 So. 426 (1931); People v. Belanger, 243 Cal. App. 2d 654, 52 Cal. Rptr. 660 (1966); Barrentine v. State, 18 Ga. App. 726, 90 S.E. 372 (1916); State v. Moriarty, 74 Ind. 103 (1881); Rosenstein v. State, 9 Ind. App. 290, 36 N.E. 652 (1893); Wellman v. Commonwealth, 218 Ky. 807, 292 S.W. 467 (1927); Thompson v. State, 153 Miss. 593, 121 So. 275 (1929); Stateham v. State, note 30 *supra;* Walker v. State, 171 Tex. Crim. 379, 350 S.W.2d 561 (1961); Byrom v. State, 126 Tex. Crim. 640, 73 S.W.2d 854 (1934); State v. Mullins, 135 W. Va. 60, 62 S.E.2d 562 (1950) (dictum); State v. Younger, 130 W. Va. 236, 43 S.E.2d 52 (1947).

[33] Walker v. State, note 32 *supra. Contra,* Finch v. State, note 28 *supra* (the court found that since the list of public places in the statute did not include the side of the road, there was no offense). *See also* cases in which the accused was arrested while standing intoxicated on the highway at the scene of an automobile accident, *e.g.,* Kelley v. Yearwood, 204 Miss. 181, 37 So. 2d 174 (1948); State v. Byron, 16 Utah 2d 47, 395 P.2d 539 (1964); courts have generally agreed in these situations that a charge of public drunkenness is in order, since the defendant was on a public highway and the offense is completely distinct from driving while intoxicated.

[34] Wilhite v. State, 225 Ind. 45, 71 N.E.2d 925 (1947); Lewis v. Commonwealth, note 31 *supra* (dictum); Stewart v. State, 38 Tex. Crim. 627, 44 S.W. 505 (1898); *see* MD. ANN. CODE art. 27, § 123 (1957).

[35] Pratt v. Brown, 80 Tex. 608, 16 S.W. 443 (1891).

[36] *In re* Zorn, note 31 *supra.*

[37] State v. Shirlen, 269 N.C. 695, 153 S.E.2d 364 (1967).

[38] State v. Fenner, 263 N.C. 694, 140 S.E.2d 349 (1965). *Contra*, Strickland v. State, 37 Ga. App. 382, 140 S.E. 524 (1927). (result of the application of *ejusdem generis* to statute).

[39] State v. Sowers, note 30 *supra;* State v. Tichner, 21 Ind. App. 142, 51 N.E. 943 (1898).

[40] It has generally been held that a greater degree of intoxication is required under the public intoxication statutes than under the motor vehicle statutes prohibiting drunken driving, *e.g.*, State v. Painter, 261 N.C. 332, 134 S.E.2d 638 (1964); State v. Bradbury, 118 Vt. 380, 110 A.2d 710 (1955). Consequently, no court has as yet accepted the results of a chemical test as evidence of intoxication in a public drunkenness prosecution.

Nevertheless, clinical studies have already shown that such use is not only feasible, but also more trustworthy. The alcohol content of the blood of 1150 patients admitted to the Buffalo City Hospital with a pre-admission diagnosis of acute alcoholism was determined. Of these, 72 were found suffering from other conditions which may be confused with alcoholic intoxication; 78 were picked up for intoxication, but their blood was alcohol free; and the remaining 1,000 cases were alcohol positive. Clinical criteria used for admission were positive results in at least three of the following: (1) gross abnormality of gait or inability to walk; (2) abnormality of speech; (3) flushed face; (4) dilated pupils; and (5) alcohol odor on the breath.

These criteria, the same used to prove intoxication under the public intoxication statutes, were thus found less dependable than the chemical analysis of the accused's blood.

Jetter, *The Diagnosis of Acute Alcoholic Intoxication by a Correlation of Clinical and Chemical Findings*, 196 AM. J. MED. SCI. 475 (1936).

[41] *E.g.*, State v. Mullins, 135 W. Va. 60, 62 S.E.2d 562 (1950).

[42] Clark v. State, 53 Tex. Crim. 529, 111 S.W. 659 (1908).

[43] *E.g.*, Roden v. State, 136 Ala. 89, 34 So. 351 (1902); Brooke v. Morrilton, 86 Ark. 364, 111 S.W. 471 (1908); People v. Danile, 168 Cal. App. 2d 788, 337 P.2d 247 (1959); State v. Pierce, 65 Iowa 85, 21 N.W. 195 (1884); People v. Bevilacqua, 12 Misc. 2d 558, 170 N.Y.2d 423 (Essex County Ct. 1958).

[44] *E.g.*, Brooke v. Morrilton, 86 Ark. 364, 111 S.W. 471 (1908); People v. Weaver, 188 App. Div. 395, 177 N.Y.S. 71 (1919); People v. Lane, 8 Misc. 2d 325, 32 N.Y.S.2d 61 (Middletown City Ct. 1942); Murchinson v. State, note 31 *supra.*

[45] Finch v. State, note 28 *supra;* Duluth v. Oberg, note 26 *supra;* Boydstun v. State, 152 Tex. Crim. 273, 213 S.W.2d 825 (1948); Clark v. State, note 42 *supra.*

[46] Berry v. Springdale, note 31 *supra;* State v. Heller, 4 Conn. 174, 228 A.2d 815 (1966); Dryden v. State, 81 Ga. App. 171, 58 S.E.2d 519 (1950); Winters v. State, 200 Ind. 48, 160 N.E. 294 (1928); Duluth v. Oberg, note 26 *supra;* Deskin v. State, 94 Okla. Crim. 107, 230 P.2d 939 (1951); Walker v. State, note 32 *supra;* Boydstun v. State, note 45 *supra.*

[47] State v. Heller, note 46 *supra;* Winters v. State, note 46 *supra;* Deskin v. State, note 46 *supra.*

[48] Burke v. Tidwell, 211 Ala. 673, 101 So. 599 (1924); Winters v. State, note 46 *supra;* State v. Hamilton, 149 Me. 218, 100 A.2d 234 (1953); Stewart v. State, note 34 *supra.*

[49] Tackett v. Commonwealth, 261 S.W.2d 298 (Ky. 1953).

[50] Tronsdale v. State, 25 Ala. App. 174, 142 So. 684 (1932).

[51] Presnell v. State, 305 P.2d 595 (Okla. Crim. 1957).

[52] *See* Appendix A, Chart II, *Criminal Prohibitions Against Public Drinking*, infra.

[53] GA. CODE ANN. § 58-605 (1965); S.C. CODE ANN. § 16-557 (1962).

[54] MICH. STAT. ANN § 436.202 (1967); N.C. GEN. STAT. § 14-333 (Supp. 1967); TEX. PEN. CODE art. 478.205 (1952).

55 MD. ANN. CODE art. 27, § 123 (b) (1957); N.Y. REV. STAT. § 2A:170-25.3 (1953).

56 *See* Appendix A, Chart II, *infra.*

57 VA. CODE ANN. § 18.1-237 (1964); W. VA. CODE ANN. § 61-8-15 (1966).

58 GA. CODE ANN. § 58-605 (1965); MO. ANN. STAT. § 562.260 (1) (Supp. 1967); NEB. REV. STAT. § 53-186 (1960); TENN. CODE ANN. § 39-2518 (1955).

59 ARK. STAT. ANN. § 48-943 (1964); KY. REV. STAT. ANN. § 244.020 (1) (1959); NEB. REV. STAT. § 53-186.01 (1960); OKLA. STAT. ANN. tit 37, § 8 (1958).,

60 GA. CODE ANN. § 58-605 (1965); MO. ANN. STAT. § 562.260 (1) (Supp. 1967); S.C. CODE ANN. § 16-557 (1962); TENN. CODE ANN. § 39-2518 (1955).

61 *See* Chandler v. State, 36 Ga. App. 121, 135 S.E. 494 (1926); Dixon v. State, 28 Ga. App. 559, 112 S.E. 159 (1922); People v. Jensen, 54 Misc. 2d 807, 283 N.Y.S.2d 530 (Suffolk County Ct. 1967); State v. Dew, 248 N.C. 188, 102 S.E.2d 774 (1958); State v. Myrick, 203 N.C. 8, 164 S.E. 328 (1932); State v. Bradbury, 118 Vt. 380, 110 A.2d 710 (1955).

62 ARIZ. REV. STAT. ANN. § 13-379 (Supp. 1967); LA. REV. STAT. ANN. § 14:103 (Supp. 1967).

63 ALA. CODE tit. 14, § 120 (1958).

64 VT. STAT. ANN. tit. 7, § 562 (1959).

65 CAL. PENAL CODE § 647 (West Supp. 1967); N.M. STAT ANN. § 40A-20-2 (1964); NEV. REV. STAT. § 207.030 (1967); N.Y. PENAL LAW § 240.40 (McKinney 1967).

66 ALA. CODE tit. 14, § 120 (1958); ARK. STAT. ANN. § 48-943 (1964); ME. REV. STAT. ANN. tit 35, § 1170 (1964); OHIO REV. CODE ANN. § 3773.22 (Baldwin 1964); ORE. REV. STAT. § 166.160 (1965).

67 GA. CODE ANN. § 58-608 (1965).

68 OKLA. STAT. ANN. tit 37, § 8 (1951).

69 GA. CODE ANN. § 58-608 (1965).

70 VT. STAT. ANN. tit 7, § 663 (1959); the pledge form reads, "As evidence of my appreciation of the opportunity given me to become a sober and better citizen, in staying the fine imposed upon me this day, I hereby freely and voluntarily sign the following: PLEDGE—I will abstain from the use of intoxicating liquors of every kind and character as a beverage for the period of . . ."

71 Ford v. State, 10 Ga. App. 442, 73 S.E. 605 (1912).

72 Lovett v. State, 13 Ga. App. 71, 78 S.E. 857 (1913).

73 Finch v. State, note 28 *supra;* Pogue v. State, 84 Ga. App. 595, 66 S.E.2d 647 (1951); Ramey v. State, 40 Ga. App. 658, 151 S.E. 55 (1929).

74 Jeffery v. State, 94 Ga. App. 434, 95 S.E.2d 290 (1956).

75 Davis v. State, 14 Ga. App. 569, 81 S.E. 906 (1914); Peterson v. State, 13 Ga. App. 766, 79 S.E. 927 (1913).

76 *See* note 65 *supra.*

77 ALA. CODE tit. 14, § 437 (1958); ARIZ. REV. STAT. ANN. § 13-991 (1956); CONN. GEN. STAT. ANN. § 53-340 (1960); FLA. STAT. ANN. § 856.02 (1965); HAWAII REV. STAT. § 772-1 (1968); IDAHO CODE ANN. § 18-7101 (1948); MONT. REV. CODE ANN. § 94-35-248 (1947); N.D. CENT. CODE § 12-42-04 (1959); N.H. REV. STAT. ANN. § 570:25 (1955); R.I. GEN. LAWS ANN. § 11-45-1 (Supp. 1967); UTAH CODE ANN. § 76-61-1 (1963); *cf.* ME. REV. STAT. ANN. tit. 17, § 3758 (1964); WASH. REV. CODE ANN. § 9.87.010 (1961).

78 IOWA CODE ANN. § 746.1 (Supp. 1969); LA. REV. STAT. ANN. § 14:107 (1950); OKLA. STAT ANN. tit. 21, § 1141 (1951).

79 *See* Appendix A. Chart I, *infra.*

80 OKLA. STAT. ANN. tit 21, § 1141 (1951).

81 ALA. CODE tit. 14, § 437 (1958); NEV. REV. STAT. § 207.030 (1957); WASH. REV. CODE ANN. § 9.87.010 (1961).

82 N.D. CENT. CODE § 12-42-04 (1959); OKLA. STAT. ANN. tit. 21, § 1141 (1951).

83 R. I. GEN. LAWS ANN. § 11-45-1 (Supp. 1967).

84 *E.g.,* the appellate courts of Alabama in Tatum v. State, 32 Ala. App. 128, 22 So. 2d 350 (1945), then Prince v. State, 36 Ala. App. 529, 59 So. 2d 878 (1952); *cf.* successive Massachusetts interpretations of a similar statute recently repealed, Commonwealth v. Boon, 68 Mass. (2 Gray) 74 (1854); Commonwealth v. Whitney, 71 Mass. (5 Gray) 85 (1855); Commonwealth v. Conley, 83 Mass. (1 Allen) 6 (1861); Commonwealth v. McNamee, 112 Mass. 285 (1873).

85 *See, e.g.,* LA. REV. STAT. ANN. § 9:1001 (1965), which applies to certain civil actions.

86 *See, e.g.,* Patton v. Commonwealth, 273 Ky. 307, 308, 116 S.W.2d 652 (1938) and Sowder v. Commonwealth, 261 Ky. 610, 612, 88 S.W.2d 274, 275 (1935) (illegal sale of intoxicating beverages); Magahay v. Magahay, 35 Mich. 210 (1876) (divorce).

87 Prince v. State, 36 Ala. App. 529, 59 So. 2d 878 (1952).

88 *In re* Newbern, 53 Cal. 2d 786, 350 P.2d 116, 3 Cal. Rptr. 364 (1960).

89 *Id.,* 53 Cal. 2d at 793-95, 350 P.2d at 121, 122, 3 Cal. Rptr. at 369, 370.

90 R.I. GEN. LAWS. ANN. § 11-45-11 (Supp. 1967).

91 *Id.,* § 11-45-1.

92 *Id.*

93 Robinson v. California, 370 U.S. 660 (1962).

94 Perkins, *The Vagrancy Concept,* 9 HAST. L.J. 237, 250-53 (1958).

95 Lacey, *Vagrancy and Other Crimes of Personal Condition,* 66 HARV. L. REV. 1224 (1953); Note, *The Vagrancy Concept Reconsidered: Problems and Abuses of Status Criminality,* 37 N.Y.U.L. REV. 102, 116-18 (1962); Note, *Vagrancy: A Constitutional Battle,* 16 SYR. L. REV. 646, 661 (1965).

96 *See* Foote, *Vagrancy Type Law and Its Administration,* 104 U. PA. L. REV. 613 (1956); Note, *The Vagrancy Concept Reconsidered: Problems and Abuses of Status Criminality,* note 95 *supra.*

97 MODEL PENAL CODE § 207.1, Comment (Tent. Draft No. 4, 1955).

98 Perkins, *supra* note 94 at 250-53.

99 "The Revolving Door" is the name used by Pittman and Gordon for a process they observed at work upon public intoxication offenders, a Deviancy Reinforcement Cycle. The constantly reincarcerated drunkard, usually already disadvantaged socio-economically, finds coping with society to be even more difficult. This leads, in turn, to more drinking, alcoholism, and more arrests. D. PITTMAN & W. GORDON, REVOLVING DOOR, A STUDY OF THE CHRONIC POLICE CASE INEBRIATE (1958).

100 Powell v. Texas, 392 U.S. 514 (1968).

101 Driver v. Hinnant, 356 F.2d 761 (4th Cir. 1966).

102 Easter v. District of Columbia, 361 F.2d 50 (D.C. Cir. 1966).

103 TASK FORCE REPORT: DRUNKENNESS, *supra* note 1, at 73.

104 "Quite probably this deterrent effect can be largely attributed to the harsh moral attitude which our society has traditionally taken toward intoxification and the shame which we have associated with alcoholism. Criminal conviction represents the degrading public revelation of what Anglo-American society has long condemned as a moral defect, and the existence of criminal sanctions may serve to reinforce this cultural taboo, just as we presume they serve to reinforce other, stronger feelings against murder, rape, theft, and other forms of antisocial conduct." Powell v. Texas, *supra* note 100, at 531.

[105] Chambliss, *Types of Deviance and the Effectiveness of Legal Sanctions,* 1967 WIS. L. REV. 703 (1967).

[106] G. THOMPSON, ALCOHOLISM 40 (1956); Rubington, *The Chronic Drunkenness Offender,* 315 ANNALS 65-67 (1958).

[107] PRESIDENT'S COMM'N ON CRIME IN THE DISTRICT OF CO-LUMBIA, REPORT 476 (1966) reported that 16 persons arrested for intoxication died while in police custody in 1964-1965.

[108] TASK FORCE REPORT: DRUNKENNESS, *supra* note 1, at 1. An FBI check of 4,043 law enforcement agencies—embracing 125 of the nation's people—revealed more than $1\frac{1}{2}$ million drunkenness arrests in 1965; projections based upon these figures would indicate that there were 2 million arrests that year. *Id.* at n. 1.

[109] "The police do not arrest everyone who is under the influence of alcohol. Sometimes they will help an inebriate home. It is when he appears to have no home or family ties that he is most likely to be arrested and taken to the local jail." *Id.* at 2.

[110] "It is often the express policy of a police department to refrain from arresting a person for drunkenness in cases in which he may be placed in a taxicab or if he is with friends who are able to escort him home" (citing a Columbus, Ohio, police training bulletin and a letter from the D.C. Chief of Police). *Id* at 2, n. 12.

[111] "The picture of the penniless drunk propelled aimlessly and endlessly through the law's 'revolving door' of arrest, incarceration, release and re-arrest is not a pretty one. But before we condemn the present practice across-the-board, perhaps we ought to be able to point to some clear promise of a better world for these unfortunate people. Unfortunately, no such promise has yet been forthcoming." Powell v. Texas, *supra* note 100, at 530.

CHAPTER 2

Emergency Treatment Of Intoxicated Persons As A Substitute For Criminal Arrest

HISTORICAL BACKGROUND

The procedures of the criminal law to protect the public against persons who became publicly intoxicated—and, incidentally, to provide some limited shelter care and an opportunity for detoxification to the inebriate—were virtually the only methods of dealing with intoxicated persons until a few years ago. Authorities in law and penology and in the treatment of alcoholism had long stigmatized the prosecution of inebriates as worse than useless.[1] They reasoned in part that a person who was intoxicated primarily needed protection from the danger and discomfort of intoxication, intense medical care for the treatment of acute bodily injuries, or more typically, food, shelter and minor medication administered in a supervised setting to prevent the development of a medical emergency. Their pleas and demands for treatment alternatives went unheeded until the early sixties. The break in the pattern can be traced back to the case of *Robinson v. California*,[2] decided in 1962, which involved an appeal to the Supreme Court from a conviction under a statute which made it unlawful to be "addicted to narcotics." In reviewing the conviction the Supreme Court found that drug addiction was an illness, and held that to penalize an addict was thus a violation of the Eighth Amendment provision against cruel and unusual punishment because the conviction was not based upon anything he had done, but upon his illness. The progeny of *Robinson* will be discussed at considerably greater length in Chapter 10[3] in connection with the criminal responsibility of alcoholics. For the present it is enough to say that the doctrine of the *Robinson* case—namely, that a person could not be punished for a crime of status, i.e., for being an addict—was soon applied to the field of alcoholism.

In 1965 Joe B. Driver, who had been convicted of public intoxication at least two hundred times, appealed his most recent conviction to the Court of Appeals for the Fourth Circuit, and in *Driver v. Hinant*,[4] that Court found that he was a chronic alcoholic, that alcoholism was a disease, and that the Eighth Amendment protected Driver against criminal prosecution. The court held that Driver could not be convicted of a crime because public intoxication was "symptomatic of the disease of alcoholism." Shortly thereafter a similar case arose in Washington, D.C. In *Easter v. District of Columbia*[5] the conviction of DeWitt Easter for public intoxication was reversed upon proof that he was a chronic alcoholic (he had been arrested for public intoxication in excess of one hundred times). The court relied on the earlier decision in the *Driver* case; and in addition drew some support from a statute passed some time ago but hardly ever used in Washington, D.C.,[6] which stated that it was the policy of the District to substitute treatment of alcoholics for jailing them.

A number of similar cases soon followed in other parts of the country. There was a widespread belief among lawyers and mental health authorities that a holding by the Supreme Court was imminent that would follow the *Robinson* case and would render unconstitutional any arrest of a chronic alcoholic for public intoxication as violative of the Eighth Amendment. Ultimately, in *Powell v. Texas*,[7] decided in 1968, the Supreme Court refused to follow its holding in the Robinson case; however, in the two years intervening between the decision of the lower court cases and the decision in *Powell* a number of states had begun to move in the direction of establishing procedures for the management of intoxicated persons through methods of treatment rather than correction. A number of such laws were passed—notably in Hawaii,[8] Maryland,[9] the District of Columbia, and most recenty in North Dakota.[10] In varying degrees, they abolish or limit criminal prosecution of persons charged with public intoxication offenses, and provide for treatment services instead. A number of other states—such as Kentucky, Pennsylvania, Massachusetts, New York and North Carolina—also considered treatment legislation; and Minnesota passed a law permitting "inebriates" to obtain treatment on an informal (guest status) basis, or on more formal "voluntary admission" basis in state and local institutions.[11]

RECENT LEGISLATION TO PROVIDE FOR EMERGENCY TREATMENT OF INTOXICATED PERSONS

The treatment laws that emerged shortly after the decisions in *Easter*[12] and *Driver*[13] are too new[14] to allow any definite conclusions to be drawn about their operation. In fact, it appears that in some instances these laws were not implemented by appropriations adequate to permit the establishment of satisfactory treatment facilities.[15]

It is clear that a shift from the handling of intoxicated persons through the procedures of the criminal law to a management which is oriented toward treatment and service carries with it a major shift in public policy. The process of arrest, prosecution, criminal conviction and jailing of intoxicated persons is designed to protect the public, although it may incidentally provide temporary shelter to the intoxicated person. A treatment program, however, expressly shifts the emphasis from protection of the public to protection of the intoxicated person,[16] who is no longer treated as an offender but as a patient. If, in the course of his treatment, he is removed from the public, and if the public is benefited, such a benefit is largely incidental to the main purposes to be served: the treatment, protection and cure of the intoxicated patient.

The laws which grew out of the decisions in the *Easter* and *Driver* cases were largely a response to a crisis. There was considerable concern about what would happen if persons found drunk in the streets could no longer be arrested. Thus, even though the legal approach shifted from protection of the public to protection of the intoxicated person, it remained nonetheless an important purpose of the laws to provide a method whereby the large number of intoxicated persons (and particularly skid row derelicts) could be handled by the police and dealt with so as not to offend the sensibilities of the public.

While the emergency treatment approach to public intoxication avoids many of the problems of the criminal law referred to previously,[17] it presents a number of serious Constitutional and legal difficulties of its own which must be resolved before truly effective treatment legislation can be devised. Before dealing with the general problem of emergency treatment legislation, a review of one or two of the new treatment laws will provide a basis for further discussion. It should be noted that all of the new treatment laws combine provisions for emergency treatment with more far-reaching provisions on the voluntary and involuntary treatment of alcoholics. The summary here will be restricted mainly to the portions of the law that deal with emergency treatment.

The Maryland law,[18] which became effective on July 1, 1968, contains a detailed set of findings and declaration of purposes in which dealing with public inebriates as criminals is condemned as "expensive, burdensome and futile."[19] It calls for the "removal of public intoxication from the criminal system and establishment of a modern public health program for the detoxification of inebriates. . . ."[20] The law abolishes public intoxication as a criminal category and provides instead that "any person who is intoxicated in a public place may be taken or sent to his home or to a public or private health facility by the police or other authorized personnel."[21] Alternatively, such a person who is "either incapacitated or whose health is in immediate danger" may be taken to a detoxification center.[22] A person is to be deemed incapacitated when he is unable to make a rational decision about accepting assistance.[23] Detoxification centers may also be used by intoxicated persons on a voluntary basis by simply applying for treatment.[24] The physician in charge of the detoxification center determines whether a person is to be admitted as a patient, referred to another facility for care and treatment, or whether he should be denied referral and admission.[25] If he is admitted as a patient he may be required to remain there until he is sober and no longer incapacitated, but in no event may he be detained for longer than five days unless he himself consents to a longer stay.[26] At the conclusion of a person's stay at the detoxification center he may voluntarily request transfer to a long-term treatment facility, or, if proper grounds appear, a proceeding may be instituted to commit him for treatment.[27] Since public intoxication is no longer a crime in Maryland[28] a police officer cannot "arrest" an intoxicated person, but the law protects the officer by providing that he acts within his official duty in taking an intoxicated person to a detoxification center or to his home.[29]

The Maryland law also requires that an intoxicated person who has been taken into custody by the police for a criminal offense (unconnected with drunkenness) be taken to a detoxification center or other medical facility whenever "his condition appears to be or becomes such as to require emergency medical treatment."[30] This procedure may raise some questions with respect to the requirement that a person charged with a crime be taken before a magistrate as soon as reasonably possible.[31] The judgment of how soon it may be reasonably possible to take the arrested person before a magistrate is made dependent on a determination of his continued need for emergency medical treatment. When the arrested offender has had the necessary medical care, he is then returned to the authorities for further proceedings on the criminal charge.[32]

The law provides that while in a detoxification unit the patient is to be encouraged to consent to an intensive diagnosis for possible alcoholism, and, where indicated, to consent to treatment at an appropriate inpatient or outpatient facility.[33] Thus the detoxification unit is viewed in the law as an effective intake facility for the alcoholism treatment program. It should be noted that—like earlier criminal statutes that deal with public intoxication—the Maryland law fails to define what constitutes sufficient "intoxication" to justify taking a person into protective detention under the law.

The provisions of the "District of Columbia Alcohol Rehabilitation Act of 1967"[34] with respect to emergency treatment of intoxicated persons are in the main similar to the Maryland law. Unlike the Maryland legislature, however, Congress in the District of Columbia statute gave the prosecutor an option whether to file charges against a chronic alcoholic who had been brought to the detoxification center when taken into custody for an intoxication offense. In any event, prosecution of such a patient is purely an added step toward his civil commitment for treatment.[35] A person detained at the detoxification center when taken into custody for an intoxication offense, and who is found *not* to be a chronic alcoholic, will then be prosecuted for the offense after release from the detoxification facility. The law further differs from the Maryland one in that in Washington, D.C., a person may be detained at the detoxification unit for no longer than three (rather than five) days.[36]

The North Dakota law, in contrast to the District of Columbia and Maryland legislation, abolishes prosecution for intoxication and authorizes a peace officer to take an intoxication person to jail, to a hospital or to his home. If taken to a jail a person may be held for 24 hours; if taken to a hospital he may held by the physician in charge for up to 72 hours. While so held, he is considered to be in "protective detention."[37]

DEVELOPMENT OF ADEQUATE EMERGENCY TREATMENT LEGISLATION

The brief summaries of the new Maryland, District of Columbia and North Dakota emergency treatment statutes show that such legislation involves difficult issues of policy and law. Effective emergency treatment legislation must provide for both voluntary and compulsory treatment since an intoxicated person who needs medical attention may be unwilling to agree to submit to treatment or, because of the impairing nature of intoxication, incapable of actually consenting. Moreover, because the need for medical attention and care is immediate, it must provide for such treatment without prior recourse to judicial proceedings to determine the need for such treatment.

Compulsory treatment of any kind—whether for a physical, mental or behavioral illness—always involves some form of detention as well as an invasion of personal integrity. Compulsory treatment of any kind is clearly a deprivation of liberty which is Constitutionally permissible only if undertaken within the requirements of due process of law.[38] The circumstances that render compulsory treatment (or any treatment without the express consent of the patient) permissible *without* prior protective judicial procedures are limited, and they usually involve situations that demonstrably involve a highly valued social interest.[39] A mentally competent person whose appendix is about to rupture is within his rights to refuse the operation that will save his life[40]—yet a woman who is equally competent but who is in an advanced stage of pregnancy may be compelled to undergo a blood-transfusion needed to preserve her life and that of the unborn child.[41] In either case if the situation involved an incompetent or a minor, there would be no question that compulsory treatment is permissible.[42] On the other hand, in both cases a physician would have acted at his peril had he proceeded to give the life-saving treatment without prior court order.[43]

An effective and Constitutionally valid law for the emergency treatment of publicly intoxicated persons will require a solid rationale to support their protective detention and compulsory treatment, and this problem had to be faced in the development of the Model Alcoholism and Intoxication Treatment Act. In constructing such a rationale heavy reliance will need to be placed both upon the older laws that deal with the detention of mentally ill persons prior to formal commitment, and upon other existing laws that provide for such detention, either for the protection of the person detained or for the protection of the public.[44]

It is an accepted doctrine of Constitutional law that the requirements of due process are neither formal nor rigid. Due process—*i.e.,* the Constitutional guarantee of essential fairness—is a flexible requirement that responds to the exact factual circumstances of the legal situation.[45] In the context of the compulsory detention of intoxicated persons, the inquiry into significant facts will include questions relating to the nature of intoxication, to the nature of the dangers facing the intoxicated person and the public, to the extent of possible and of permissible treatment at emergency treatment facilities, and to the maximum time necessary to complete emergency treatment; these considerations will provide some measure for the maximum permissible period of detention.

DETENTION FOR TREATMENT AT EMERGENCY FACILITY OR DETOXIFICATION UNIT

Both as a matter of law and policy, treatment voluntarily incurred or consented to is preferable to compulsory care. In establishing emergency treatment facilities for intoxication, it clearly remains the hope that most intoxicated persons will simply enter the facility and request treatment. Early results of the Manhattan Bowery project in New York,[46] as well as experience under the District of Columbia law,[47] show that most intoxicated persons sought out in the street by police or roving emergency patrols will consent to come along to the treatment facility if the availability of help is made clear to them. Once consent has been given by a patient who is capable of making a rational decision, treatment may proceed.[48]

In the cases where consent to come to the emergency facility for treatment is refused, the question will be raised as to the power to compel the intoxicated person—even, perhaps, to the use of force— to attend the emergency facility and to undergo treatment. It is clear from other medical situations that a person who has the capacity to make rational decisions cannot be compelled to undergo any kind of treatment against his will, no matter how benign the purpose of the compulsion.[49] Just as a mentally competent patient cannot be compelled to undergo a necessary appendectomy against his will, a person who is intoxicated but who still has the capacity to make rational decisions about his need for treatment cannot be subjected to compulsory treatment for intoxication simply because the policeman or a member of the roving patrol thinks that it will be good for him. "Danger to himself" is not an adequate ground for compulsory treatment unless at least one other factor is present, namely lack of capacity to make a rational decision about the need for treatment. Just as the state *will* make treatment decisions for the protection of incompetents who cannot make such decisions themselves, it ought to be able to make such decisions for intoxicated persons who are similarly disabled, though only temporarily.

Since alcohol is an anesthetic which affects the functioning of mental processes,[50] it is likely that many persons who have consumed more than moderate amounts of beverage alcohol are impaired in their decision-making processes. The issue whether persons who are unable to make a rational decision about their need for help may be detained irrespective of their stated wishes will therefore have to be faced quite regularly. While there are no decisions that involve intoxicated persons, authority for holding such persons is furnished by the decisions which allow emergency medical treatment, regardless of consent, when the patient is unconscious or otherwise unable to make a treatment decision, if such treatment is necessary for the preservation of life, limb or health.[51] Such cases typically involve surgical procedures, and even in those situations it is not entirely clear just what dangers to life and limb are sufficient to justify compulsory treatment.[52] Yet the underlying rationale which justifies treatment regardless of consent in an acute medical emergency is applicable, too, in emergencies affecting intoxicated persons who lack judgmental capacity by reason of their drunkenness. Such a person, in consequence of intoxication, may also lack muscular control and is likely to suffer from impaired vision;[53] his potential peril is as great as that of a person who has sustained a fracture or an acute attack of appendicitis.

Useful analogies are supplied, too, by a number of decisions that permit emergency restraint of the mentally ill—even in the absence of statutory authority—when such detention is necessary for the care and safety of the individual or for the protection of society.[54] These decisions are based on the danger to the public which may result from the person's lack of capacity to act rationally. The degree of danger that is necessary to justify emergency restraint has not, however, been precisely defined.[55] An intoxicated person is not mentally ill, but he does suffer from a somewhat similar impairment of judgment.

Thus intoxicated persons can be brought to emergency treatment facilities if they agree, or if they require emergency medical treatment and are intoxicated to the point of being incapable of making a rational decision as to their need for treatment. Normally, an inability to make such a judgment is likely to be evidenced by cognitive deficiencies, generally confused thinking or other manifestations of disorientation. For emergency detention, an immediate determination must be made as to whether or not the intoxicated person lacks capacity to make such rational decisions. Ultimately, this is a medical determination; however, for immediate purposes this determination—as for instance medical determinations relating to the need for quarantine—need not be based on certainty but only on reasonable cause.[56] The visible medical symptoms of incapacitating intoxication are staggering, slurred speech and diplopia.[57] Observation of such symptoms can supply reasonable cause for the belief that the intoxicated person is irrational, so that he may be detained for involuntary treatment.

Emergency detention for compulsory treatment, based on need for treatment coupled with apparent incapacity of the intoxicated person for making rational decisions relating to his own need for treatment, is less than a perfect solution. One significant draw-back is that the initial determination of this judgmental incapacity will have to be made in the street by a policeman or other medically untrained personnel. While less than perfect, and while undoubtedly susceptible to errors of judgment, it is the only possible way in which a system oriented to care and treatment can operate at all. The proposed scheme—which is similar to that operative in Maryland and in the District of Columbia—appears to be Constitutionally acceptable because it seeks to balance fairly the interests of the intoxicated person in his own liberty with the interests of society in protecting both itself and the inebriate. It is also acceptable because any errors are subject to prompt correction—an intoxicated person will be promptly conveyed to the emergency treatment facility, where he will be examined by a physician. If it appears that he was detained for reasons that are medically (and therefore legally) inadaquate, he will be released.

Selection, and Transportation of Persons to Care-giving Facilities

All persons who are involuntarily detained for emergency treatment should be brought to treatment facilities. Only a physician can determine both the justification for detention and the intoxicated persons's medical needs. There will be situations when the intoxicated persons needs will be adequately met simply by helping him to return to his home. But the objective of providing adequate medical care for all intoxicated persons who need it could not be met if detention for treatment were based in part on extraneous criteria. If homeless men were treated differently from intoxicated persons who have a home, or if the fact that the inebriate has enough money in his pocket for a taxi ride home were determinative, the result would be to characterize the entire procedure as removal operation rather than an effort to provide treatment for the effects of intoxication.[58] The treatment facility should not be allowed to become a place for the involuntary treatment of only the poor and homeless; discriminatory detention practices might well provide the basis for challenge based on a denial of equal protection.[59]

Further, the law should not merely authorize treatment detention for intoxicated persons; it should *require* it for all who are incapacitated by reason of intoxication—*i.e.* in immediate need of emergency medical attention, or unable to make a rational decision about their need for care. If not, the treatment laws are likely to be administered in the same selective fashion as the criminal laws prohibiting public intoxication—authority to detain will be used only to hold for treatment lower class inebriates and skid row inebriates.[60] In addition, if there is authorization to bring intoxicated persons to treatment facilities but no requirement to do so, it is possible that persons who are intoxicated will simply be ignored and left to fend for themselves in the street.[61] In the beginning the police should have the duty to detain intoxicated persons who are subject to involuntary treatment and to take them to a treatment facility.

At present the police force is the only public agency equipped to carry out this task—it has the organization and the conveyances to bring intoxicated persons to emergency treatment facilities, and it is staffed to function in all areas of the city. Over a period of time, however, it may be wise to de-emphasize police management of inebriates, and to utilize other public employees to perform the task of bringing inebriates to help-giving facilities. Eventually, it would be best to establish special civil emergency service patrols for the purpose of collecting intoxicated persons and conveying them to treatment facilities.[62] The advisibility of such a course depends upon practical considerations, such as the number of persons in a given area who are likely to be in need of assistance or subject to detention, and the funds available for staffing such emergency service patrols. It should be pointed out that such civilian (non-police) emergency patrols may find useful application in other areas of service to mentally ill or behaviorally disordered persons.

In addition to public employees, private citizens certainly may assist intoxicated persons to treatment facilities. A citizen's right to assist should, however, be limited to situations in which the intoxicated person has consented; if he refuses assistance, only the police or designated public employees should be allowed to act. The citizen's role in law enforcement—as well as in the voluntary rendition of services—traditionally has been restricted in order to guard against mistakes and improperly motivated actions.[63]

Treatment at the Facility

A person who has voluntarily enterd or who has been brought to a treatment facility should be examined by a physician as soon as possible,[64] in order to determine, first, if there are sufficient grounds for detaining him, and, second, the type of treatment he requires. If an intoxicated person is not seen by a physician in a relatively short time, the program will meet neither the medical objective of prompt and adequate treatment, nor the legal objective of proper Constitutional protection against unwarranted detention. A physician's examination provides a check on the initial curb-side determination that a particular person is incapable of deciding about his treatment needs. This check is particularly important since no judicial review is available to restrain improper action, as there is in the case of arrest and in other situations where emergency restraint is authorized.[65]

The physician will first have to decide whether the person requires intensive medical treatment and whether he is intoxicated to the point of irrationality so that he may be detained irrespective of his consent. If the person is not so intoxicated as to be incapable of forming a judgment as to his need for treatment, he should be released immediately, unless he agrees to stay on and consents to undergo recommended treatment. When a person has recovered his judgmental capacity, he should be released, regardless of whether he himself initially consented to submit to treatment, or whether he was involuntarily detained. The medical determination that a person is again rational may release some people who would benefit from further medical attention, but this price must be paid; benign intentions will not outweigh the Constitutionally protected interest in personal freedom.

A person should also be released—even where the proper grounds exist for retention—if the physician has good reason to believe that he will be properly attended elsewhere; for example, the physician should have authority to release a patient to a private physician or to a family member.[66]

Thus after the initial examination only those intoxicated persons will remain at the emergency treatment facility who have asked for, or consented to, care; and those who are in need of medical treatment, incapable of making a rational decision, and in the physician's judgment unfit for immediate release. As has already been pointed out, if the intoxicated person requires hospitalization and is unable to consent, there is no legal impediment to administering the requisite treatment; the emergency situation overrides the strong interests in protecting the person from physical interference without agreement.[67] If the person were rational and competent to understand the situation, he would, the law presumes, consent. This doctrine probably goes far enough to authorize the treatment of an intoxicated person who is not in need of major medical attention, but who, in addition to food and shelter, requires the administration of vitamins and tranquilizers, or of other minor medications.[68]

Length of Detention at Emergency Treatment Facility

From a medical view it may be desirable to detain a person at a treatment facility until he is fully detoxified. Depending upon the definition of "full detoxification," this may take up to six weeks. Such a lengthy detention, however useful it might be for treatment purposes, would not be contenanced without judicial review. The proper measure of emergency detention is the length of the emergency—which ends when the person is again able to make a rational decision about his need for care. No plausible argument can be made to support involuntary detention without judicial review beyond the time when the patient's faculties are impaired. Of course, he can consent to stay longer, but he must be allowed to leave when from a medical point of view he is again capable of making a rational decision.

In practice, the intoxicated person's right to liberty might be best protected by a time limit on involuntary emergency detention, such as the five-day limit under the Maryland law[69] or the three-day limit in the District of Columbia.[70] To be valid and defensible, such a fixed maximum term for detention should be supported by medical evidence that indeed it will not take substantially less than the three or five days specified to detoxify the patient sufficiently to restore his judgmental capacity.[71] By this test, even three days is probably too long, and five days is even harder to defend.[72] It is possible that a test which measures the level of alcohol in the blood may be used if it can be reasonably related to the point at which a person becomes capable of making rational decisions.[73] The Supreme

Court has upheld the use of such tests in criminal prosecutions in a manner which obviates any Constitutional problem, even if the person who is given a blood level test is irrational at the time the test is administered.[74] Until objective tests of rationality prove feasible, it is probably best to consider a 48 hour time limit on involuntary detention as a reasonable time for detoxification, sufficient to produce a return to rationality; it is the time limit which has been proposed in the Model Alcoholism and Intoxication Treatment Act.

Few decided cases speak directly to the issue of release from emergency detention. Where an insane person was detained without statutory authorization courts have held that he could no longer be held once the object of assuring the immediate safety of the patient and of his family had been met.[75] Other instances of permissible emergency detentions without judicial order may be cited. A prisoner who has been arrested and is so intoxicated as not to be conscious of what is passing may be retained without a magistrate's approval until sober,[76] and statutes have been upheld that expressly provide that a drunk can be held without court order until the morning after arrest.[77] Cases relating to emergency detention of the mentally ill generally emphasize strict compliance with the statutory procedures, but some necessary time intervals between detention and hearing have been upheld.[78] However, in the situation of a criminal arrest, as well as in the case of emergency detention of the mentally ill under statutory authority, judicial intervention is required at some early point so that the propriety of the initial detention may be promptly reviewed. Since the need for emergency treatment makes judicial review prior to detention at emergency facilities impossible to achieve, emergency detention must be for very brief periods only and must be limited to situations where it is essential.

The Role of Emergency Treatment of Intoxicated Persons in an Alcoholism Treatment Program

Mandatory emergency treatment with proper protection against undue deprivation of personal liberties will do little by itself to deter repeated intoxication, nor will it provide long-range treatment for intoxicated persons who are alcoholics. Yet even though emergency treatment services must first be aimed at reducing the immediate medical and other dangers that arise from intoxication, they provide an important starting point for a more extended alcoholism program. Emergency treatment facilities provide a point of intake for voluntary referral for long-range help, and they may also furnish a convenient starting point for involuntary commitment proceedings in the few instances in which such commitments may be warranted.[79]

Properly managed, an emergency treatment facility can significantly advance the aims of an alcoholism treatment program that relies on voluntary participation. The emergency treatment facility can provide systematic referral to available longer-term care-giving facilities, and it may also arrange for more elaborate diagnostic procedures at the facility itself or at another convenient location. The emergency facility may also offer a short-term treatment program to detoxify fully and to counsel those who consent to a somewhat longer stay and who could benefit from such brief and limited therapy. When a person is ready for release he may be advised of available alcoholism treatment programs and facilities and may be encouraged to utilize them. However, release must not under any circumstances be conditioned on the patient's "voluntary" acceptance of a subsequent treatment program, for to do so would put in question the whole validity of the emergency detention. It would also jeopardize the voluntariness of the treatment, and this in turn may well have adverse consequences on the success of the treatment itself.

There is, of course, no way of accurately predicting how many alcoholics will voluntarily use the recommended treatment facilities. The limited statistics available from the VERA Foundation's Manhattan Bowery Project show that two-thirds of the men who completed the short-term detoxification program afforded by the Project accepted referral to one of the Project's associated longer term care agencies.[80] More generally, current theories support the belief that treatment which promises results will be accepted on a voluntary basis,[81] and more alcoholics are likely to accept treatment when it is offered in a crisis situation.[82]

To link emergency treatment to involuntary commitments raises more complex issues. To use the emergency treatment facility as a regular starting point for initiating commitment procedures is undesirable. The possibility—or even likelihood—that the emergency treatment facility is the first stop on the way to long-term commitment may dissuade intoxicated persons, and particularly alcoholics, from using the facility, and may detract from the help-giving atmosphere which should prevail. However, the alcoholic who is truly disoriented cannot be held indefinitely without judicial approval, nor should he be released. To provide for this limited situation, the administrator of the emergency treatment facility must be authorized to commence proceedings for commitment.

The emergency treatment program may properly be used for the identification of alcoholics in need of treatment. To the fullest possible extent, however, any initiation of commitment proceedings should wait until after release from the emergency treatment facility. In any event, the time of release from emergency detention cannot be delayed beyond the statutory maximum without court order. Emergency detention should not be extented to suit the convenience of the government merely to allow enough time to process a petition for involuntary commitment.

Conclusion

In order to meet the needs of an intoxicated person humanely, the law should not subject him to arrest and prosecution. Rather, treatment facilities should be provided. Because intoxication frequently causes a person to lose his capacity to make a rational decision about his treatment needs, legislation should authorize involuntary short-term detention under the supervision of a physician so that an intoxicated person who is unable to make a rational decision about out by past experience, is that most intoxicated persons will voluntarily avail themselves of the opportunity for treatment.
his need for care can be properly treated. The expectation, borne
tarily avail themselves of the opportunity for treatment.

CHAPTER 2 NOTES

[1] *See, e.g.*, PITTMAN & GORDON, REVOLVING DOOR, A STUDY OF THE CHRONIC POLICE CASE INEBRIATE (1958); Rubington, *The Chronic Drunkenness Offender*, 315 ANNALS 65, 66-67 (1958).

[2] 370 U.S. 660 (1962).

[3] *See* pp. 233-36 *infra.*

[4] 356 F.2d 761 (4th Cir. 1966).

[5] 361 F.2d 50 (D.C. Cir. 1966).

[6] Act of Aug. 4, 1947, ch. 742, § 1, 61 Stat. 744.

[7] 392 U.S. 514 (1968).

[8] HAWAII REV. STAT. §§ 334-1—334-86 (1968).

[9] MD. ANN. CODE art. 2c (Supp. 1968) and art. 27, §§ 122, 123 (Supp. 1968).

[10] D.C. CODE ANN. §§ 24-521—535 (Supp. II 1969); N.D. CENT CODE §§ 5-01—05.1, 5-01—05.2 (Supp. 1969).

[11] *See, e.g.*, Ky. House Bill 603, Mar. 6, 1968; Pa. Bill 200, Feb. 29, 1968, and MINN. STAT. ANN. § 253 A .03 (Supp. 1969).

[12] Note 4 *supra.*

[13] Note 5 *supra.*

[14] None became effective until 1968: the Hawaii law in January, the Maryland law in July, and the District of Columbia law in November.

15 *See* Baltimore Sun, Sept. 16, 1968, at B 10, col. 4.

16 *See, e.g.,* D.C. CODE ANN. § 24-521 (Supp. II 1969) ; MD. ANN. CODE art. 2c, § 102 (i) (Supp. 1968) ; PRESIDENT'S COMM'N ON LAW ENFORCE-MENT & ADMINISTRATION OF JUSTICE, TASK FORCE REPORT: DRUN-KENNESS 54, 59, 75 (1967).

17 *See* pp. 26-30 *supra.*

18 A "Comprehensive Intoxication and Alcoholism Control Act" was enacted along with laws relating to disturbance of the public peace and drunkenness and disorderly conduct. They are codified as MD. ANN. CODE art. 2c (Supp. 1968) and art. 27, §§ 122, 123 (Supp. 1968), respectively.

19 MD. ANN. CODE art. 2c § 102 (b) (Supp. 1968).

20 *Id.* § 102 (c).

21 *Id.* § 303 (a) ; *see also* § 102 (h).

22 *Id.* § 303 (b).

23 *Id.* § 303 (b) (1).

24 *Id.* § 303 (b) (2) ; however, incapacitated persons and those in immediate medical danger are given priority.

25 MD. ANN. CODE art. 2c, § 303 (b) (3) (Supp. 1968).

26 *Id.*

27 *Id.* §§ 304 (a), 306 (a).

28 *Id.* § 102 (c). *But cf.* art. 27, § 123.

29 MD. ANN. CODE art. 2c, § 303 (c) (Supp. 1968).

30 *Id.* § 303 (d).

31 *Cf.* Annot., 98 A.L.R.2d 966 (1964). 14th Amend. issues of due process and speedy trial might also be raised.

32 MD. ANN. CODE art. 2c, § 303 (d) (Supp. 1968).

33 *Id.* §§ 304 (a), 305 (a).

34 D.C. CODE ANN. §§ 24-521—24-535 (Supp. II 1969).

35 *Id.* § 24-524 (b) (1).

36 Id. § 24-524 (a) and (b) (1).

37 N.D. CENT. CODE §§ 5-01—05.1 and 5-01—05.2 (Supp. 1969).

38 U.S. CONST. amend. XIV.

39 *See* Jacobson v. Massachusetts, 197 U.S. 11 (1905) (upholding compulsory vaccination law) ; People *ex rel.* Wallace v. Labrez, 411 Ill. 618, 104 N.E.2d 769, *cert. denied,* 344 U.S. 824 (1952) (compulsory treatment of child over religious objection). *Compare* Application of Pres. & Directors of Georgetown Col., Inc. 331 F.2d 1000, 1008 (D.C. Cir.), *cert. denied,* 377 U.S. 978 (1964) (blood transfusion ordered over refusal to consent on basis of religion), *with In re* Estate of Brooks 32 Ill. 2d 361, 369, 205 N.E.2d 435, 440 (1965) (blood transfusion order refused, distinguishing the 1964 result on the tenuous ground that the patient there was the mother of a minor child, so that there was an overriding public interest in her welfare and in avoiding the burden of making the child a public ward).

40 *In re* Estate of Brooks, *supra* note 39.

41 Raleigh Fitkin-Paul Morgan Mem. Hosp. v. Anderson, 42 N.J. 421, 201 A.2d 537, *cert. denied,* 377 U.S. 985 (1964).

42 PROSSER, TORTS 104 & n. 51 (1964).

43 *See, e.g.,* Application of Pres. & Directors of Georgetown col., Inc., note 39 *supra. But see* PROSSER, note 42 *supra,* at 104.

44 *E.g.,* MINN. STAT. ANN. § 253A.04 (Supp. 1969) ; N.Y. MENTAL HYGIENE LAW § 75 (McKinney Supp. 1968) ; N.C. GEN. STAT. § 122-59 (Supp. 1967) ; *See also* the discussion at 54, *infra.*

[45] U.S. CONST. amend. XIV. *Cf.* the agreement on this point in the various interesting opinions in Burns v. Lovett, 202 F.2d 335, 341 (D.C. Cir. 1952), *aff'd sub nom.* Burns v. Wilson, 346 U.S. 137, 142, etc., *rehear'g denied* (with separate opinion of Frankfurter, J.), 346 U.S. 844 (1953).

[46] MANHATTAN BOWERY PROJECT, 1ST ANNUAL REPORT (April 1969).

[47] D.C. CODE ANN. §§ 24-521—24-535 (Supp. II 1969).

[48] PROSSER, note 42 *supra*, at 102.

[49] Note 40 *supra*. *But see* notes 39, 41 *supra*.

[50] HAGGARD & JELLINEK, ALCOHOL EXPLORED 111 (1954).

[51] *E.g.*, Preston v. Hubbell, 87 Cal. App. 2d 53, 196 P.2d 113; Delahunt v. Finton, 244 Mich. 226, 221 N.W. 168 (1928); McGuire v. Rix, 118 Neb. 434, 225 N.W. 120 (1929); King v. Carney, 85 Okla. 62, 204 P. 270 (1922); *see* Powell, *Consent to Operative Procedures*, 21 MD. L. REV. 189 (1961); annot., 26 A.L.R. 1032 (1923).

[52] *Cf.* Lefourneau, *Legal Aspects of the Hospital Emergency Room*, 16 CLEV.-MAR. L. REV. 50 (1967), *citing* FLINT, EMERGENCY TREATMENT AND MANAGEMENT 3 (3d ed. 1965).

[53] HAGGARD & JELLINEK, *supra* note 50, at 115.

[54] Forsythe v. Ivey, 162 Miss. 471, 139 So. 615 (1932) states that at common law an officer was authorized to arrest an insane person without legal process where it was reasonably necessary to do so, 162 Miss. at 478, 479, 139 So. at 617. *See* Christansen v. Weston, 36 Ariz. 200, 284 P. 149 (1930); Emmerich v. Thorley, 35 App. Div. 452, 54 N.Y.S. 791 (1898). *See also* 92 A.L.R.2d 571 (1963); and Powell v. Texas, 392 U.S. 514, 554 n. 5 (1968) (concurring opinion) which recognizes:

> . . . the power of the state to remove a helplessly intoxicated person from a public street, although against his will and to hold him until he has regained his powers. The person's own safety and the public interest require this much.

Likewise, statutes providing for emergency restraint of narcotics addicts have been upheld. *In re* Rover, 59 Cal. 2d 635, 381 P.2d 638, 30 Cal. Rptr. 814 (1963). *See also* Application of Hoffman, 131 Cal. App. 2d 758, 281 P.2d 96 (1955); Felix v. Hall-Brooke Sanitarium, 140 Conn. 496, 101 A.2d 500 (1953).

[55] *See* ch. 6 *infra* (discussing the meaning of danger in the context of involuntary commitments).

[56] *Cf.* cases relating to quarantine, *e.g.*, People *ex rel.* Barmore v. Robertson, 302 Ill. 422, 134 N.E. 815 (1922); *Ex parte* Dillon, 44 Cal. App. 239, 186 P. 170 (1919); *Ex parte* Johnston, 40 Cal. App. 242, 180 P. 644 (1919); State v. Rackowski, 86 Conn. 677, 86 A. 606 (1913). In some serious instances arrest without warrant is allowed upon reasonable cause; *e.g.*, N.Y. CODE CRIM. PROC. § 177 (Mc Kinney Supp. 1968) allows such arrest on a felony charge.

[57] HAGGARD & JELLINEK, *supra* note 50, at 115.

[58] D.C. CODE ANN. § 24-524 (1), 524 (2), (Supp. II 1969) and MD. ANN. CODE art. 2c, § 303 (a) (Supp. 1968) suggest selective criteria.

[59] U.S. CONST. amend. XIV. *Cf.*, *e.g.*, United Enterprises v. Dubey 128 F.2d 843 (5th Cir. 1942) and cases cited in n. 5 therein, 128 F.2d at 845.

[60] *See* ch. 1 *supra*.

[61] In Maryland the police are merely empowered but not mandated to bring public drunks to emergency facilities; note 11 *supra* and accompanying text. In part because of lack of facilities, police have simply ignored drunks, whom they are no longer obligated to arrest; note 15 *supra*.

[62] The VERA Foundation Project uses citizen reserve teams; TASK FORCE REPORT: DRUNKENNESS 58, 59. *See also* Alcoholism Treatment and Rehabilitation Bill § 3, filed for Mass. 1969 Legislative Session.

63 *Cf.* N.Y. CODE CRIM. PROC. §§ 183-185 (McKinney Supp. 1968).

64 To require that a person must be examined within a specified number of hours, rather than "as soon as possible," may increase protection somewhat; however, such specification might unduly hamper proper medical administration.

65 *Cf.* emergency commitment statutes; *e.g.*, MINN. STAT. ANN. § 253A.04 (1967); N.C. GEN. STAT. § 122-59 (1964); N.Y. MENTAL HYGIENE LAW § 75 (McKinney 1951). *But cf. In re* Coates, 9 N.Y.2d 242, 249, 173 N.E.2d 797, 801, 213 N.Y.2d 74, 79 (1961) (temporary confinement of an insane persons may be valid without hearing).

66 *See, e.g.*, FLA. STAT. ANN. § 394.201(4) (Supp. 1969).

67 *See* note 51 *supra.*

68 *E.g.*, the plan for a St. Louis Detoxification Center, TASK FORCE REPORT: DRUNKENNESS, *supra* note 16, at 50, 52.

69 MD. ANN. CODE art. 2c, § 303 (Supp. 1968).

70 D.C. CODE ANN. § 24-524 (Supp. II 1969).

71 The term for detention should be related to the time needed for detoxification. *See* Nebbia v. New York, 291 U.S. 502, 537 (1934) (holding that due process requires a substantial relation to obtaining a proper legislative purpose). *Cf.* People *ex rel.* Baker v. Strautz, 386 Ill. 360, 54 N.E.2d 441 (1944) (term must not be arbitrary, oppressive or unreasonable).

72 Gross, *Management of Acute Alcohol Withdrawal States*, 28 Q.J. STUD. ALCOHOL 655 (1967) (2-4 days of chemotherapy for alcoholics); Greenberg, *Intoxication and Alcoholism: Physiological Factors*, 315 ANNALS 22 (1958) (10 hours to 2 days for complete detoxification); Nason, *A Safe Method of Detoxificating the Acutely Ill Alcoholic*, 8 Q.J. STUD. ALCOHOL 43 (1947) (30 hours to 2 days for detoxification of alcoholics).

73 *See* DONIGAN, CHEMICAL TESTS AND THE LAW (1966); Harger, *"Debunking" the Drunkometer*, 40 J. CRIM. L. 497 (1949); Newman, *Proof of Alcoholic Intoxication*, 34 KY. L.J. 250 (1946); Ladd & Gibson, *Legal-Medical Aspects of Blood Tests to Determine Intoxication*, 29 VA. L. REV. 749 (1943); Ladd & Gibson, *Medico-Legal Aspects of the Blood Test to Determine Intoxication*, 24 IOWA L. REV. 191 (1938).

74 Breithaupt v. Abram, 352 U.S. 432, 435 (1957); in considering whether the results of a blood level test should be excluded from evidence, the Court held that the test was neither brutal nor offensive, and that the absence of consent did not render its taking the violation of a Constitutional right.

75 *E.g.*, Forsythe v. Ivey, note 54 *supra;* Colby v. Jackson, 12 N.H. 526 (1842).

76 *Cf.* Gilbert v. State, 164 Tex. Crim. 290, 284 S.W.2d 906 (1955) and authorities cited therein.

77 *Cf.* Wilson v. Hellard, 333 S.W.2d 777 (Ky. 1960), applying KY. CODE CRIM. PRAC. § 396 (1959). *See also* Scircle v. Neeves, 47 Ind. 289 (1874), reaching a similar result without statutory authority.

78 Felix v. Hall-Brooke Sanitarium, note 54 *supra* (30-day emergency confinement); Belger v. Arnot, 183 N.E.2d 866 (Mass. 1962) (10 days); Warner v. State, 297 N.Y. 395, 79 N.E.2d 459 (1948) (2 weeks).

79 *See* ch. 6 *infra.*

80 VERA FOUNDATION, MANHATTAN BOWERY PROJECT REPORT #9 (May 9, 1968). The report notes that such acceptance of referrals dropped to one half in the mid-March to mid-April period, and it hypothesizes that the variation may be related to changing weather and the opening of the summer job market in the mountains.

81 *Cf.* pp. 96-98 *infra.*

82 *See* Maurer, *The Beginning of Wisdom About Alcoholism*, FORTUNE, May, 1968, at 176, 211.

PART II

LEGAL APPROACHES TO THE TREATMENT OF ALCOHOLISM

CHAPTER 3

The State Alcoholism Program And Its Target; Definition Of Alcoholic

With an estimated five to six million alcoholics in the population, the fact that alcoholism is a major health and social problem, and that it is a proper matter for state concern and state action need hardly be demonstrated. It is, moreover, a problem that involves every branch of the state government in its management. As a legislative matter, it involves the state legislature in the consideration and passage of laws for its control and treatment. It involves the judicial branch, both in the criminal context of prosecution for drunkenness offenses, and in the context of civil commitment proceedings. Finally, it involves the executive and the administrative branches in the form of police authorities, institutional confinement, treatment services, as well as in the form of a variety of social services.

ALCOHOLISM LEGISLATION; GENERAL COVERAGE

Indeed, the laws of almost all states do give statutory recognition to the problem of alcoholism.[1] In a few states this recognition is limited to a general direction to study the problem or to the establishment of a purely advisory commission.[2] Typically, however, the law establishes a division within an existing department or a commission which is empowered to study the problem, educate the citizenry, improve treatment, and, somewhat less often, establish and administer treatment facilities.[3] The problem is not whether alcoholism should be an area for state action but rather how states should respond.

Modern alcoholism legislation must, at the least, deal with such essential subjects as research into the causes and treatment of alcoholism and education about the appropriate and inappropriate uses of alcoholic beverages which will contribute to the prevention of the disorder, and treatment of alcoholism that will restore as many alcoholics as possible to adequate functioning.

As has been previously pointed out, this work accepts as a working hypothesis that alcoholism is a behavioral disorder or medical-social problem. It follows that the problem of alcoholism and the treatment of alcoholics, though unique in some of its aspects, may draw for experience and guidance on other areas that present a number of legal analogies. These areas are areas of treatment of other behavioral disorders, such as drug addiction and sexual psychopathy, as well as the treatment and control of mentally ill persons. In short, it is to be expected that a number of recommendations arising from an analytical consideration of legal problems in the management of alcoholics may find application in other treatment areas as well.

Without anticipating later chapters, the general conclusion may here be stated that most of the existing state laws that deal with alcoholism are in need of major revision. There is need for a more comprehensive definition of the class to whom the legislation should apply; for a statutory specification of the facilities that should be available; for a statement of guidelines to regulate admission to treatment programs. Moreover, treatment laws should provide for a more restricted use of involuntary commitment and treatment, and should, instead, reflect a more liberal policy toward persons who are willing to undergo treatment voluntarily.

ALCOHOLISM LEGISLATION; THE IMPACT OF DEFINITIONS ON COVERAGE AND TREATMENT

This chapter focuses on the problem of defining the "alcoholic." The definition of the term is of great significance in the development of effective alcoholism legislation, because it sets the limits on the category of individuals who are to be regulated—or served—by the alcoholism program. Thus the definition of the category of "alcoholics" effectively sets some of the limits of what can be done under the law. As will presently appear, moreover, the impact of the definition is even more far-reaching, because the nature of the definition—whether it stresses behavioral or physiological aspects for instance—has definite implications on the nature of treatment alternatives. Subsequent chapters in this part of the study focus primarily on the legal problems related to treatment for alcoholism, both those encountered in voluntary treatment and in involuntary commitment and its implementation. The final chapter in this part highlights organizational, administrative and structural matters involved in shaping an alcoholism program and considers the enumeration of necessary powers and duties of the agency entrusted with the task. The functions of an alcoholism treatment agency relating to education and research are discussed in that context. The legal problems relating to treatment will take up the bulk of this part of the study, because they are many and complex. Education and research, though of enormous importance to the field, raise few legal issues and their discussion in the context of agency powers and duties can therefore be brief.

WHO IS AN ALCOHOLIC?

The definition of "alcoholic" is, in a sense, the starting point for alcoholism legislation, since it describes who will come within the purview of the programs and facilities to be established. Drawing a definition poses special difficulty because there is no generally accepted definition of alcoholic. The non-legal definitions reflect many conflicting views; moreover, the different views may have different legal implications.

One aspect of the definitional problem is the nature of the ailment, which clearly has physiological as well as psychological components. The symptomatology of the disorder is physiological, to a considerable degree—both in the acute stages of intoxication, and in advanced stages of the disorder, where it may manifest itself in polyneuropathy, gastritis, cirrhosis of the liver, increased tissue tolerance to alcohol, adoptive cell metabolism and withdrawal symptoms, including delirium tremens. On the other hand, the etiology of the disorder can be more readily described in psychological or sociopsychological terms. Hence, by concentrating either on symptoms, or on causes, or on particular phases of the progressive disorder, alternative definitions may be devised that stress the physical or the psychological nature of the disorder.

The alternative emphases have significant implications in terms of treatment laws and organization of treatment services. If the alcoholic is characterized as a physically ill person who has a number of psychological symptoms, then treatment will be directed to physical symptoms, and because of this, is likely to be essentially anti-psychiatric. For such treatment, no special facilities are needed in addition to the general hospital. On the other hand, a basic physiological orientation ought to come close to defining alcoholism in terms of a non-communicable chronic disease, thereby relieving the victim of any moral disapprobation whatever. A primarily physiological characterization of alcoholism would also work in favor of attaching treatment services to general departments of health, rather than to departments of mental hygiene.

A predominantly psychological, or socio-psychological definition of the nature of alcoholism, on the other hand, has the result of shifting treatment emphasis from the medical to the social adjustment side. In terms of necessary legal provisions, it argues for provision for treatment of a more extended nature, because of the general experience that problems of socio-psychological adjustment take longer to work out, particularly in alcoholics, than the treatment of acute medical problems. As a socio-psychological problem, alcoholism is not unlike many other behavioral problems, in that there may be a variety of causes that lead to excessive drinking, which in turn leads to secondary physical and psychological difficulties. With this definitional emphasis on socio-psychological aspects, the treatment of alcoholism becomes clearly the business of a department of mental health. One of the curious consequences of a socio-psychological definition of alcoholism is that, in spite of all good intentions it is often reminiscent in language, if not in tone, of earlier characterizations of alcoholism that defined it in terms of a moral weakness. References to "lack of control of his drinking," or "inability to abstain," or "interference with economic and interpersonal relationships" translate easily into "weakness of the will" and "inability to take care of his own affairs." This has readily given rise to the charge that much of the modern treatment approach to alcoholism merely substitutes concepts of social maladjustment and disease for moral weakness and evil.[4] In this regard, early legislation to provide for the commitment of alcoholics parallels legislation for the commitment of the mentally ill, in placing primary stress on protection of the public, and only secondary emphasis on treatment.

A few selected examples of definitions of alcoholism with their distinctive emphases will demonstrate some of the points made earlier. One of the few purely physiological definitions is found in a fairly recent edition of a medical dictionary:

> Alcoholism is alcohol poisoning; the morbid effects of excess in alcoholic drinks . . . .[5]

This definition clearly is not a definition that is usable for statutory or treatment purposes. Other medically oriented definitions may be less simplistic, but they stress the physiologically addictive or habituating properties of alcohol as much as they stress the psychogenic origin of the desire to drink to excess:

> Alcoholism is a psychogenic dependence on or a physiological addiction to ethanol (or similar intoxicants), manifested by the inability of the alcoholic consistently to control either the start of drinking or its termination once started, owing to (or caused by) . . . .[6]

The author goes on to say that the definer may add personality deviation, or immature or deviant personality development, or injury to the brain by alcohol, or nutritional defect, or whatever he believes to be the causative agency or agent; or he may prefer to say "owing to undetermined causes."[7]

A definition that stresses socio-psychological factors is the following:

> Alcoholism is a chronic illness, psychic or somatic, or psychosomatic, which manifests itself as a disorder of behavior. It is characterized by the repeated drinking of alcoholic beverages, to an extent that exceeds customary dietary use or compliance with the social customs of the community and that interferes with the drinker's health, or his social or economic functioning.[8]

Note that this definition is primarily behavioral and descriptive—it makes no mention of loss of control over drinking behavior which, in the opinion of many specialists, is the essential characteristic of alcoholism.

The classical analytical and descriptive definitions of Alpha through Delta alcoholism by Jellinek[9] require mention because, in spite of the behavioral emphasis, they place considerable stress on physiological components. They also demonstrate another definitional difficulty—namely, that alcoholism is a progressive disorder, and that physiological and psychological components of the definition will differ, depending on the stage of the disease the definition focuses on.

It would be inappropriate in a legal study to express judgments of a medical or socio-psychological nature. However, in arriving at a proper provision for the class of persons to whom legislation is to be directed, the basic orientation that regards alcoholism as a behavioral disorder or medical-social problem has been accepted as a working hypothesis for this report.

Existing legislation seldom adequately solves the definitional problem.[10] Alcoholism legislation most frequently defines "alcoholic" as follows:

> Alcoholic means any person who chronically and habitually uses alcoholic beverages to the extent that said person has lost the power of self-control with respect to the use of such beverage, or while chronically and habitually under the influence of alcoholic beverages endangers public morals, health, safety or welfare.[11]

Some states, however, do not include the element of loss of control within the definition.[12] One state relies on this definition but also includes as an alcoholic anyone convicted five times of intoxication.[13] Several other states emphasize drinking which interferes with personal, social or family life, inter-personal relations or economic funcioning, or which results in danger to health, either in conjunction with, or as an alternative to, loss of self-control.[14] Other states reflect an older but similar view, by defining the "inebriate" as one who has formed the inveterate habit of getting drunk so as to have lost self-control and to be incapable of taking care of his person and estate.[15] One state relates alcoholism to a physical compulsion coupled with a mental obsession.[16] Most of the remaining states which set out a definition define the alcoholic as one "addicted" to the use of alcoholic beverages or to the intemperate use of spirits or intoxicating liquor.

Although some of these definitions can be subjected to very specific criticism—for example, there is no firm medical agreement that anyone is really "addicted" to beverage alcohol[17]—most of them are inadequate because they are too limited for the multitude of functions they are to serve. The primary purpose of defining "alcoholic" in the context of a treatment-oriented law is to determine broadly the class of persons at which the alcoholism division's treatment—and research—activities ought to be directed. To some extent, the cases that have equated being an "alcoholic" with exculpation from drunkenness offenses[18] have confused the definitional problem for the purposes of a broader alcoholism treatment program. The definitions of an alcoholic should not serve to define who should be excused from criminal responsibility,[19] or to define the category of persons suitable for compulsory treatment.[20] In instances where the law is aimed at any such special group, that group must be further defined, and the particular provisions should be made applicable only to alcoholics who show the special characteristics that may be relevant. So, for instance, one category of alcoholics appropriate for civil commitment might be "alcoholics who are likely to cause physical harm to others . . . ."

Viewed from the point of view of the need to devise such a workable legal definition, the emphasis should be on alcoholism as a social-medical disorder, allowing the greatest definitional latitude for the purposes of a treatment law. The singular purpose of defining "alcoholic" should be to set out the class of persons to whom treatment facilities should be available, and who are the special concern of research relating to causes and cures of alcoholism.

A good start toward such a definition is that proposed by Plaut for problem drinking as "a repetitive use of beverage alcohol causing physical, psychological, or social harm to the drinker or others";[21] it includes the condition of alcoholism, "in which an individual has lost control over his alcohol intake in the sense that he is consistently unable to refrain from drinking before getting intoxicated or to stop drinking before getting intoxicated."[22] Indeed, Plaut makes a persuasive case for differentiating between the alcoholic and the problem drinker. He suggests that inclusion of many varied conditions under the head of alcoholism "may lead to stereotyping and gross oversimplification of highly complex phenomena."[23] Yet the distinctions are sometimes difficult to diagnose and from a legislative view serve no useful purpose—in practice most programs admit almost anyone suffering from any form of an alcohol problem,[24] unless the person has been otherwise diagnosed as mentally ill.[25]

Another useful beginning, too, is the recent statutory definition under Maryland's new treatment law, which clearly derives from Plaut and earlier similar definitions, defining a chronic alcoholic as

> any person who chronically and habitually uses alcoholic beverages (1) to the extent that it injures his health or substantially interferes with his social or economic functioning or (2) to the extent that he has lost the power of self-control with respect to the use of such beverages.[26]

However, even this definition is not entirely workable. There is no need, for the purpose of establishing to whom treatment facilities should be available, to modify the term alcoholic by the equally elusive phrase "chronic." Secondly, the persons who are encompassed in the second part of this definition, persons who have lost control over the use of beverage alcohol, would almost certainly come within the class whose drinking interferes with social functioning or injures health, and is probably superfluous. Finally, the limitation of the term alcoholic to a person who drinks chronically or habitually may eliminate the "weekend" or "spree" drinker who also is likely to have serious problems because of his drinking, and who may well benefit from appropriate treatment.

Thus, for the purpose of determining to whom legislation should apply, the term alcoholic should be broadly defined. A definition is most workable when the definition is in terms of the effects, injury to health or interference with social or economic functioning, and when it is general enough to include habitual, chronic, or periodic drinking to intoxication.

One definition which is sufficiently broad is that proposed in the Model Alcoholism and Intoxication Treatment Act, as follows:

> "Alcoholic" means any person who chronically, habitually or periodically uses alcoholic beverages to the extent that they injure his health or substantially interfere with his social or economic functioning.[27]

With the target group appropriately delimited, treatment alternatives may now be considered.

CHAPTER 3 NOTES

[1] Only Missouri and Wyoming do not (see Appendix B, Chart I); however, according to questionnaire responses, both states do have special facilities for alcoholics. (Appendix C.)

[2] E.g., ARIZ. REV. STAT. ANN. § 36-141 (Supp. 1969); COLO. REV. STAT. ANN. § 66-1-7 (23) (1963).

[3] Infra.

[4] Szasz, Alcoholism: A Socio-Ethical Perspective, 6 WASHBURN L.J. 255, 259 (1967); see Davis, Mental Hygiene and the Class Structure, 4 PSYCHIATRY 55 (1938); Swartz, Compulsory Legal Measures and the Concept of Illness, 19 S.C.L. REV. 372, 386 (1967); Wooton, The Law, the Doctor, and the Deviant, 2 BRIT. MED. J. 197 (1963); Wooton, Sickness or Sin, 159 20TH CENT. 433 (1956).

[5] DORLAND'S ILLUSTRATED MEDICAL DICTIONARY (23rd ed. 1957).

[6] Keller, Definition of Alcoholism, 21 Q.J. STUD. ALCOHOL 125, 128 (1960).

[7] Id.

[8] Keller & Efron, Alcoholism, in 1 ENCYCLOPEDIA AMERICANA 348 (1956).

[9] E. JELLINEK, THE DISEASE CONCEPT OF ALCOHOLISM 36-38 (1960).

[10] Appendix B, Chart I.

[11] ARK. STAT. ANN § 83-703 (c) (1960); GA. CODE ANN. § 88-402 (a) (Supp. 1968); IND. ANN. STAT. § 22-1502 (b) (1964); IOWA CODE ANN. § 123A.1 (Supp. 1969); KY. REV. STAT. § 222.110 (2) (1959); MICH. COMP. LAWS ANN. § 436.47a (1967); MISS. CODE ANN. § 436-01 (a) (1956); N.Y. MENTAL HYGIENE LAW § 301 (a) (McKinney Supp. 1968); R.I. GEN. LAWS ANN. § 40-12-2 (1956); TENN. CODE ANN. § 33-803 (Supp. 1968); TEX. REV. CIV. STAT. ANN. art. 5561c, § 3 (c) (Supp. 1968); W. VA. CODE ANN. § 27-1A-11 (1966).

[12] NEV. REV. STAT. § 458.010 (2) (1968) (*but cf.* § 433.28 (1) (1967) which defines alcoholic for commitment purposes as requiring loss of control); IDAHO CODE ANN. § 67-3109 (Supp. 1967); UTAH CODE ANN. § 55-13-3 (1963).

[13] KAN. GEN. STAT. ANN. § 74-4401 (1964).

[14] HAWAII REV. LAWS § 334-1 (1968); MD. ANN. CODE art. 2c, § 130 (b) (Supp. 1968); MONT. REV. CODES ANN. § 80-2404 (2) (a) (Supp. 1967); WASH. REV. CODE ANN. § 70.96.020 (1963). (*See* Appendix B, Chart I.)

[15] LA. REV. STAT. ANN. § 9.1001 (1965); MINN. STAT. ANN. § 253A.02 (Supp. 1969); N.C. GEN. STAT. § 122-36 (c) (Supp. 1967); W. VA. CODE ANN. § 27-1-4 (1966).

[16] ALASKA STAT. § 47.30.500 (3) (1966) (although the definition of alcoholic is typical).

[17] *See* T. PLAUT, ALCOHOL PROBLEMS 43-45 (1967).

[18] Easter v. District of Columbia, 361 F.2d 50 (D.C. Cir. 1966); Driver v. Hinant, 356 F.2d 761 (4th Cir. 1966).

[19] *See* ch. 10 *infra.*

[20] *See* ch. 6 *infra.*

[21] PLAUT, *supra* note 17, at 37-38.

[22] *Id.,* at 39.

[23] *Id.,* at 41.

[24] R. GLASSCOTE, T. PLAUT, D. HAMMERSLEY, F. O'NEILL, M. CHAFETZ & E. CUMMING, THE TREATMENT OF ALCOHOLISM 18 ff. (1967).

[25] A typical policy is that of the West Virginia Division of Alcoholism, which will admit any alcoholic except those with serious organic damage, psychosis, or mental deficiency. TREATMENT OF ALCOHOLISM, *supra* note 24, at 33. Similar exclusions for psychosis, chronic brain syndromes and similar disorders are made in most programs. *Id.,* at 47, 59, 115. However, some programs do admit almost anyone. *Id.,* at 18 ff., 101. *See also* NATIONAL INSTITUTE OF MENTAL HEALTH, ALCOHOL AND ALCOHOLISM 37 (Public Health Service Pub. No. 1640, 1968) in reference to the makeup of the alcoholic population. The VERA Foundation's Manhattan Bowery project has diagnosed 33% of the men admitted to their detoxification center as schizophrenic, 17.5% as suffering from depression and 32% as having character-disorders. This high rate of mental illness, however, may be attributable to the population from which the men were drawn (New York City's skid row). VERA FOUNDATION, FIRST ANNUAL REPORT OF THE MANHATTAN BOWERY PROJECT 30, 58, 59 (1969).

[26] 1968 LAWS OF MARYLAND, ch. 146, § 103 (b); MD. ANN. CODE art. 2c, § 103 (b) (Supp. 1968).

[27] MODEL ALCOHOLISM AND INTOXICATION TREATMENT ACT § 3 (1) (1969).

CHAPTER 4

Legal Implications Of Available Methods Of Treatment For Alcoholism

The idea that alcoholics are not persons who are morally abandoned and of evil and unprincipled disposition is now generally accepted.[1] While there may be differences of opinion regarding the nature and causes of alcoholism, there is also general acceptance of the idea that alcoholics are persons in need of help. It is one of the main purposes of alcoholism legislation to provide for the ways in which such help is to be rendered.

While many alcoholics will voluntarily seek treatment if it is available, others will not. Laws that provide for treatment of alcoholics thus have to provide both for the treatment of persons who want to be treated, and for those who resist treatment, but who—for reasons to be discussed later—ought to be compelled to get treatment whether they want it or not. Moreover, in the light of the enormous number of persons afflicted with alcoholism, and in the light of the present scarcity of treatment facilities, choices have to be made whether some treatment resources ought to be primarily used for the treatment of the voluntary or the involuntary category, and what priorities, if any, there ought to be within either of these.

Another policy matter that must be considered is whether treatment-oriented laws ought to stress inpatient or outpatient care, and ought to take fixed positions on length of commitment, or length of treatment generally. Clearly the law itself should not support one school of treatment over another. Whether moneys are to be made available for one kind of therapy rather than another—for drug therapy or for psychoanalysis, or, even more specifically, for Freud or for Pavlov is a question which the treatment services will have to answer, guided by the conclusions reached with respect to the treatment of alcoholism by the physician, the psychiatrist, the psychologist and by others involved in the provision of services to alcoholics.

TREATMENT FOR ALCOHOLISM AND ITS IMPLICATION FOR TREATMENT LAWS

Just there is no single generally accepted cause for the disorder of alcoholism, there is no standard generally accepted method of treating alcoholics.[2] There is not even a consensus on what constitutes a "cure" for alcoholism. Most treatment programs for alcoholism are based on some form of psychotherapy,[3] usually a form of group therapy.[4] Most psychotherapeutic approaches to alcoholism tend to be more directive and symptom-oriented than traditional psychotherapy.[5] Many programs are didactic, expatiating on the evils of excessive drinking while also attempting to treat psychological problems.[6] On the common assumption that alcoholism is caused in whole or in part by psychological problems, psychotherapy is likely to continue to play a major part in treatment programs although it has not always been successful.[7]

Psychotherapy is often combined with some form of drug therapy.[8] The most commonly used drug is Antabuse (Disulfiram) which causes severe nausea when a person drinks alcohol.[9] Frequently used at the beginning of psychotherapy, Antabuse enables alcoholics to remain sober long enough to begin or to continue other treatment.[10] Antabuse has also been successfully used alone and has helped alcoholics remain abstinent for long periods.[11] Other drugs such as tranquilizers, sedatives or LSD-25 have also been used in conjunction with psychotherapy.[12] There have been some claims for success,[13] as well as assertions that controlled experiments have indicated that their use does not significanly raise the success rate of a treatment program.[14] Frequently, it seems, such drugs will be used only to induce a psychological state in which the alcoholic can accept therapy.[15] Potential disadvantages of drug therapy—including suicide attempts through overdoses, new drug dependence and other problems—have also been alleged.[16]

Another treatment approach is aversion therapy or conditioned response treatment. It consists of having the patient take a drink while subjecting him at the same time to an extremely painful experience, such as electric shock, so as to associate the unpleasant reaction with a drinking experience. Successful cures have been claimed for aversion therapy, though it has few advocates at this time.[17] Another similar type of therapy, little used today, is hypnotic conditioning against drinking alcoholic beverages.[18] Neither post-hypnotic suggestion nor aversion therapy are used frequently[19] possibly because of the assertion that they ignore the underlying causes of the patient's drinking in the course of treatment. Aversion therapy bears some similarity also to Antabuse therapy previously mentioned in that Antabuse, too, will associate drinking with the unpleasant experience of nausea.

Although there has always been a school of thought that alcoholism is primarily a physiological disorder caused by genetic or constitutional abnormalities,[20] no clear physiological cause of alcoholism has been found.[21] Research has shown, however, that alcoholics frequently suffer from biochemical abnormalities. Whether there is a causal relationship between these abnormalities and alcoholism—or vice versa—is not known.[22]

Lastly, lay treatment, such as the program of Alcoholics Anonymous, should be mentioned. It has been asserted that more alcoholics are treated and "cured" by Alcoholics Anonymous than by any other form of treatment.[23] Based on a system of mutual spiritual support by other members of the group, the Alcoholics Anonymous lay treatment provides the alcoholic with continuing group support both before and after he has accomplished abstinence. While the record of the Alcoholics Anonymous is on its face impressive,[24] it is clear that the Alcoholics Anonymous attracts mainly middle-class members with a strong sense of guilt who interact easily in small groups.[25] Since the only criterion for membership in Alcoholics Anonymous is the admission that one is an alcoholic, there is no way of knowing how much of its success is due to its methods and how much is due to the characteristics of its self-selected members.

Although each of the treatment approaches mentioned can point to a significant rate of "cures," i.e., 30-40 percent,[26] this rate must be compared with the rate of spontaneous cures. One study of 500 alcoholics reports that this rate may be as high as 20 percent.[27] Similar spontaneous cure rates are indicated by other studies.[28]

In addition to treatment methods that attack the disease of alcoholism directly, there are a number of other methods and approaches that seek to resolve the alcoholic's drinking problem by attacking certain social and environmental aspects of his life and by attempting to return him to a normal role in society. These efforts include the location of skid row inhabitants,[29] the establishment of a comprehensive diagnostic and social referral system,[30] the establishment of a program of vocational rehabilitation,[31] and the use of a controlled and supportive environment such as halfway houses.[32] Therapy for members of the alcoholic's family, often a source for his difficulties, has been suggested.[33] All such constructive efforts to improve the alcoholic's environment have met with some limited success.

In the light of the wide variety of current treatment approaches, in the light of the absence of any standard uniformly successful method of treating alcoholics, and in the light of the fact that different methods of treatment will be appropriate for different kinds of alcoholics, it is clear that an alcoholism treatment law should not endorse any particular treatment method, but should rather permit a variety of treatments, and encourage experimentation and research to develop new, successful methods of therapy. Although it is not common for state statutes to limit treatment approaches, a few states—including Nebraska and Utah—do endorse or suggest particular treatment methods.[34] This is unduly limiting a field in which future development will have to supply significant answers.

Another insight which is gained from a review of available treatment methods is that they ought not to become solely the property and vested area of interest of any single department or division of a department. Much of the success of treatment programs depends on follow-up[35] that may involve a whole system of social services, in an outpatient, or semi-institutional setting.[36] To be fully successful, an alcoholism program should, therefore, be based on statutory provisions that permit the involvement of many departments or agencies, public and private, that have care or social services to offer.

"MOTIVATION" AND THE QUESTION OF COMPULSORY TREATMENT

In assessing the different treatment methods most researchers have been unable to agree on why some individuals can be cured and others cannot. There is disagreement as to whether objective factors such as length of treatment, socio-economic factors, age, or education are significantly related to the success of treatment.[37] The only factor which many experts agree is connected with the likelihood of cure is an elusive quality called "motivation," which generally is interpreted to mean an admission of an alcohol problem and a desire to do something about it. Many, or most, experts feel that a patient must come to treatment with "motivation for cure" if any treatment is to succeed.[38]

"Motivation" or readiness to be cured is hard to spot. Often it is determined by hindsight—those who are cured are said to have been motivated, and those who are not cured are said to have lacked motivation.[39] Thus, many experts blame the failure of their treatment methods on the lack of motivation of their patients instead of critically appraising their methods.[40] Treatment programs often accept only patients judged to be "motivated," screening out those alcoholics who appear to be more difficult to treat, but who nevertheless might respond to treatment.[41]

Another troublesome aspect of "motivation" is that it is frequently said to come about only after an alcoholic has "hit bottom."[42] This is reflected in the doctrine of Alcoholics Anonymous.[43] Motivation has also been connected with taking the initiative to be cured.[44] However, many, if not most, alcoholics are not "motivated" in that rather narrow and simplistic sense, and it is accepted that denial of a drinking problem, hostility and suspiciousness are symptoms of alcoholism.[45] There is a question whether the lack of such a specific motivation should be used to exclude some persons from treatment or whether any system which attempts to treat a majority of alcoholics should not accept the aloholic's general desire to improve his situation as sufficient, and should then itself seek to create motivation or receptiveness to cure as part of the treatment.

Several attempts have been made to provide or facilitate motivation, with notable success,[46] and studies have shown that "unreachable" and unmotivated persons can be motivated to accept treatment.[47] The apparent lack of motivation of many alcoholics therefore seems to result partly from the failure of treatment facilities to encourage alcoholics seeking treatment.[48]

A good example of the creation of motivation is found in industrial alcoholism programs. In such programs a supervisor who notices symptoms of alcoholism in an employee suggests that the employee accept treatment. If the employee does not willingly accept treatment, he is offered a choice of treatment or losing his job (generally on the grounds of poor job performance). Under such pressure 60-70 percent choose treatment and are cured (at least to the extent that they become able to function adequately in their jobs).[49] This is a much higher cure rate than is claimed by any other treatment program.

Because of a feeling that an alcoholic must be "self-motivated" in order to benefit from treatment, many experts do not believe that involuntary treatment methods can be successfully employed.[50] Yet court referrals to treatment clinics of individuals arrested for public drunkenness have in a number of instances yielded good results; in some cases involuntary (court-committed) patients in alcoholism programs have had as high a success rate as the voluntary patients.[51]

It should also be kept in mind that many so-called "voluntary" alcoholic patients have been coerced into seeking treatment by their families or employers.[52] Also most lower-class alcoholics, who tend not to be particularly verbal or "psychologically minded," are unlikely to appear "self-motivated" to most treatment professionals.[53]

In the light of the desirability of recognizing motivation where it exists—as well as in the light of a proper preference for liberty and free choice as against compulsion—alcoholism treatment legislation should express a preference for voluntary over involuntary treatment. Moreover, it is only fair to recognize that compulsory treatment for diseases or disorders is always legally and constitutionally circumscribed,[54] and that compulsory treatment is difficult to sustain as a legal matter when the success of treatment is as problematical as it still appears to be for alcoholics. Thus, while the law must provide for compulsory commitment for persons who lack the judgmental capacity to determine that they need treatment, or for persons who create a danger to their families or to the public, the major emphasis of contemporary alcoholism legislation should be on opportunities for voluntary treatment. This, indeed, has occurred in the most recently enacted alcoholism treatment laws.[55]

The emphasis on voluntariness of treatment leads as well into another direction. Past emphasis on involuntary commitment has led to stressing the inpatient hospital as primary treatment facility. There is good evidence that most alcoholics will respond to treatment as well, or even better, in an outpatient situation that does not remove them from their homes and familiar environs, and that permits them to function as well as they may be able in their jobs or occupations.[56] Since adequate social and economic functioning is a major problem of alcoholics, maintaining existing ties would seem to be particularly important. From the state's point of view, moreover, outpatient care is better because it is far less costly.[57] Treatment-oriented alcoholism legislation should, therefore, express a clear preference for outpatient treatment. This preference, too, is implicit in recent federal legislation to support the states' efforts in the provision of adequate treatment opportunities through the Community Mental Health Centers Act.[58]

THE LEGAL IMPLICATIONS OF THE CONCEPT OF "CURE" FOR ALCOHOLISM

A consideration of current treatment methods for alcoholism, and a review of treatment results lead to the conclusion, that the concept of "cure" is an inappropriate one for alcoholism programs, at least for the present. There is not, at present, any consensus on what constitutes a "cure" for alcoholism.

Traditionally, the goal of most alcoholism treatment programs was complete abstinence. Although it is still listed as the ultimate goal of many programs, including Alcoholics Anonymous,[59] it is now clear that many alcoholics can never achieve total abstinence. Although it is still widely believed that an alcoholic has only two choices—hopeless and incapacitating addiction or complete abstinence—there is an increasing amount of evidence that some alcoholics can control their drinking enough to allow them to hold a job and function within a family situation[60] and that some may even be able to return to a normal social drinking pattern.[61] In addition, merely achieving abstinence will not necessarily cure the underlying or accompanying psychological and social problems of the alcoholic, who may be just as neurotic and maladjusted when abstinent as he was when drunk.[62]

Many alcoholism programs are now revising their goals. Often improved drinking behavior and improved ability to function within a job or family is sufficient for treatment to be considered at least a partial success,[63] and an alcoholic who has been rehabilitated to this extent may today be regarded as "cured." The goals of improved drinking behavior and improved ability to function within a job or family situation are both realistic and sufficiently definite to measure success. They are also flexible enough to recognize success in terms of the particular problem of each individual alcoholic.

The clear implication of current concepts of successful treatment is that treatment legislation should not seek unrealistic goals of complete recovery or complete abstinence. Legislation should specifically recognize the high probability of relapse, for it is frequent, and relapse should not be penalized.[64] Under no circumstances should legislation respond to the problem of relapse—as indeed it does in a number of states[65]—by denying admission or readmission to treatment programs to alcoholics who have "failed" before. So, too, even alcoholics who volunteer for treatment may decide to leave a treatment institution against medical advice, and this, also, must be expected. Again, a treatment-oriented law should not deny treatment to such a lapsed alcoholic, should he again, voluntarily, seek admission.

CHAPTER 4 NOTES

1 Strong residual feelings against drinking and treatment still remain; T. PLAUT, ALCOHOL PROBLEMS 35, 36 (1967). For discussions of the history of drinking and societal attitudes toward drunkenness *see* Conger, *Perception, Learning, and Emotion: The Role of Alcohol,* 315 ANNALS 31 (1958) and NATIONAL INSTITUTE OF MENTAL HEALTH, ALCOHOL AND ALCOHOLISM 1-8 (Public Health Service Pub. No. 1640, 1968). (hereinafter cited as NIMH).

2 Powell v. Texas, 392 U.S. 514, 518, 522 (1968) ; *see* R. GLASSCOTE, T. PLAUT, D. HAMMERSLEY, F. O'NEILL, M. CHAFETZ & E. CUMMING, THE TREATMENT OF ALCOHOLISM 6-8, 13 (The Joint Information Service 1967) (hereinafter cited as GLASSCOTE).

3 78% of state mental hospitals use psychotherapy for alcoholics; Moore & Buchnan, *State Hospitals and Alcoholism: A Nation-wide Survey of Treatment Techniques and Results,* 27 Q.J. STUD. ALCOHOL 459, 461 (1966). *See* NIHM, *supra* note 1, at 33; GLASSCOTE, *supra* note 2, at 16.

4 Group therapy is very commonly chosen for treatment of alcoholics; Vogel, *Psychiatric Treatment of Alcoholism,* 315 ANNALS 99, 106 (1958) ; GLASSCOTE, *supra* note 2, at 15. "Group counselling is a practical and economical method of treating a large number of persons"; Soden, *Constructive Coercion and Group Counselling in the Rehabilitation of Alcoholics,* 30 FED. PROBATION, No. 3, Sept. 1966, at 56, 60. Group therapy has been found particularly useful in treating Skid Row alcoholics; Rubington, *The Chronic Drunkenness Offender,* 315 ANNALS 65, 66-69 (1958).

5 GLASSCOTE, *supra* note 2, at 15. For specific examples see Margolis, Krystal & Siegel, *Psychotherapy with Alcoholic Offenders,* 25 Q.J. STUD. ALCOHOL 85, 88-89 (1964) ; HARRISON TREATMENT & REHABILITATION CENTER, PROGRESS REPORT: SEPTEMBER 2 - DECEMBER 31, 1967 (UPDATE MAY 15, 1968) 6 (College of Osteopathic Medicine & Surgery, Des Moines, Iowa) ; PLAUT, *supra* note 1, at 84.

6 Moore & Buchanan, *supra* note 3, at 461. 38% of state mental hospitals include alcohol education in their treatment programs; however, some therapists have found that too much exhortation or urging of a patient to use will power can be destructive; NIMH, *supra* note 1, at 34. *See* Ingraham, *Test Class for Drunken Drivers Is Making the Grade in Phoenix,* N.Y. Times, Sept. 28, 1968, at p. 65 col. 2.

7 Moore & Buchanan, *supra* note 3, at 463. Some studies have concluded that improvement is unrelated to the amount of therapy; Robson, Paulus & Clarke, *An Evaluation of the Effect of a Clinic Treatment Program on the Rehabilitation of Alcoholic Patients,* 26 Q.J. STUD. ALCOHOL 264, 276 (1965) ; Saenger & Wile, *The Abstinent Alcoholic,* 6 ARCH. GEN. PSYCHIATRY 83, 94-95 (1962) ; Wedel, *Involving Alcoholics in Treatment,* 26 Q.J. STUD. ALCOHOL 468, 474-75 (1965). Success frequently may be due to unknown or unrelated factors; Bruun, *Outcome of Different Types of Treatment of Alcoholics,* 24 Q.J. STUD. ALCOHOL 280, 284 (1963) ; Hill & Blanc, *Evaluation of Psychotherapy with Alcoholics: A Critical Review,* 28 Q.J. STUD. ALCOHOL 76 (1967). But others have found a relationship between successful treatment and the number of therapy sessions; *e.g.,* Jackson, Fagan & Burr, *The Seattle Police Department Rehabilitation Project for Chronic Alcoholics,* 22 FED. PROBATION, No. 2, 1958, at 36, 39. One study reported that short-term therapy (1-5 sessions) can significantly help a substantial number of alcoholics; Krimmel & Falkey, *Short-term Treatment of Alcoholics,* 7 SOC. WORK 102 (1962).

8 75% of state mental hospitals use some from of psychochemotherapy; Moore & Buchanan, *supra* note 3, at 461.

9 22% of state mental hospitals use Antabuse in treating alcoholics; *id.*

10 *Hearing on H.R. 6143 Before a Subcomm. of the House Comm. on the District of Columbia*, 90th Cong., 1st Sess., at 30 (1967). Antabuse can also be used alone.

11 In a study of use of Antabuse (both voluntary and compulsory) by chronic drunkenness offenders in Atlanta, nearly 50% of the users remained abstinent over a period of nine months. Interestingly, of the voluntary users, blacks had a significantly higher success rate than whites; Bourne, *Treatment of Skid Row Alcoholics with Disulfiram*, 27 Q.J. STUD. ALCOHOL 42, 45, 47 (1966). Antabuse is sometimes administered successfully as a precondition of employment on an outpatient basis; HARRISON TREATMENT & REHABILITATION CENTER, *supra* note 5, at 7. Similarly successful results have been achieved with use as a condition of probation or parole. In a group of chronic drunkenness offenders who were ordered to take daily doses of Antabuse as a condition of suspended sentence, 46% were still taking it after nine months; Bourne, *supra* this note, at 45. *See also* PRESIDENT'S COMM'N ON LAW ENFORCEMENT & ADMINISTRATION OF JUSTICE, TASK FORCE REPORT: DRUNKENNESS 103 (1967); Davis & Ditman, *The Effect of Court Referral and Disulfiram Motivation of Alcoholics*, 24 Q.J. STUD. ALCOHOL 276, 278 (1963).

12 GLASSCOTE, *supra* note 2, at 16. There is disagreement and uncertainty as to the effectiveness of such treatment.

13 *E.g.*, reports by wives of alcoholics treated with LSD showed marked improvement by their husbands at first (as compared with a control group), but the improvement lessened after six months; Sarett, Cheek & Osmond, *Reports of Wives of Alcoholics of Effects of LSD-25 Treatment of Their Husbands*, 14 ARCH. GEN. PSYCHIATRY 171 (1966).

14 Charnoff, *Long-term Treatment of Alcoholism with Amitriptyline and Emcyclamate: A Double-blind Evaluation*, 28 Q.J. STUD. ALCOHOL 289 (1967); Van Dusen, *Treatment of Alcoholism with Lysergide*, 28 Q.J. STUD. ALCOHOL 295, 300 (1967).

15 *E.g.*, Van Dusen, *supra note* 14, at 303. Antabuse also has been said to give a patient "mental sobriety" which allows him to accept treatment.

16 *E.g.*, Bartholomew, *A Long-acting Phenothiazine in the Treatment of Alcoholics in an Outpatient Clinic*, 27 Q.J. STUD. ALCOHOL 510 (1966); Smilde, *Risks and Unexpected Reactions in Disulfiram Therapy of Alcoholism*, 24 Q.J. STUD. ALCOHOL 489-94 (1963).

17 *See* PLAUT, *supra* note 1, at 70; Lemere & Voetglin, *An Evaluation of the Aversion Treatment of Alcoholism*, 11 Q.J. STUD. ALCOHOL 199-204 (1950); *cf.* N.Y. Post, Sept. 24, 1968, at 37, col. 3.

18 PLAUT, *supra* note 1, at 70.

19 GLASSCOTE, *supra* note 2, at 16.

20 *See, e.g.*, JELLINEK, THE DISEASE CONCEPT OF ALCOHOLISM 82-110 (1960); Williams, *Identifying and Treating Potential Alcoholics*, 49 J. CRIM. L.C. & P.S. 218 (1958).

21 PLAUT, *supra* note 1, at 51.

22 A substance to which alcohol reacts specifically has been found more prevalent in alcoholics than in non-alcoholics; Armstrong, *The Search for the Alcoholic Personality*, 315 ANNALS 40, 46 (1958).

23 88% of state mental hospitals reportedly use Alcoholics Anonymous to treat alcoholics, compared to 78% that use psychotherapy; Moore & Buchanan, *supra* note 3, at 461. In 1967 there were 405 AA groups in U.S. prisons; MacCormick, *Correctional Views on Alcohol, Alcoholism, and Crime*, 9 CRIME & DELINQUENCY 15, 22 (1963). An estimate of 200,000 members was made more than a decade ago; Trice, *Alcoholics Anonymous*, 315 ANNALS 108, 111 (1958). A more recent claim is that AA has *cured* 400,000 alcoholics; Maurer, *The Beginning of Wisdom About Alcoholism*, FORTUNE, May, 1968, at 176, 211.

24 *See, e.g.*, Brown, *An Aftercare Program for Alcoholics*, 9 CRIME & DE-LINQUENCY 77, 79-83 (1963) ; Maxwell, *Alcoholics Anonymous: An Interpretation* in SOCIETY, CULTURE AND DRINKING PATTERNS 577, 581 (D. Pittman & C. Snyder eds. 1962) ; Otten, *Politics and People: Iowa's Outspoken Governor, Harold Hughes*, The Wall St. J., July 19, 1968, at 8, col. 3.

25 Brown, *supra* note 24, at 79; Palola, *Alcoholism and Suicidal Behavior* in SOCIETY, CULTURE AND DRINKING PATTERNS 511, 528 (D. Pittman & C. Snyder eds. 1962) ; Trice, *supra* note 23, at 113.

26 Pattison, *A Critique of Alcoholism Treatment Concepts*, 27 Q.J. STUD. ALCOHOL 49 (1966). All state mental hospitals averaged an improvement rate of about 33% in a recent study, but hospitals with special alcoholism programs averaged only 31% improvement; Moore & Buchanan, *supra* note 3, at 463. Industrial programs have claimed cure rates of 65-70%; however, such high rates may be in part accounted for by the fact that only employed (and therefore relatively stable and well-adjusted) alcoholics and problem drinkers enter such programs; Maurer, *supra* note 23, at 176.

27 Lemere, *What Happens to Alcoholics*, 109 AM. J. PSYCHIATRY 674 (1953).

28 *E.g.*, Bailey, *Some Issues in Epidemiologic Surveys of Alcoholism*, 57 AM. J. PUB. HEALTH 987, 988 (1967).

29 *See* Otten, *supra* note 24.

30 *E.g.*, the proposals for the District of Columbia in VISITING COMM. OF THE WASHINGTON, D.C., AREA COUNCIL ON ALCOHOLISM, FIRST REPORT ON THE CURRENT STATUS OF ALCOHOLISM PROGRAMS AND FACILITIES 47-54 (1967) (hereinafter cited as WACA).

31 *E.g.*, STEERING COMM. ON TREATMENT & REHABILITATION OF CHRONIC ALCOHOLIC COURT OFFENDERS, A COMPREHENSIVE PLAN 6 (Atlanta, Ga. 1968).

23 *E.g.*, WACA, *supra* note 30, at 32-37; Katz, *The Salvation Army Men's Social Service Center*, 25 Q.J. STUD. ALCOHOL 324, 325 (1964) ; Martinson, *The California Recovery House: A Sanctuary for Alcoholics*, 48 MENT. HYG. 432 (1964) ; Rubington, *supra* note 4, at 70-71.

33 Jackson, *Alcoholism and the Family*, 315 ANNALS 90, 91 (1958).

34 NEB. REV. STAT. 83-307.01 (1943) ; UTAH CODE ANN. 55-13-2 (1953).

35 Brown, *supra* note 24; Meyerson & Mayer, *Origins, Treatment and Destiny of Skid Row Alcoholic Men*, 19 S.C. L. REV. 332, 338 (1967) ; Trice, *supra* note 23; GLASSCOTE, *supra* note 2, at 140.

36 *E.g.*, WACA, *supra* note 30, at 31; Weil & Price, *Alcoholism in a Metropolis*, 9 CRIME & DELINQUENCY 60, 67 (1963) (day work-release program for involuntary alcoholic inpatients) ; HARRISON TREATMENT & REHABILITA-TION CENTER, *supra* note 5, at 9-10 (day-patient arrangements in inpatient facilities) ; Weil & Price, *supra* this note, at 66-67; TASK FORCE REPORT: DRUNKENNESS, *supra* note 11, at 19 (halfway houses and foster homes) ; GLAS-SCOTE, *supra* note 2, at 62 (outpatient clinics provide follow-up care for former inpatients). *Id.* (Alcoholics Anonymous for aftercare). *See also*, TASK FORCE REPORT: DRUNKENNESS, *supra* note 11, at 5.

37 One study found the number of visits to an outpatient alcoholism clinic to be related to the success of treatment, but to a lesser extent than motivation and attendance at AA meetings. In addition, 37% of those patients receiving no significant treatment at the clinic or at Alcoholics Anonymous showed improvement; Robson, Paulus & Clarke, *supra* note 7, at 274-276. Other studies report no relationship between the number of therapy sessions (over one) and success of treatment; Wedel, *supra* note 7, at 474-475. A follow-up study of alcoholics who had undergone treatment found abstinence generally unrelated to treat-ment (not caused by treatment). It also found that most of those who were abstinent were still emotionally disturbed. The authors concluded that treat-ment benefited very few patients; Saenger & Wile, *supra* note 7, at 83. One study found that among skid row men, those who were younger, better educated,

and more occupationally skilled had a better chance of successful treatment. Meyerson & Mayer, *supra* note 35, at 339-340. The amount of counselling in another project was related to success; Jackson, Fagan & Burr, *supra* note 7.

38 A survey of institutions treating alcoholism revealed that 75% felt motivation was important, and 50% thought it "absolutely essential" for successful treatment; 48% thought of motivation as a static attribute or quality which an alcoholic either had or not; Sterne & Pittman, *The Concept of Motivation: A Source of Institutional and Professional Blockage in the Treatment of Alcoholics,* 26 Q.J. STUD. ALCOHOL 41, 44-45, 48 (1965). *See* GLASSCOTE, *supra* note 2, at 16.

39 76% of one group of experts surveyed took the outcome of treatment into account in determining if a patient had been motivated; Sterne & Pittman, *supra* note 38, at 46.

40 In a survey of the staff of state mental hospital alcoholism programs, 73% blamed their "poor results" on lack of motivation of the patients, whereas only 44% blamed it on a lack of proven techniques for curing alcoholism; Moore & Buchanan, *supra* note 3, at 463. *See* Soden, *supra* note 4; GLASSCOTE, *supra* note 2, at 14-15.

41 GLASSCOTE, *supra* note 2, at 14.

42 For example, it has been found that persons arrested for public drunkenness do not admit they are alcoholics unless there has been "complete devastation" in their lives; *Social and Psychological and Demographic Characteristics of Arrested Drunk Offenders,* Ohio Dept. of Health, Alcoholism Unit. 33-34 (1967).

43 In the first of AA's "Twelve Steps," a member admits he is powerless over alcohol and that his life has become unmanageable. Often an alcoholic comes to AA as a last resort after everything else has failed. Trice, *supra* note 3, at 112, 114; PLAUT, *supra* note 1, at 80. But recently it has been reported that more alcoholics, an estimated 50% of those who join AA, join in the early and middle stages of alcoholism; Maurer, *supra* note 23, at 178.

44 Sterne & Pittman, *supra* note 38, at 53.

45 *E.g., id.* at 53-54; Soden, *supra* note 4. Only 32% of a sample of persons arrested for public drunkenness considered themselves alcoholics, although more could have been so diagnosed; Ohio Dept. of Health, Alcoholism Units supra note 42, at 31.

46 *E.g.,* Chafetz *et al., Establishing Treatment Relations with Alcoholics* 134 J. NERV. & MENT. DISEASE 395 (1962); GLASSCOTE, *supra* note 2, at 15.

47 Demone, *Experiments in Referral to Alcoholism Clinics,* 24 Q.J. STUD. ALCOHOL 495, 498-500 (1963) (experiments with women and with juvenile alcoholics); Wedel, *supra* note 7.

48 Similar effects have been observed on non-alcoholic patients in most mental health clinics, too.

49 Maurer, *supra* note 3; *see Supervisor's Guide to Alcoholism,* N.Y. Dept. of Civil Service, Dept. of Ment. Hyg., 6, 7 (1968).

50 Sterne & Pittman, *supra* note 38, at 44-45; *see* Cowen, *A Six-year Follow-up of a Series of Committed Alcoholics,* 15 Q.J. STUD. ALCOHOL 413-416 (1954).

51 Davis & Ditman, *supra* note 11; Cowen, *supra* note 50, at 416-422; Mills & Hetrick, *Treating the Unmotivated Alcoholic,* 9 CRIME & DELINQUENCY 46, 47-78; Jackson & Fagan Burr, *supra* note 7, at 38-39.

52 Strayer, *The Social Worker's Role in Handling the Resistances of the Alcoholic,* 9 CRIME & DELINQUENCY 39, 41 (1963); Soden, *supra* note 4.

53 Mills & Hetrick, *supra* note 51, at 50-51.

54 Ch. 6 *infra.*

55 D.C. CODE ANN. § 24-525 (Supp. II 1969); MD. ANN. CODE art. 2c, § 307 (Supp. 1968); VT. STAT. ANN. tit. 18 §§ 7503 8403 (1968).

56 Ch. 5 *infra.*

[57] Ch. 8 *infra*.

[58] 42 U.S.C. §§ 2681-2688q (Supp. IV 1965-1968).

[59] Bacon, *Alcoholics Do Not Drink*, 315 ANNALS 55, 56 (1958); Vogel, *supra* note 4, at 104-105.

[60] Kendell, *Normal Drinking in Former Alcohol Addicts*, 26 Q.J. STUD. ALCOHOL 247 (1965); Bailey & Stewart, *Normal Drinking by Persons Reporting Previous Problem Drinking*, 28 Q.J. STUD. ALCOHOL 305 (1967).

[61] GLASSCOTE, *supra* note 2, at 13-14.

[62] Saenger & Wile, *supra* note 7.

[63] Abstinence should not be the sole criterion for a cure. Pattison, *supra* note 26, at 65-66; GLASSCOTE, *supra* note 2, at 13.

[64] *See, e.g.*, MD. ANN. CODE art. 2c, § 304 (a) (1) (d) (Supp. 1968).

[65] ARK. STAT. ANN. § 83-713 (1960); TEX. REV. CIV. STAT. ANN. art. 5561c, Sec. 13 (Supp. 1968).

CHAPTER 5

Legal Aspects Of Voluntary Treatment

In view of the express preference for voluntary over involuntary treatment, the law should not place obstacles in the way of an alcoholic who seeks help. In actual practice, however, depending on the particular jurisdiction, an alcoholic may find that obtaining treatment for alcoholism calls for much more procedural effort than, say, obtaining treatment for an intestinal ailment or a broken limb. The main difference appears to be that the person with the ulcer is accepted as a patient, free to leave the hospital where he enjoys guest status, while traditionally—and presently still in many jurisdictions—the situation of the alcoholic who seeks voluntary treatment is analogized to that of the mentally ill person who is not simply a patient, but who must "commit" himself in order to get treatment.[1] While there appears to be some difference of opinion on the subject, most persons involved in the treatment of alcoholics seem to prefer ordinary patient "guest" status for alcoholics in treatment institutions, with formal application, restraints on leaving the institution and limits on the patient's freedom of movement reduced to a minimum.[2]

Most of the legal limitations on voluntary treatment deal with inpatient treatment. There are hardly any restrictions on voluntary treatment as on outpatients in a clinic or similar open facility, for all that the law needs to do in that context is to authorize the facilities and the service, and to provide the appropriations necessary for their management.

The subject of "motivation" and its relationship to treatment for alcoholism has been referred to earlier.[3] It is clear that most alcoholics have great personal barriers to overcome before they will take steps to seek treatment, and most of them need encouragement and personal support before they will take decisive action. Any legal barriers and any procedural obstacles placed in their way will not only discourage the alcoholics themselves, but will ultimately have

adverse effects on the state's program. The alcoholic who is discouraged too long from seeking voluntary treatment is likely to need
involuntary treatment in the future—when he will have further
deteriorated, and when treatment is likely to be more difficult, less
hopeful, more prolonged and, therefore, more expensive. Consequently, the admission process should actively encourage alcoholics to
proceed to treatment, and should insure that anyone who may benefit
from treatment will be admitted.

APPLICATION FOR TREATMENT

More than half the states, including most of those which provide
for involuntary commitment, expressly provide by law for the admission of voluntary patients to inpatient institutions, and, in addition, there are several states that admit voluntary patients under
departmental regulations based on general legal powers.[4] The relevant
legal provisions usually set out where application for treatment is
made, and provide in some instances for conditions or standards that
must be met for voluntary admissions. Some states also set out the
minimum which the applicant must agree to stay.

In most states requests for treatment may be made either to the
alcoholism division or other responsible agency,[5] or directly to a
particular state facility.[6] In two states applications can be addressed
to either,[7] and in a few states applications must, or may be made to
the court.[8] Where courts are involved in the procedure, admissions
usually take the form of voluntary commitment. Application to the
court, even if the proceduce involves only formal filing of papers, is
unnecessarily rigid, and because it is complex and foreboding it is
likely to discourage applicants; it should be eliminated as serving no
useful purpose. Application to a division of alcoholism may enhance
the likelihood of proper matching of treatment facility and program
to the patient's needs, if there is more than one facility available.
On the other hand, application to the facility is the most direct
method; it is likely, moreover, to provide the quickest action. It is
desirable that voluntary applicants be permitted to apply directly
to any facility, but the division should be authorized to transfer
patients within the system so as to accomplish a proper matching of
patient needs to available programs.

A few states require that a voluntary application be accompanied
by a medical affidavit or other written evidence that the person is
competent to make the request and that he is an alcoholic.[9] Some

states seek to limit voluntary commitments by providing that admission shall be allowed only if the person is unable to care for himself and is a burden to the public;[10] or "if the person is suitable and it is in his best interests"[11] or "if the person is in need of care and treatment."[12] Two states go so far as to permit a refusal of admission if the person has been discharged from treatment within the last 12 months.[13] The provision that allows admission only if the patient is a "burden on the public" is clearly too restrictive. Suitability and need of treatment are relevant standards in determining who should be admitted, but these matters should be determined after diagnosis at the treatment facility, rather than in advance of admission. The imposition of prerequisites will work only to discourage application. So, too, requirements for medical certifications may be justifiable as screening devices, but they too make admission cumbersome and in most instances they do not provide the facility with information which it could not obtain more effectively through its own observation and diagnosis. Admissions provisions should not require prior examination or rigid classification. An effective voluntary admission law should provide that any applicant can be admitted for diagnosis and evaluation as well as for treatment, and it should authorize the administrator of the facility to discharge a patient whenever he deems it appropriate.

DURATION OF VOLUNTARY INPATIENT TREATMENT

Many states require that a person who has applied for inpatient care remain for a period specified in the law, ranging from 13 days to 4 months,[14] or for a period of time set by the court.[15] Some states which require voluntary commitment for a specified time permit a patient to leave on notice after a waiting time from 3 to 15 days, though the most common provision allows him to leave 10 days after he has given notice.[16]

To assure a meaningful opportunity for treatment success, the patient's agreement to stay for a predetermined length of time may make good sense—but it is likely that the requirement of an advance agreement to stay for a specified time deters many applicants. Moreover, in many states the requirement of notice and waiting period prior to release is a transparent device to allow enough time to permit the state to obtain a court order for a patient's involuntary commitment. The convenience of the state is not a sufficient reason for detaining a voluntary patient against his will. Voluntary admission and release procedures should parallel normal hospital procedures; the patient arrives and departs at will, subject at most to minor delays resulting from administrative considerations.

REGULATING DEMANDS FOR TREATMENT

Although ideally any alcoholic should be allowed to apply for treatment wherever and whenever he wishes, it is clear that existing facilities are inadequate to meet the needs of an estimated 5 to 6 million alcoholics.[17] Existing statutes seldom make any explicit provision for allocation of resources—a few states specify that admissions for voluntary patients should be according to division policies[18] or rules[19] or that there must be adequate facilities[20] or that space must be available before patients are accepted;[21] Virginia suggests that admission to its university-related facility be limited to those persons to whom care is of value or whose treatment will serve research purposes.[22] The recent District of Columbia law specifically provides that preference be given to voluntary patients unless the involuntarily committed person is found dangerous.[23]

Although it is a difficult task, some standards must be set to determine whose needs will be served first when the demand for services exceeds the supply. The method which presently seems to be used in many states is to accept applicants in the order of application.[24] This seems simple on its face, but if the state runs several different treatment programs and wants to assign patients to the program best suited to these needs, even this approach can become unworkable. Another choice in regulating admissions is to allow each facility to make decisions on a case-to-case basis, but this will impede effective coordination and a unified approach. It may be suggested that legislative priorities for admission, requiring the alcoholism division to establish rules regulating admissions within the legislature guide lines, should be considered. Even though such rules may to some extent rigidify a treatment system, the requirement that priorities be established compels a consideration of the purposes of an alcoholism program and an evaluation of the allocation of its resources.

Some of the legislative guidelines suggested have already been discussed: there should be a preference for outpatient treatment and for voluntary treatment, and persons should not be denied treatment because they suffered a relapse or left earlier treatment against medical advice. It would also be possible to provide for a preference for alcoholics who have lost control over drinking over other alcoholics in order to insure care for those who are most in need, and for the law to require special preference for young persons, persons with dependents, and persons whose prospects for successful treatment are good over persons who are the older, less likely to cause serious damage to the lives of others, and less likely to benefit from treatment.[25] To avoid an overly rigid system of priorities, these ought to be incorporated in departmental regulations that may be changed from time to time to reflect available treatment resources. Ultimately, the aim of a treatment law should be to provide treatment to all alcoholics who seek it and who may benefit from it. The problem of treatment priorities is a difficult one that deserves further study before rigid treatment categories are frozen into law. Broad guidelines and flexible departmental regulations would provide an opportunity to test a variety of approaches.

CHAPTER 5 NOTES

[1] *E.g.,* KAN. STAT. ANN. § 74-4410 (1953); N.M. STAT. ANN. § 46-12-9 (1949); *see* Appendix C, Chart I, *esp.* n. 6.

[2] Ch. 4 *supra.*

[3] *Id.*

[4] *See* Appendix B, Charts I, III.

[5] *E.g.,* ARK. REV. STAT. § 83-713 (1960); CONN. GEN. STAT. ANN. § 17-155e (Supp. 1969); GA. CODE ANN. § 88-409 (Supp. 1968); HAWAII REV. STAT. § 334-52 (1968); N.H. REV. STAT. ANN. § 172:13 (Supp. 1967); R.I. GEN. LAWS ANN. § 40-12-14 (1956); TEX. REV. CIV. STAT. ANN. art. 5561c, Sec. 13 (Supp. 1968); VT. STAT. ANN. tit. 18, § 8459 (a) (1968); WASH. REV. CODE ANN. § 70.96.100 (1962); W. VA. CODE ANN. § 27-1A-11 (1966). *See* Appendix B, Chart III.

[6] *E.g.,* CONN. GEN. STAT. ANN. § 17-155j (Supp. 1969); MASS. GEN. LAWS ANN. ch. 111, § 4C (1967); MINN. STAT. ANN. § 253A.03 (2) (Supp. 1969); MONT. REV. CODES ANN. § 38-406 (1961); N.Y. MENTAL HYGIENE LAW § 306 (McKinney Supp. 1968); N.C. GEN. STAT. § 122-56 (1964); N.D. CENT. CODE § 25-03-01 (1960); TENN. CODE ANN. § 33-806 (Supp. 1968). *See* Appendix B, Chart III.

[7] IND. ANN. STAT. § 22-1504 (1957); IOWA CODE ANN. § 229.41, 42 (Supp. 1969).

[8] *E.g.,* KY. REV. STAT. § 222.180 (1) (1959); PA. STAT. ANN. tit. 50, § 2105 (a) (Supp. 1969); WIS. STAT. ANN. § 51.09 (3) (Supp. 1969). *See* Appendix B, Chart III.

[9] *E.g.,* KY. REV. STAT. § 222.150 (1959) (medical statement by licensed physician that applicant is an alcoholic and mentally competent); WIS. STAT. ANN. § 51.09 (3) (Supp. 1969) (certificate that confinement advisable for health and for public welfare). *See* Appendix B, Chart III.

[10] MASS. GEN. LAWS ANN. ch. 111, § 4C (1967).

[11] N.Y. MENTAL HYGIENE LAW § 306 (McKinney Supp. 1968) ("found suitable for care and treatment"); VA. CODE ANN. § 32-374 (1969) (". . .care will be of value both individually and/or for research purposes").

[12] *E.g.,* PA. STAT. ANN. tit. 50, § 2105 (a) (Supp. 1969) (". . .in need of care and will benefit from such treatment").

[13] ARK. STAT. ANN. § 83-713 (1960); TEX. REV. CIV. STAT. ANN. art. 5561c, Sec. 13 (Supp. 1968).

14 *E.g.,* HAWAII REV. STAT. § 334-52 (1968) (agree to remain for not less than 90 days); N.H. REV. STAT ANN. § 172:13 (I) (Supp. 1967) (not less than 60 days or more than 1 year); MONT. REV. CODES ANN. § 38-406 (1961) (at least 4 months but early release); N.Y. MENTAL HYGIENE LAW § 306 (McKinney Supp. 1968) (15 days, maximum consecutive 12 months); PA. STAT. ANN. tit. 50, § 2107 (1954) (1 year or earlier); WASH. REV. CODE ANN. § 70.96.100 (1962) (120 days if required by dept.). *See* Appendix B, Chart III.

15 *E.g.,* KY. REV. STAT. ANN. § 222.180 (1962). *See* Appendix B, Chart III.

16 *E.g.,* ARK. REV. STAT. § 83-713 (1960) (10 days notice); CONN. GEN. STAT. ANN. § 17-155j (Supp. 1969) (10 days notice); GA. CODE ANN. § 88-409 (Supp. 1968) (15 days notice); IOWA CODE ANN. § 229.41 (Supp. 1969) (3 days notice); MASS. GEN. LAWS ANN. ch. 123, § 86 (1965) (3 days notice); MINN. STAT. ANN. § 253A.03 (2) (Supp. 1969) (3 days notice); N.C. GEN. STAT. § 122-56 (1964) (10 days notice but can require 30 days agreement at admission); N.D. CENT. CODE § 25-03-06 (1960) (5 days notice); TEX. REV. CIV. STAT. ANN. art. 5561c, Sec. 13 (Supp. 1968) (10 days notice). *See* Appendix B, Chart III.

17 PRESIDENT'S COMM'N ON LAW ENFORCEMENT & ADMINISTRATION OF JUSTICE, TASK FORCE REPORT: DRUNKENNESS 30 (1967).

18 R.I. GEN. LAWS ANN. § 40-12-13 (1956).

19 *E.g.,* N.H. REV. STAT. ANN. § 172:131 (1964); N.D. CENT. CODE §§ 25-03-02, 54-38-08 (1957); VT. STAT. ANN. tit. 18, § 8459 (a) (1968); VA. CODE ANN. §§ 32-373, 374 (1969).

20 *E.g.,* IOWA CODE ANN. § 229.41 (Supp. 1969).

21 *E.g.,* MASS. GEN. LAWS ANN. ch. 123, § 86 (1965).

22 VA. CODE ANN. §§ 32-373, 374 (1969).

23 D.C. CODE ANN. § 24-525 (1967).

24 *See* Appendix C, Chart II.

25 Such a guideline, if adopted, should not be interpreted to focus treatment on "nice" alcoholics; it would merely reflect a determination that the choices which must be made will weigh relative benefits to the individual and society.

CHAPTER 6

Involuntary Treatment For The Alcoholic; Grounds For Commitment And Other Emergency Measures

It is a paradox that in a work that advocates voluntary treatment of alcoholics in preference to involuntary treatment, the largest number of pages should be devoted to the subject of involuntary commitment. Yet the reasons for this seeming inconsistency are not hard to find. Involuntary treatment has been the traditional legal response to much deviant behavior, including drug addiction, sexual psychopathy and alcoholism. Moreover, involuntary treatment for any behavioral disorder invariably involves a conflict between treatment considerations on the one hand, and the constitutionally protected values of individual liberty and free choice on the other.

Involuntary commitment to an institution is similar in many respects to a prison sentence. It deprives the person committed of his personal liberty, it subjects him to a routine and regimen not of his own choosing, and it places the decision of his release to rejoin society in the hands of others. Moreover, unlike the case of a person convicted of a crime, the person committed to an institution for treatment is deprived of his liberty not because he has harmed society by breaking its laws, but rather because he is ill—and because in somebody else's judgment, his illness creates a risk. Unlike the "prisoner," who can look forward to release when he has served his sentence, the committed "patient" has no such assurance—he may be held until, in somebody else's judgment, he is well again, or at least sufficiently well to reduce the risk of leaving him at large.

The only justification for depriving a person who has not committed a criminal offense of his liberty is that the risk of leaving him at large is substantial, and that everything will be done to make him well again so that his liberty may again be restored to him. The law surrounds all deprivations of liberty by the state with considerable constitutional safeguards, and an important preliminary question that must be posed in connection with the involuntary commitment of alcoholics is whether substantial numbers of them ever do create any major risk to society so as to justify their commitment—and so as to justify, too, legislative emphasis on the involuntary treatment of alcoholics.

In spite of the need for substantial legal grounds for the deprivation of an alcoholic's liberty, commitment laws have generally failed to spell out clear guidelines, and often are quite vague.

In reaching a decision about the circumstances that justify the commitments of alcoholics, it is instructive to examine the criteria and objectives of existing commitment laws, as well as the legal and constitutional limitations on the use of involuntary confinements generally. Such a study clarifies the need for carefully drawn statutes which authorize commitment only when deprivation of liberty and compulsory treatment are fully justified by the circumstances.

THE BACKGROUND—SOCIAL CONTROL OF THE BEHAVIORALLY DISORDERED

The evident symptom of any behavioral disorder—be it drug addiction, sexual psychopathy or alcoholism—is conduct which oversteps the line of socially accepted norms. The traditional method of dealing with persons who transgress in this fashion has been the penal law.

Penal law specifies what conduct is prohibited and what sanctions will be imposed if the prohibitions are violated. All penal sanctions include a punitive ingredient and a consequent social stigma;[1] in most instances the sanction is a deprivation of liberty through incarceration. Application of the penal law requires that no accused person's liberty be restrained unless he is convicted of a crime in a proceeding characterized by due process, which is composed of an expanding list of procedural safeguards.[2]

Penal law, however, does not include in its prohibitions all behavior which violates society's norms, nor can all persons be held responsible for transgressions of the criminal law. Moreover, there are persons, who, though technically within the purview of the penal law, should not be dealt with (in the view of some) by invoking penal sanctions. The legislative response to persons who offend social norms but are not, or should not be, criminally prosecuted increasingly has been to provide for what may be generalized as status adjudication. A status adjudication is simply a determination that a person comes within a legislatively established class. Existing legal provisions for status adjudications share the theoretical absence of a punitive ingredient, the frequent substitution of "treatment" for correctional sanctions, and the frequent practical consequence of a deprivation of liberty through civil commitment.[3]

The underlying theoretical framework for status adjudication and resulting civil commitment has been discussed extensively. The point of departure for the examination, however, is to look at the major groups of persons subject to status adjudication and to see in each instance the reason for resort to this device.

There are presently laws which provide for status adjudication and civil commitment in the case of the mentally ill, the sexual psychopaths, the narcotic addicts and alcoholics. This listing generally reflects the order in which the procedures were adopted.

What all of these groups share is the fact that there is no assured "cure" for any of their maladies or disorders,[5] that for most of them there are few reliable treatment methods and often fewer facilities.[6] This is important since all civil commitment laws have, in at least some degree, the avowed goal of helping, curing, or rehabilitating the subject.[7] Of course, in each instance in which civil commitment is used the underlying behavior gives rise to fear, so that the public draws comfort from the fact that the afflicted individuals are not only treated, but are being removed so as to pose no further threat. Indeed, it has been said that such legislation is "felicitous," because it satisfies strivings of both the treatment minded and the punishment minded.[8]

Mental Illness

Confinement of the mentally ill has a long history; it is a history that precedes both the establishment of special institutions for confinement and the emergence of effective, or in fact, any treatment methods.[9] The initial purpose of restraint of the mentally ill was at best clear-cut —it was a removal of the "furiously insane" and those who were deemed "dangerous to be permitted at large."[10] The typical place of confinement was the local jail, or for the affluent, strong rooms, cellars, and outhouses.[11] At a somewhat later point, the laws expanded to allow institutionalization of the poor, but less dangerously insane;[12] they were confined with other paupers, rogues and vagabonds at almshouses and asylums, undoubtedly as much for pauperism as for illness.[13]

Finally, increased knowledge led to the establishment of special institutions for "lunatics" and insane persons. As treatment methods were developed, the purposes of confinement shifted from mere restraint to an interest in helping and rehabilitating the afflicted.[14] The dominant philosophy was that the mentally ill should be treated and cared for, regardless of their expressed wishes. Thus, institutional confinements came to replace restraint for all mentally ill persons who were adjudged in need of hospitalization.

The goals of present laws for the confinement of the mentally ill are either protective of the public—removal of the dangerous—or beneficent—treatment for persons in need of care. The express goals vary from state to state, and current legal criteria for commitment are neither clear nor uniform. For example, new laws in two states allow commitment on a mere showing that a person is "insane or suffering from a mental disease";[15] in another state a person can be committed if he is "in need of care and treatment"[16] and "mentally ill to a degree which warrants hospitalization."[17] One state has adopted the more restrictive rule that a commitment can be obtained only if the person "because of his illness or retardation is likely to injure himself or others if allowed to remain at liberty."[18] A comprehensive survey undertaken some years ago suggests that in five states dangerousness is the sole criterion for confinement; in seven the only criterion is the need for care and treatment; in twelve states either criterion will suffice; and in six states no criteria are set out.[19]

Sexual Psychopathy

Commitment for the disorders of psychopathy and drug addiction does not have the long history of confinements for mental illness. However, the statutes providing for civil commitments in these cases reflect the same lack of clarity and diversity of objectives as the laws relating to the mentally ill.

There are essentially two types of statutes which reflect somewhat different goals. The most common type comes into operation either after criminal conviction, or less frequently, after a criminal charge has been lodged. In either instance the crime usually is a sex crime. Sexual psychopathy laws provide for treatment rather than imprisonment in the case of the convicted offender, and for treatment in lieu of continued criminal prosecution in the case of the offender who has merely been charged.[20] Such statutes reflect an interest in removing from the criminal process those who should be subject to special treatment rather than correction; yet especially since there are few facilities and inadequate treatment methods, it is clear that the substitution of treatment for punishment is not the sole motivation. One commentator related that in Indiana the legislative enactment

> . . . was the direct result of almost mass hysteria following a series of murders. . . . The newspapers and radios kept the public fully informed . . . providing the impression that sex fiends lurked in every doorway.[21]

The "advantage" these statutes offer for the punishment minded is that confinement is usually indefinite—until cure is effected.[22]

A few statutes, however, do not require the commission of any overt act, but authorize the commitment of a person upon a mere showing of sexual psychopathy (however defined) and the likelihood of "danger" arising from it.[23] The underlying problem which these laws attempt to meet is protection of the public through removal of persons considered dangerous; but of course these laws repeat the benevolent verbiage which emphasizes treatment purposes.

Narcotic Addiction

Although provision for confinement of drug addicts is not entirely new, the more recent enactments are of special interest.[24] The recent enactments are typically comprehensive, providing in part that addicts who are charged with certain crimes may volunteer for treatment or may upon conviction be committed for treatment.[25] Of special interest and relevance here are the statutory provisions that persons can be adjudicated addicts and committed even though they are neither charged with nor convicted of crimes.[26] The nice mixture of benign treatment motives and the plain fear of the addict as a potentially dangerous person is neatly reflected in the statement of legislative intent that forms part of California's law:

> It is the intent of the Legislature that persons addicted to narcotics. . . shall be treated for such condition and its underlying causes, and that such treatment shall be carried out for non-punitive purposes not only for protection of the addict. . . against himself, but also for the prevention of contamination of others and the protection of the public. . . Persons committed. . . who are uncooperative with efforts to treat them or are otherwise unresponsive to treatment nevertheless should be kept in the program for the purpose of control.[27]

Alcoholism

As in the case of the mentally ill, the sexual psychopath and the drug addict, commitment laws for alcoholism are not uniform or consistent in purpose, but rather display a similar joinder of the goals of public protection and benevolent treatment of the person affected.

Laws which govern involuntary commitment generally contain provisions on permissible grounds for commitment, commitment procedures, duration of commitment, and place of commitment. Often these provisions form a part of the general mental health laws, and frequently the provisions for the commitment of alcoholics parallel the law on commitments for mental illness.[28] Occasionally the same provisions relate to alcoholics and drug addicts.[29] A detailed schematic analysis of commitment laws may be found in Appendix B. The purposes of the law are generally implicit in the stated grounds for commitment.

In general, the grounds for commitment either emphasize the risk of harm to others by such general standards as "danger,"[30] "protection of society;"[31] or they emphasize the alcoholic's own impairment, "unable to conduct himself or his affairs,"[32] "loss of self-control,"[33] or "needs care."[34] The laws are often quite unclear whether the requirements of risk and impairment are cumulative or alternative. In addition to the risk of danger and impairment criteria, a few states require evidence that the treatment will benefit the alcoholic.[35] Finally, in some states any "alcoholic" can be committed though, as previously shown, the definitions of the term vary widely;[36] in most, in order to authorize his commitment, the person must meet the applicable definition of "alcoholic"[37] and must also evidence some other enumerated characteristics that point to danger or impairment.[38]

Kansas furnishes an example of a comprehensive provision for civil commitment which includes most of the concepts of language used in whole or in part in other states. To commit an individual in Kansas, it must be shown:

> . . . that such a person is an alcoholic, is a resident of the county, is over eighteen years of age and is not capable of or is unfit properly to conduct himself, or to conduct and look after his affairs, or is dangerous to himself, or others, or has lost the power of self-control because of a periodic use of alcohol. Such a petition or application must show that the alleged alcoholic is in actual need of care and treatment and that his detention, care and treatment. . . would improve his health.[39]

Specific criteria for involuntary commitment are needed, but this mixed bag of alternative and cumulative criteria is unsatisfactory. To justify a person's deprivation of liberty, good intentions to improve his health are irrelevant—after all, the chain smoker is not confined to stop him from smoking, nor is the obese person civilly committed to reduce his weight. To be sure, the alcoholic is more troublesome, but provisions for commitment cannot be justified if it merely is a method for removing those who are bothersome and annoying.

The criteria for commitment in existing alcoholism statutes thus tend to be vague and confused. There appear to have been no substantial challenges to the grounds for alcoholism commitments in the recent past—for if there had been, it is very doutful whether many such statutes could have survived a well-made constitutional attack.

LEGAL LIMITATIONS ON INVOLUNTARY COMMITMENT

As a general rule, the need for care and treatment alone cannot serve as a basis for commitment. That is, just as the law recognizes no power in the state to order a person suffering from cancer, or heart disease, or any other non-communicable physical ailment, to undergo care or treatment,[40] there is no reason to find that the state has the power to compel a person whose illness is not physical to undergo treatment—or institutional confinement.

But the prohibition against compulsory care or treatment is not absolute. First there is a long-standing tradition of supervision of incompetents stemming from the powers of the feudal lord to assume jurisdiction over the person and property of one unable to manage his own affairs.[41] This power of the state as *parens patriae* gives it control over those who, because of mental illness, infancy, or other cause, are deemed unable to make a rational decision about their need for care,[42] and under this power it may compel treatment for those who need it.[43] This justifies some instances of involuntary commitment for the mentally disordered and for alcoholics.

Second, because of the high value placed on life, there is some authority which suggests that treatment can be compelled when there is imminent danger to the life itself,[44] but the authority for commitments under these circumstances is scant, inconclusive and unreliable.

Moreover, quite apart from the alcoholic's need for care and treatment, society has the clear right to protect itself. The police power enables the state to confine or otherwise regulate a person who presents a danger to the health, safety or welfare of others,[45] even when such person has not violated any law. For example, the police power is a proper base for civil restraint of those who are ill with communicable diseases.[46]

. Legislative constraints, as well as court decisions, however, have been relied on in an indiscriminate and sometimes improper mixture of grounds for commitment. Judicial opinions often reflect a merging of separate purposes, some of which are, and some of which may not be, individually valid. For example, an older case notes:

> Nothing can be clearer than the duty of the state to restrain and confine the insane, not only for their own safety and protection, but for the safety and protection of the public. . . .[47]

Likewise, a recent case upholding narcotic addiction commitment in New York states:

> The enforced separation of narcotic addicts from the general population is the only humane and benevolent means to succor and rescue these victims from the mire of their own mental and physical deterioration, while at the same time protect the bulk of our citizenry from the perils of the depredation of those uncontrolled and insatiable needs for drugs.[48]

Thus, in the individual case it may be impossible to determine whether the person was committed because the court decided that he was a danger to the public, or merely because the court thought that treatment would be good for him.

The confusion stems from the fact that the behaviorally disordered who present a danger to society are often persons who also need care and treatment. Moreover, an illness which goes untreated is likely to cause some danger to the victim, and some persons who are in need of treatment are also likely to present some danger to society. Further, the general tendency to conformity supports the removal of all deviants from society. And finally, the humane urge to help those who need care is intensified when failure to do so may create even a remote chance of injury to the public. All this has been merged in laws that base a deprivation of liberty on the dual grounds of protection and benevolence.

Involuntary treatment can today be legally justified only 1) if the alcoholic or other behaviorally disordered person needs treatment and his mental processes are so impaired that he cannot recognize his need, or 2) if his conduct is such as to present a clear danger to society. It has been suggested that a person who is physically or mentally so deteriorated that his life is in immediate danger also may be committed, but this point of view is not likely to be upheld.

A person who may need care but is not so dangerous as to be adjudged a danger to society, nor so deprived of "judgment" as to be found unable to make a rational decision, may not be committed, even though some elements of danger to others and to self, and some damage to judgmental capacity are present. The idea that some risk to society, or slight judgmental impairment, are insufficient to authorize compulsory treatment may be disturbing to treatment-minded persons, because often treatment may be more successful before the condition reaches the stage where any of the proper bases for commitment may be invoked.

Recent Supreme Court cases provide an instructive framework for considering when civil commitment is permissible. The emphasis is increasingly on strict procedural due process, and the cases clearly indicate that the Court will no longer permit civil commitment based solely on the expression of benevolent treatment purposes. In *Robinson v. California*,[50] the Court suggests a broad endorsement of the use of civil commitment in lieu of criminal prosecution of addicts, although it was not an issue in that case.[51] In *Lynch v. Overholser*,[52] involving a commitment after acquittal based on lack of responsibility, the Court, on very technical procedural grounds, struck down the challenged commitment, and indicated a sense of discomfort with the practical aspects of civil restraint,[53] seeking practical distinction between penal confinement and civil commitment. Moreover, in three other recent cases, the Court struck down commitments in decisions which, like *Lynch,* rested on particular procedural deficiencies.[54] Finally, in the *Powell* case,[55] where again confinement was not in issue, but where the alternative of civil commitment laws was very much in the Court's mind, there is a warning against "hanging a new sign reading 'Hospital' over one wing of the jail house"[56] as well as a suggestion that a "coherent approach"[57] providing effective treatment might more readily lead to the abandonment of penal sanctions.

The Concept of Danger as a Basis for Commitment

There is common agreement that danger to the public is a proper criterion for commitment. The difficulty is to determine what kind of behavior is encompassed within the term, or under what circumstances can a person be considered dangerous? It would be easy to say that any threatened conduct that would violate criminal law constitutes sufficient "danger" to justify commitment—but obviously not all illegal conduct poses sufficient danger for preventive confinement. The person who is shown to be likely to stab or assault another is clearly dangerous. Is the person who is likely to forge a $20 check, however, so dangerous to society as to justify commitment? And what about the person who is merely likely to loiter or panhandle? Unfortunately, court decisions are not very helpful in giving content to the concept of danger for two reasons: testimony in support of commitment is not always fully reported, and, as has been pointed out earlier, commitments frequently are ordered on multiple grounds. It is often difficult, therefore, to determine whether in a given case the evidence of danger alone would have been sufficient for commitment, absent testimony concerning a need for treatment.

Some instances where courts have held proof of danger insufficient are: where the only deficiency recorded was "strange fancies,"[58] where the proof showed only poetical mysticism and nuisance but no hallucinations, homicidal or suicidal tendencies,[59] where the proof of danger was that the intelligence level of the subject was that of a 6-year old,[60] where there was "only a possibility" of danger[61] and, finally, where the subject was just a "weak and unfortunate" habitual drunkard.[62]

Examples of cases where courts accepted the evidence as sufficient to prove danger are: where the person had previously been convicted of larceny and robbery, and while institutionalized had been disciplined for fighting, possession of contraband and for homosexual activity,[63] where the person shot a fellow student, and was found to be delusional and probably hallucinating,[64] and where the person had committed a robbery and an assault and was likely to repeat the conduct.[65]

The cases have been uniform in finding danger where there had been aggressive, assaultive behavior[66] accompanied by evidence of likelihood that the conduct would be repeated. Courts have not found danger where there had been a mere showing of eccentricity but no commission of a specific aggressive act.[67] Decided cases fail, however, to answer the difficult question whether persons who are likely to commit only property damage or crimes that cause no actual harm but consist mainly of annoying conduct are sufficiently "dangerous" to justify commitment.[68] Some years ago, in a case in which the Supreme Court upheld Minnesota's sexual psychopathy law, the Court gave a broad sweep to the danger concept.[69] Danger under that state's sexual psychopathy statute as interpreted by the state court was apparently proven by evidence that persons, as a result of "utter lack of control" of sexual impulses, were:

> likely to attack or otherwise inflict injury, loss, pain, or other evil on the objects of their uncontrolled and uncontrollable desire.[70]

The opinion clearly covers the real danger of sexually assaultive behavior, but it may also suggest that the threat of *any* illegal behavior will prove danger sufficient to justify commitment once a person has been shown to suffer from sexual psychopathy.

Except in cases involving a threat of physical assault, it is difficult to assess who may be considered dangerous. There is support for the view that the concept should always be limited to physical assault-ivenness, since non-penal confinement was initially used only for restraint of the violent,[71] and since "society's interest in preserving property is not great enough to justify confining someone solely on a prediction that he is likely to damage property."[72] On the other hand, there may be broader implications arising from the decision on the Minnesota law,[73] possibly supporting the view that since a behavioral disorder has been shown, a wide variety of lesser threats may suffice to justify commitment; such a reading of the decision is possible, but would be both unfortunate and out of keeping with contemporary attitudes.

A statute which offers danger to the public as a ground for commitment should state explicitly what is to be considered dangerous conduct. If it does not, it is probable that the statute will not be uniformly applied. It is possible, moreover, that a statute which allows for commitment based on proof of danger without any greater specificity can be attacked as being void for vagueness.

Finally, regardless of what may suffice as proof that a particular individual creates danger to the public, it is not acceptable to categorize an entire class of persons as "dangerous" for commitment purposes without evidence that the particular member of the class presents a risk. For example, a recent scientific discovery links certain abnormal genetic patterns and violent crimes.[74] Nevertheless, a law providing for the commitment of persons with this specific genetic defect, prior to any manifestation of antisocial or criminal behavior, and in the absence of evidence of the particular individual's posing any danger to the public, would not be upheld.[75] Yet the laws which allow commitment for narcotics addiction seem to point the other way. Commitment laws for drug addicts may be distinguished, however, from laws authorizing commitment of other special classes of persons, such as alcoholics. The basis for the distinction is as follows: (1) there is a legal prohibition against the use of narcotics; (2) any person found to be an addict must have violated the prohibition; (3) any violation of the law is proof of danger.[76] The syllogism is lopsided but thus far seems to have sufficed as a rationale for addict commitment statutes. It would not, however, well support a commitment statute which equated alcoholism with dangerousness, simply because the consumption of alcoholic beverages is not itself a crime.

Membership in a class of behaviorally disordered persons coupled with the danger that the individual member creates for the public, has, on the other hand, been quite clearly accepted as a ground for commitment by the Supreme Court. In the case[77] discussed earlier, where an argument against classification under the Minnesota sexual psychopathy statute was made, the Court responded:

> As we have often said, the legislature is free to recognize degrees of harm, and it may confine its restrictions to those classes of cases where the need is deemed to be clearest.[78]

Classification for purposes of commitment of a particular group of persons as dangerous to society is also justified by the need for providing them with special facilities. The Supreme Court has indirectly suggested this:

> . . . classification of mentally ill persons as either insane or dangerously insane of course may be a reasonable distinction for purposes of determining the type of custodial or medical care. . . .[79]

Clearly, any law that makes provisions for the commitment of alcoholics cannot rest on an assumption that all alcoholics are dangerous—because this assumption is not borne out by the facts—nor should it merely provide for commitment on proof of "danger" without further amplification of proof of danger to the public that will meet the objective.

Impairment of Judgmental Capacity and the Need for Treatment

Just as in the case of commitments based on danger to the public, there has been little discussion of the precise boundaries of impairment of judgmental capacity as a ground for commitment. In this instance, however, the problem is different. Judgmental impairment, unlike danger, is primarily a matter for medical determination—the law can decide what conduct is sufficiently dangerous to justify commitment, but it cannot, except in a very general fashion, describe when a person has or lacks the capacity for decision-making. If a person's mental state is such that he believes himself sane but suffers from the delusion that others are plotting against him, then he may be a proper subject for commitment.[80] On the other hand, refusal to undergo treatment for a disorder should not alone be proof of the requisite judgmental impairment. There are, after all, many fully accountable persons who refuse treatment for physical ailments for a variety of reasons— including religious ones—and no compulsion is exercised to compel a cure. Moreover, a distinction should be made between those who have lost control of certain of their actions and those who have lost control and are unable to recognize that they need treatment or supervision.[81] Both the "peeping Tom" who cannot stop looking and the gambler who cannot stop gambling show evidence of loss of control, but neither has necessarily lost his ability to decide about his need for treatment.[82] Similarly, the alcoholic who is unfit to regulate his own conduct or to attend to his affairs is not necessarily a person whose judgment is impaired.[83] A statute cannot attempt to describe the precise nature of the evidence upon which the medical determination of judgmental incapacity should be made except to require more than the existence of an illness coupled with a refusal to undergo treatment. On the other hand, evidence of total disorientation may not be necessary before commitment is justified.

When impairment of judgmental capacity, rather than danger to others is the ground for commitment, some showing ought to be required that the person to be committed is indeed capable of benefiting from treatment—otherwise there would be no justification for detaining him. This point will again be considered in Chapter 7, in the context of the discussion of "right to treatment."

Danger to Self

Danger to self is a fairly frequent statutory ground for civil commitment, but in spite of this, it is unlikely that, as a general rule, it can provide a constitutionally valid base. In the special circumstances where it may do so, the danger must be imminent. There are cases which uphold compulsory treatment for children,[84] but because children are by definition incapable of making legally binding decisions and because they are specially protected by law, these do not seem relevant to setting adult standards.

The only affirmative support for the doctrine of danger to self as a ground for compulsory treatment is derived from a case in which a blood transfusion was ordered for an adult over her objection on religious grounds.[85] The judge was clearly concerned with the imminent danger to life and the irreversible consequences of not granting the order. He reasoned that since the patient was a mother, her death would deprive her children of care, thus attempting to bring the situation within the rule of treatment for children. One year later another court reached a contrary conclusion,[86] and decided that a person whose mental and physical faculties are weakened but not totally impaired cannot be compelled to accept treatment over his religious objection.[87]

Of course, it is probable that if a person is "dangerous to himself" and will not agree to treatment in spite of imminent risk of the loss of his life, he may be found to lack judgmental capacity. Danger to self, absent proof of judgmental impairment, is unlikely to be held to be a proper base for civil restraint, and there is no good reason for including it as a separate ground for commitment.

USE OF INVOLUNTARY TREATMENT FOR ALCOHOLICS

Even though many of the existing statutes are not satisfactory, they are applied with some frequency for the commitment of alcoholics.[88] With an increasingly greater emphasis on treatment for alcoholism—rather than jailing for intoxication—it becomes likely that there will develop an increasing tendency to utilize involuntary commitment more fully in the case of alcoholics than it has been used in the past. It is clear that that has been the result of greater treatment emphasis in the field of narcotics addiction.

Serious questions have been raised whether involuntary commitment procedures of any kind should be used in the treatment of medical problems. Dr. Szasz, an articulate opponent of the use of involuntary hospitalization, has said in speaking of alcoholics:

> If we regard alcoholism as a disease, we ought to let the alcoholic accept or reject treatment for it. The involuntary hospitalization and treatment of the alcoholic should be morally abhorrent to all who believe that individual freedom under the Rule of Law is more important than the dubious benefits that might be derived from the coercive medical control of the problem drinker. In our time, one of the most insidious dangers to individual liberty in America lies in the steadily increasing use of medical rhetoric and the ostensibly therapeutic actions justified by it.

Alcoholism cannot be controlled or eradicated like malaria or pellagra can. Like all conduct, drinking may be regulated either by external rules, laid down and enforced by society; or by internal rules, acquired from parents or other value ideals, and enforced by the self. There is often a reciprocal relationship between these two types of controls of individual behavior. Accordingly, if our ultimate aim is a society where individuals are self-disciplined, rather than controlled by external authority, we cannot expect to advance toward that goal by proliferating laws for the coercive medical control of an ever-increasing variety of behaviors, among them the proper use of alcoholic beverages.[89]

This declaration against well-intentioned, though possibly oppressive official interference with essentially private decisions is also supported by more practical factors which should be kept in mind in the development of an alcoholism treatment law. The relevant considerations, most of which have already been discussed in other contexts, are: (1) it is generally agreed by persons knowledgeable in the field that voluntary treatment is more effective than involuntary treament;[90] (2) there is no general agreed upon cure for alcoholism, nor is there a uniformly reliable method for the rehabilitation of alcoholics;[91] (3) known and promising methods of treatment and rehabilitation are at present inadequately employed because of a shortage of resources, facilities, and personnel.[92] Widespread resort to involuntary commitment is therefore unlikely to result in equally widespread rehabilitation of alcoholics. On the other hand, procedures for involuntary commitment are necessary, because not all alcoholics have the capacity to make the requisite decisions regarding treatment and some of them manifest their untreated disorder by conduct which is dangerous to the rest of society.

A rational alcoholism treatment law should not rely on routine involuntary commitment, nor should it fully reject its use. An alcoholic should be subject to involuntary commitment if he is actually dangerous, or if he needs treatment and is so impaired in judgment that he cannot get it for himself, or make any rational decision about it. If, as has been recommended, "alcoholic" is defined broadly so as to include any person whose drinking behavior has resulted in the interference with social or economic functioning—so as to include as large a group as possible for voluntary treatment purposes—then the determination that someone is an alcoholic should not, by itself, be sufficient to justify commitment. The category of persons who can be committed should be further limited to those who have lost control over the use of beverage alcohol, in addition to meeting the other criteria of danger or loss of judgmental capacity. The use of civil commitment in the treatment of alcoholics should thus be strictly circumscribed and carefully defined. Involuntary commitment should be regarded as an extraordinary rather than a routine remedy.

In this context commitment of an alcoholic based on dangerousness should be limited to danger of physical assaultiveness. Evidence should be required that the person whose commitment is sought has attempted, threatened or actually assaulted another *and* that he is likely to commit future assaults, unless committed. Although it may be constitutionally permissible to define danger more broadly, to do so would be unwise because it would open up the possibility of overuse of commitments in circumstances that do not require such a drastic remedy.

In providing for commitment based on need for treatment, it should always be coupled with a requirement of impairment of judgmental capacity. It should be clear, however, that refusal to undergo treatment should not be equated with a loss of capacity to make a rational decision with respect to treatment. The determination of such judgmental impairment should be based on expert medical opinion. Commitment would not be warranted merely because the person is an alcoholic and is in need of treatment, or because he is an alcoholic and likely to commit property crimes, or likely to appear repeatedly in public intoxicated, or has disturbed his family or other social relationships. Commitment would be warranted, however, when the alcoholic exhibits cognitive deficiencies, generally confused thinking or other manifestation of disorientation which show an inability to make judgments about areas of behavior that do not directly relate to his drinking problem.[93]

THE ROLE OF EMERGENCY COMMITMENT

In addition to providing for involuntary treatment on a long-term basis, legislation that authorizes treatment should also provide for emergency commitments. The kind of provision here proposed differs both in purpose and procedure from the provisions for short-term detention in emergency facilities of persons who are severely intoxicated, previously discussed in Chapter 2. The emergency commitment procedure here referred to would apply in cases of alcoholics who are undergoing a serious crisis, probably involving assaultive behavior, where the emergency makes it unsafe or inadvisable to take the time necessary to follow the regular commitment procedure and to obtain judicial approval prior to the temporary confinement. Whether or not the criteria for short-term emergency commitment can be or should be the same as those for judicial long-term commitment must also be considered.

There is rather wide authority for emergency restraint. At common law an "insane" person could be temporarily restrained without judicial intervention if he was dangerous to others or likely to commit suicide, and if there was an urgent need for his confinement.[94] In some states the power of restraint was also allowed when proper medical treatment so required[95] or when the person was so mentally irresponsible that he was unable to care for and protect himself.[96] Statutes for emergency restraint typically allow emergency commitment if a person is in imminent danger of inflicting serious harm on himself or others;[97] some are less restrictive, permitting emergency restraint when there is a need for immediate care[98] or when the need for care and treatment develops suddenly.[99] Such statutes have been assumed to be valid by the courts,[100] and usually they have been held to supersede common law rules.[101]

The central issue for alcoholism legislation is how the power should be exercised. Emergency restraint should be carefully circumscribed to cases of clear necessity. There is no sufficient reason for emergency restraint merely because of a need for treatment or even because of impairment of judgmental capacity. The appropriate circumstance for short-term restraint without judicial interference is where the person is dangerous, as evidenced by a threat of physical injury, or by an act of physical assault. It can be utilized regardless of whether the person was intoxicated or sober if the danger of physical assaultiveness relating to alcoholism existed. There are many instances of threats and actual assaults by intoxicated alcoholics upon members of their families during prolonged drinking bouts. When such drinking behavior is not public, but is carried on in the home, other statutory remedies may not suffice because the police are notoriously unwilling to make arrests or to interfere in "family quarrels" until after a serious crime has been committed. A short emergency commitment sought by the family or peace officer—possibly pending judicial commitment after full consideration of all of the issues—may serve as a necessary protective measure. A statute which meets this need would offer protection in drastic cases without significantly extending or encouraging the use of other involuntary procedures.

CHAPTER 6 NOTES

[1] *See* Wechsler, *The Criteria of Criminal Responsibility*, 22 U. CHI. L. REV. 367, 374 (1955); MODEL PENAL CODE § 4.01, Comment (Tent. Draft No. 4, 1955).

[2] *See, e.g.,* Duncan v. Louisiana, 391 U.S. 145 (1968) (jury trial in serious criminal cases); Klopper v. North Carolina, 386 U.S. 213 (1967) (speedy trial); Pointer v. Texas, 380 U.S. 400 (1965) (right to confrontation); Malloy v. Hogan, 378 U.S. 1 (1964) (no self-incrimination); Gideon v. Wainwright, 372 U.S. 335 (1963) (right to counsel); Mapp v. Ohio, 367 U.S. 643 (1961) (no illegally seized evidence).

[3] Typically the person adjudicated into a status is confined to an institution but the deprivation of liberty can also include a more limited supervision; *e.g.,* CAL. WELF. & INST'NS CODE §§ 3151, 3152 (West Supp. 1968), which allows for release of narcotic addict to outpatient status. *See* N.C. GEN STAT. § 122-11.6 (1964), which provides authorization for outpatient facilities; N.C. GEN. STAT. § 122-7.1 (1964), which sets up local community alcoholism programs.

[4] However, many commentators, especially the earlier ones, emphasized the procedural problems; *e.g.,* Curran, *Hospitalization of the Mentally Ill*, 31 N.C.L. REV. 274 (1953); Kadish, *A Case Study in the Signification of Procedural Due Process—Institutionalizing the Mentally Ill*, 9 W. POL. Q. 93 (1956); Ross, *Commitment of the Mentally Ill: Problems of Law & Policy*, 57 MICH. L. REV. 945 (1959); Whitmore, *Comments on a Draft Act for the Hospitalization of the Mentally Ill*, 19 GEO. WASH. L. REV. 512 (1951); Comment, *Analysis of Legal and Medical Considerations in Commitment of the Mentally Ill*, 56 YALE L.J. 1178 (1947). More recent works give more consideration to the problem; *e.g.,* Aronowitz, *Civil Commitment of Narcotic Addicts*, 67 COLUM. L. REV. 405 (1967); Note, *Civil Commitment of the Mentally Ill: Theories and Procedures*, 79 HARV. L. REV. 1288 (1966); Note, *The Plight of the Sexual Psychopath: A Legislative Blunder and Judicial Acquiescence*, 41 NOTRE DAME LAW. 527 (1966); Note, *Due Process for All—Constitutional Standards for Involuntary Civil Commitment and Release*, 34 U. CHI. L. REV. 633 (1967); Note, *Civil Restraint, Mental Illness, and the Right to Treatment*, 77 YALE L.J. 87 (1967); Note, *Civil Commitment of Narcotic Addicts*, 76 YALE L.J. 1160 (1967).

[5] *See, e.g.,* A. DEUTSCH, THE MENTALLY ILL IN AMERICA xii (2d ed. 1949).

[6] *See, e.g.,* Comment, 56 YALE L.J., *supra* note 4, at 1178-1179; Ross, *supra* note 4, at 946.

[7] Pp. 126, 128, 129 *infra*.

[8] Hacker & Frym, *The Sexual Psychopath Act in Practice: A Critical Discussion*, 43 CALIF. L. REV. 766, 767 (1955) (the authors were referring particularly to the California Psychopath Law).

[9] *See generally* DEUTSCH, *supra* note 5.

[10] *Id.,* at 419.

[11] *Id.,* at 40-42.

[12] *Id.,* at 116.

[13] *Id.,* at 420.

[14] The first judicial expression of interest in "helping" the insane is attributed to a Massachusetts case, which stated:

> "'The question must then arise in each particular case, whether a patient's own safety, or that of others, requires that he should be restrained for a certain time, and whether restraint is necessary for his restoration, or will be conducive thereto. . . .'"

In re Oakes, 8 Law Rep. 122, 125 (1845) (cited in DEUTSCH, *supra* note 5, at 422). *See* AMERICAN BAR FOUNDATION, THE MENTALLY DISABLED AND THE LAW 17 (F. Lindman & D. McIntyre eds. 1961) which states, ". . . of course, once hospitals were available, hospitalization became a multi-purpose remedy."

15 MD. ANN. CODE art. 59, § 21 (1967); VA. CODE ANN. § 37.1-67 (Supp. 1969).

16 N.Y. MENTAL HYGIENE LAW § 70 (McKinney 1967).

17 *Id.*, § 72. New York provides as well for emergency commitment based on danger and immediate need for care; *id.*, § 76.

18 W. VA. CODE ANN. § 27-5-4 (1966).

19 *See* THE MENTALLY DISABLED AND THE LAW, *supra* note 14.

20 Note, 41 NOTRE DAME LAW., *supra* note 4, at 530. This note gives an excellent overview and criticism of the legislation as of April, 1966.

21 Cohen, *Administration of the Criminal Sexual Psychopath Statute in Indiana,* 32 IND. L.J. 450, 451 (1967).

22 Note, 41 NOTRE DAME LAW., *supra* note 4, at 535.

23 *Id.*, at 529.

24 *See* Aronowitz, *supra* note 4, at 406; THE MENTALLY DISABLED AND THE LAW, *supra* note 14, at 87-88, Table 11k.

25 *E.g.*, N.Y. MENTAL HYGIENE LAW § 206 (McKinney 1967); 42 U.S.C. §§ 3401 *et seq.* (Supp. III, 1968).

26 42 U.S.C. § 3413 (Supp. III, 1968); CAL. WELF. & INST'NS CODE § 3106 (West Supp. 1968); MASS. ANN. LAWS ch. 111A, § 4 (1967); N.Y. MENTAL HYGIENE LAW § 206 (McKinney 1967). Both the California and New York statutes authorize commitment of persons "in imminent danger of addiction" as well.

27 CAL. WELF. & INST'NS CODE § 3000 (West 1966).

28 *E.g.*, MASS. GEN. LAWS ANN. ch. 123, § 62 (1965); MONT. REV. CODES ANN. § 80-2404 (Supp. 1967); NEB. REV. STAT. § 83-306 (1966); N.C. GEN. STAT. §§ 122-60—122-68 (1964, Supp. 1967); WIS. STAT. ANN. §§ 51.09—51.13 (Supp. 1969).

29 *E.g.*, IOWA CODE ANN. §§ 224.1—224.5 (Supp. 1969); MICH. COMP. LAWS ANN. § 330.18 (1967); MISS. CODE ANN. § 436-01 (1956); NEV. REV. STAT. § 433.248 (1967); VT. STAT. ANN., tit. 18, §§ 8401-8405 (Supp. 1968).

30 *E.g.*, ARK. STAT. ANN. § 83-709 (Supp. 1967); KAN. GEN. STAT. ANN. § 74.4408 (1964); KY. REV. STAT. § 222.130 (1959); MISS. CODE ANN. § 436-02 (1956); TEX. REV. CIV. STAT. ANN. art. 5561c, Sec. 9 (b) (Supp. 1968); *see* Appendix B, Chart II.

31 *E.g.*, CONN. GEN. STAT. ANN. § 17-155 (e) (Supp. 1969); MINN. STAT. ANN. § 253A.07, subd. 17 (a) (Supp. 1969); *see* Appendix B, Chart II.

32 *E.g.*, ARK. STAT. ANN. § 83-709 (Supp. 1967); KAN. GEN. STAT. ANN. § 74.4408 (1964); KY. REV. STAT. § 222.130 (1959); LA. REV. STAT. ANN. § 9.1002 (1965); MISS. CODE ANN. § 436-02 (1956); PA. STAT. ANN. tit. 50, § 2105 (Supp. 1969); TEX. REV. CIV. STAT. ANN. art. 5561c, Sec. 9 (b) (Supp. 1968); *see* Appendix B, Chart II.

33 *E.g.*, ARK. STAT. ANN. § 83-709 (b) (Supp. 1967); CONN. GEN. STAT. ANN. § 17-155 (g) (1961); KAN. GEN. STAT. ANN. § 74-4408 (1964); KY. REV. STAT. § 222.130 (1959); MASS. GEN. LAWS ANN. ch. 123, § 62 (1965); MISS. CODE ANN. § 436-02 (1956); N.M. STAT. ANN. § 46-12-7 (Supp. 1967); TEX. REV. CIV. STAT. ANN. art. 5561c, Sec. 9 (b) (Supp. 1968); *see* Appendix B, Chart II.

34 *E.g.*, ARK. STAT. ANN. § 83-709 (Supp. 1967); KAN. GEN. STAT. ANN. § 74-4408 (1964); MICH. COMP. LAWS ANN. § 330.18 (1967); MISS. CODE ANN. § 436-02 (1956); TEX. REV. CIV. STAT. ANN. art. 5561c, Sec. 9 (b) (Supp. 1968); WIS. STAT. ANN. § 51.09 (Supp. 1969); *see* Appendix B, Chart II.

35 *E.g.*, ARK. STAT. ANN. § 83-709 (b) (Supp. 1967); KAN. GEN. STAT. ANN. § 74-4408 (1964); KY. REV. STAT. § 222.130 (1959); MISS. CODE ANN. §436.02 (1956); TEX. REV. CIV. STAT. ANN. art. 5561c, Sec. 9 (Supp. 1968); *see* Appendix B, Chart II.

[36] Ch. 3 *supra.* "Alcoholic" is the only requirement in NEV. REV. STAT. § 433.250 (1967); *see* N.H. REV. STAT. ANN. § 172:13 (Supp. 1967) (inebriate); N.J. STAT. ANN. § 30:9-12.21 (1964) ("acute alcoholism"); R.I. GEN. LAWS ANN. § 40-12-17 (1956); S.D. COMP. LAWS ANN. ch. 27-8 (1967); TENN. CODE ANN. § 33-810 (Supp. 1968); *see* Appendix B, Chart II.

[37] *See* ch. 3 *supra;* Appendix B, Chart I.

[38] *E.g.,* ARK. STAT. ANN. § 83-709 (b) (Supp. 1967); CONN. GEN. STAT. ANN. § 17-155e (Supp. 1969); KAN. GEN. STAT. ANN. § 74-4408 (1964); KY. REV. STAT. § 222.130 (1959); LA. REV. STAT. ANN. § 9.1002 (1965); MD. ANN. CODE art. 2c, § 306 (Supp. 1968); MASS. GEN. LAWS ANN. ch. 123, § 63 (1965); MICH. COMP. LAWS ANN. § 330.18 (1967); MINN. STAT. ANN. §253A.07, subd. 17 (a) (Supp. 1969); MISS. CODE ANN. § 436-02 (1956); N.Y. MENTAL HYGIENE LAW §§ 306, 307 (McKinney Supp. 1968); N.C. GEN. STAT. § 122-58 (1964); PA. STAT. ANN. tit. 50, § 2105 (Supp. 1969); TEX. REV. CIV. STAT. ANN. art. 5561c, Sec. 9 (b) (Supp. 1968); VT. STAT. ANN. tit. 18, § 8401 (Supp. 1968); W. VA. CODE ANN. § 27-6-1 (1966); WIS. STAT. ANN. § 51.09 (Supp. 1969); *see* Appendix B, Chart II.

[39] KAN. GEN. STAT. ANN. § 74.4408 (1964).

[40] *See, e.g.,* Note, 76 YALE L.J., *supra* note 4, at 1171; Jacobson v. Massachusetts, 197 U.S. 11 (1905). The Court therein recognized, ". . . the inherent right of every freeman to care for his own body and health in such way as to him seems best," *id.,* 197 U.S. at 26.

[41] Kittrie, *Compulsory Mental Treatment and the Requirements of "Due Process,"* 21 OHIO S.L.J. 28, 32 (1960).

[42] *Id.;* Note, *Civil Commitment of Narcotic Drug Addict Held Constitutional,* 8 UTAH L. REV. 367, 371 (1964); Note, 76 YALE L.J., *supra* note 4, at 1172-1174. For other interpretation *see* Note, 34 U. CHI. L. REV., *supra* note 4, at n. 98, which defines *parens patriae* as including only those who are dangerous to self; *In re* Gault, 387 U.S. 1, 16 (1967), describes the *parens patriae* doctrine: ". . . its meaning is murky and its historical credentials are of dubious relevance." The Court limits the scope of the power to person and property interests of children.

[43] Incompetent is used in this memorandum to include only those who are unable to make a rational decision about their need for help.

[44] *See* pp. 142-143 *infra.*

[45] Jacobson v. Massachusetts, *supra* note 40, at 25.

[46] *Id.;* Compagnie Francaise de Navigation A Vapeur v. State Board of Health, 186 U.S. 380 (1902) (quarantine upheld); People *ex rel.* Baker v. Strautz, 386 Ill. 360, 54 N.E.2d 441 (1944) (confinement for venereal disease upheld); Moore v. Draper, 57 So. 2d 648 (Fla. 1952) (tuberculosis confinement upheld). *See* GRAD, PUBLIC HEALTH LAW MANUAL 48-50 (1965).

[47] Hammon v. Hill, 228 F.Supp. 999, 1001 (W.D. Pa. 1915).

[48] *In re* Spadafora, 54 Misc. 2d 123, 126, 281 N.Y.S.2d 923, 927 (1967).

[49] *Infra* p. 143, which discusses the validity of danger to self as a criterion for commitment.

[50] 370 U.S. 660 (1962).

[51] *Robinson, id.,* struck down a criminal conviction for being addicted to narcotics as cruel and unusual punishment. The Court said:

> ". . . a state might establish a program of compulsory treatment for those addicted to narcotics." *Id.,* at 665.
> "A state might determine that the general health and welfare require that the victims of these [mental illness, leprosy, venereal disease] and other human afflictions be dealt with by compulsory treatment. . . ." *Id.,* at 666.
> "He [the drug addict] may of course be confined for treatment or for the protection of society." *Id.,* at 676 (Douglas, J. concurring).

52 369 U.S. 705 (1962).

53 *Id.* Lynch had been charged with negotiating $50 checks without sufficient funds; the trial court did not allow him to plead guilty, found him "insane" and then applied the D.C. automatic commitment statute. The Supreme Court held that the automatic commitment statute did not apply to one "who has maintained that he was mentally responsible"; *id.*, at 710. The Court speaks of congressional awareness of safeguarding against "improvident confinement" in arriving at this strained construction; *id.*, at 711.

54 In Baxstrom v. Herold, 383 U.S. 107 (1966), the Court struck down a commitment to a mental institution at the expiration of criminal sentence because the failure to follow New York procedures for civil commitment was a denial of equal protection. In Spect v. Patterson, 386 U.S. 605 (1967), the Court did not allow a sentence under the Colorado Sex Offenders Act without notice and a full hearing since the sentence under the Act required a new finding of fact. The Court said, "These commitment proceedings whether denominated civil or criminal are subject both to the Equal Protection Clause of the Fourteenth Amendment . . . and to the Due Process Clause." *Id.*, at 608. In *In re* Gault, *supra* note 42, the Court remanded a juvenile delinquency proceeding because of lack of adequate notice, no right to counsel, no right to cross-examination and no right to remain silent. The Court emphasized the deprivation of liberty that is the result of this type of proceeding. *Id.*, at 27.

55 Powell v. Texas, 392 U.S. 514 (1968).

56 *Id.*, at 529.

57 *Id.*, at 530.

58 *Ex parte* O'Neil, 239 Mich. 450, 214 N.W. 411 (1927); *but cf.*, Director of Patuxent Institution v. Daniels, 243 Md. 16, 221 A.2d 397 (1966).

59 *In re* Heukelekian, 24 N.J. Super. 407, 94 A.2d 501 (1953).

60 State v. Caralluszo, 49 N.J. 152, 228 A.2d 693 (1967); *In re* Alexander, 372 F.2d 925 (D.C.C.A. 1967).

61 *Ex parte* Harcourt, 27 Cal. App. 642, 150 P. 1001 (1915).

62 State *ex rel.* Larkin v. Ryan, 70 Wis. 676, 36 N.W. 823 (1888).

63 Barnes v. Director of Patuxent Institution, 240 Md. 32, 212 A.2d 465 (1965).

64 Commonwealth v. Bechtel, 384 Pa. 184, 120 A.2d 295 (1956).

65 Greenwood v. United States, 350 U.S. 366 (1956).

66 Notes 63-65 *supra*.

67 Notes 58-62 *supra*.

68 Director of Patuxent Institution v. Daniels, *supra* note 63, suggests that property damage may be considered as proof of danger, though this is not entirely clear.

69 Minnesota *ex rel.* Pearson v. Probate Court, 309 U.S. 270 (1939).

70 *Id.*, at 273.

71 Note 5 *supra* and acompanying text.

72 Note, 79 HARV. L. REV., *supra* note 4, at 1291; Note, 77 YALE L.J., *supra* note 4, at 102 n. 60.

73 Note 69 *supra*.

74 N.Y. Times, April 21, 1968, at 1, col. 3.

75 *See* cases which hold no commitment for habitual drunkenness alone, but allow commitment on other grounds; Leavitt v. Morris, 105 Minn. 170, 117 N.W. 393 (1908); *Ex parte* Schwarting, 76 Neb. 773, 108 N.W. 125 (1906); State *ex rel.* Larkin v. Ryan, supra note 62. *Cf. Ex parte* Hinkle, 33 Idaho 605, 196 P. 1035 (1921).

76 Note, 76 YALE L.J., *supra* note 4, at 1173, 1174.

77 Note 74 *supra*.

78 *Id.*, at 275.

[79] Baxstrom v. Herold, *supra* note 54, 383 U.S. at 111.

[80] Ross, *supra* note 4, at 958, 959.

[81] Note, 76 YALE L.J., *supra* note 4 ,at 1173, 1174.

[82] *Id.*

[83] *Id.*

[84] *E.g.*, People *ex rel.* Wallace v. Labrenz, 411 Ill. 618, 104 N.E.2d 769, *cert. denied*, 344 U.S. 824 (1952) (blood transfusion given to child over parent's religious objections); PROSSER, TORTS 104 & n. 51 (1964).

[85] Application of Georgetown College, 331 F.2d 1000 (D.C. Cir.), *cert. denied*, 377 U.S. 978 (1964).

[86] *In re* Estate of Brooks, 32 Ill. 2d 361, 205 N.E.2d 435, *cert. denied*, 382 U.S. 945 (1965).

[87] *Id.*

[88] *See* Appendix C, Chart IV.

[89] Szasz, *Alcoholism: A Socio-Ethical Perspective*, 6 WASH. L.J. 255, 268 (1967).

[90] GOLDFARB, ROADBLOCKS TO PROGRESS IN THE TREATMENT OF THE CHRONIC INEBRIATE, SELECTED PAPERS 41 (North American Ass'n of Alcoholism Programs 1967), *see* ch. 4 *supra*.

[91] R. GLASSCOTE, T. PLAUT, D. HAMMERSLEY, F. O'NEILL, M. CHAFETZ, E. CUMMING, THE TREATMENT OF ALCOHOLISM 13 (1967); *see* ch. 4 *supra*.

[92] *See* Appendix C, Chart V.

[93] *See* Vogel, *Psychiatric Treatment of Alcoholism*, 315 ANNALS 99 (1958).

[94] *E.g.*, Felix v. Hall-Brooke Sanitarium, 140 Conn. 496, 101 A.2d 500 (1953); Warner v. State, 297 N.Y. 395; 79 N.E.2d 459 (1948); Christiansen v. Weston, 36 Ariz. 200, 284 P. 149 (1930); Colby v. Jackson, 12 N.H. 526 (1842); Belger v. Arnot, 183 N.E.2d 866, 871 (Mass. 1962).

[95] Bisgaard v. Duvall, 169 Iowa 711, 151 N.W. 1051 (1915) (there was a claim of possible violence).

[96] Forsythe v. Ivey, 139 So. 615, 618 (Miss. 1932).

[97] *E.g.*, MINN. STAT. ANN. § 253A.04 (1967); N.Y. MENTAL HYGIENE LAW § 75 (McKinney 1951, Supp. 1968); N.C. GEN STAT. § 122-59 (1964).

[98] N.Y. MENTAL HYGIENE LAW § 75 (McKinney 1951).

[99] *Id.*

[100] Warner v. State, *supra* note 94; *In re* Coates, 9 N.Y.2d 242, 249, 173 N.E.2d 797, 801 (1961).

[101] *E.g.*, Application of Hoffman, 131 C.A.2d 758, 281 P.2d 96 (2d D., 1955); Belger v. Arnot, *supra* note 94, at 871; Warner v. State, *supra* note 94.

CHAPTER 7

Involuntary Commitment Continued; Practice And Procedure

The previous chapter explained the substantive criteria that must be met before an alcoholic may be committed for involuntary treatment. The substantive issue of who is subject to commitment having been determined, the procedural problems relating to civil commitment may be examined. Procedural issues involve a number of aspects of the formal commitment proceeding, as well as of the nature of treatment decisions, the duration of commitment, and the procedures for release.

Civil commitment involves a number of mixed problems of law and therapy. If, for example, the law states a preference for outpatient care, should the assignment to an outpatient clinic be made by the court or by the treatment agency? If the law provides that the court is to commit an alcoholic to the treatment agency, then a delegation of the choice of institution to that agency follows as a matter of course. On the other hand, a requirement that the court commit an alcoholic to a specific institution in effect requires the court, and not the agency, to make the first major decision with important treatment implications.

The treatment decision may have significant effects on a person's liberty, which may argue for judicial participation in decisions of institutional placement—reporting to an outpatient clinic a short trip from home is quite different from being sent to a far-away, strictly regimented state mental institution that serves people with a variety of disorders. The difficult task of matching the patient with the treatment program appropriate for him, however, requires detailed knowledge of treatment alternatives and a statute of sufficient flexibility to permit transfers to be made efficiently from one institution to another; proper placement and subsequent transfer can be severely hampered if court approval is required for every move.

The issue is a complex one which can only be resolved in the light of the guiding purposes of treatment legislation. The sum of recent decisions suggests that the court must play a primary role in decisions which affect personal liberty.[1] As to other matters, the legislative determination of the precise role of the treatment agency is likely to prevail.

PROCEDURES FOR INVOLUNTARY COMMITMENT

There are two major statutory patterns for civil commitment proceedings, namely commitment after a formal court or administrative hearing or commitment on medical certification. In most states which provide for involuntary commitment for alcoholics there is provision for notice to the alcoholic, a formal hearing, and often a requirement for medical evidence, or at least the opportunity for the court to require it.[2] However, a few states confine a person on the basis of medical certificaion without a hearing, subject to the patient's rights to appeal the regularity of admission and to demand a hearing on the need for continued hospitalization.[3] Both types of commitments were first used in commitments for mental illness.[4]

A new approach to the problem of involuntary commitment is reflected in California's Lanterman-Petris-Short Act on community mental health services that became effective on July 1, 1969. It allows a person who is dangerous or gravely disabled by inebriation to be taken into custody by a peace officer or a member of the attending staff of the institution, and to be placed, without court order, in an approved facility for 72-hour treatment and evaluation. He must be released after 72 hours, unless he is found a proper person to be certified for intensive treatment or for conservatorship as a person who is mentally disordered. A further certification for intensive treatment up to 14 days is signed by the person in charge of the facility that provides the evaluation services and by a psychiatrist, if one is available, and the Superior Court is officially notified of the certification. Subsequent confinement, after petition to and hearing by the court, is available for periods of 90 days at a time, if the person presents a danger of physical harm to others. Review by *habeas corpus* is, of course, available.[4a]

Commitment After Court Hearing

In the case of *In re Gault,*[5] which involved a constitutional challenge to a commitment for juvenile delinquency, the Supreme Court

held that benign social purposes do not relieve the law of the obligation to provide the "essentials" of due process in a civil commitment
proceeding. The Court emphasized the "deprivation of liberty" and
the "incarceration against one's will" resulting from commitment as
the motivating factors in its decision. Although in that case the Court
required notice, the right to counsel, the rights to confrontation and
cross-examination, and observance of the privilege against self-incrimination, it reiterated the view that the hearing need not "conform to all the requirements of a criminal trial or even an administrative hearing."[6] The decision in effect suggests a balancing test—
a weighing of claimed benefits from abandonment of a specific procedural protection against the consequences which flow from the commitment order.

A provision for a prior hearing, if accompanied by requirements
of notice and counsel and by provisions for medical evidence, clearly
meets the essentials of due process; moreover, a prior hearing insures
that a person whose commitment is sought will have an opportunity
to be heard *before* he is committed. Furthermore, where the judgments involve both social and medical determinations, use of a prior
hearing provides judicial expertise as well as a forum for medical
opinions. Yet every effort must be made to guard against turning the
hearing into a mere formality with the trappings of due process, a
sham which merely adopts the medical evidence of the state.[7] A
guarantee of counsel and provision for a physical examination should
help to satisfy this objective.

It is clear that any commitment decision must rely in large
measure on medical expertise—the required determination of the
likelihood that the person may commit physical harm, as well as a
finding of impaired judgmental capacity must be founded, as far as
possible, upon sensitive medical judgments. As a practical matter
the requisite medical evidence may not be available—a person whose
commitment is sought may refuse to be examined by a physician or
may simply not cooperate in the examination which must also
include the taking of a social history. Some doubts have also been
raised as to the medical capacity to predict dangerousness.[8] When
sufficient medical evidence is not available, the best solution is to
authorize the court to make a preliminary commitment order for a
few days' hospitalization for the purpose of observation and diagnosis,
unless the person whose commitment is sought will submit to examination by a court-appointed physician. In the long run, such a provision
will help to protect the person by insuring that longer term treatment

will not be ordered on less than full evidence. In a close case, when the court has less than full evidence, it is more likely to use caution and order commitment rather than to risk having a possibly dangerous or disoriented person at large.

At the hearing itself, the burden of proving that the person is a proper subject for commitment is undoubtedly on the state.[9] The more difficult issue is the quantum of proof required. A lesser standard than the requirement of proof beyond a reasonable doubt (as in criminal proceedings) is suggested on two grounds. The first is that, while criminal conviction and civil confinement may both result in loss of liberty, the punitive purpose and the social stigma of a criminal conviction are absent in commitment hearings.[10] The second is that, since it is essential in most commitments to rely on expert opinion both as to the degree of impairment of mental processes, and as to what is likely to occur in the future, a requirement of "proof beyond a reasonable doubt" would be unworkable.[11] Thus, a requirement of clear and convincing proof suggests itself as the best standard;[12] it is more stringent than the usual quantum of proof in civil cases, and yet not as limiting as the standard in criminal prosecutions. At present, in most jurisdictions, the quantum of proof required for commitment is that used in civil cases—"by a preponderance of evidence."

Finally, in determining whether or not commitment should be ordered some thought must be given to requiring proof that the person will benefit from or be improved by commitment. A few existing statutes do so provide.[13] It is an unassailable proposition that a person should not be confined for treatment unless he will in fact benefit from it. Yet a requirement of "proof" of benefit by "clear and convincing evidence" is unworkable—the treatment for alcoholism is more involved than the administration of a pill or the application of a routine which has been proven effective in a high percentage of cases. It is unrealistic to expect proof that benefit is likely to occur to consist of anything more than expert opinion in the nature of an educated guess. It seems desirable, however, to require evidence that a treatment program is available, and evidence, admittedly speculative, of possible benefit. This requirement need not be met, of course, when the alcoholic is shown to be likely to inflict physical harm; in this instance the interest in protecting society should be paramount, and he should be restrained regardless of the availability or potential benefit of treatment.

Commitment on Medical Certification

There is a view, shared by a number of psychiatrists and other mental health practitioners, that formal court hearings prior to a civil commitment that grows out of a mental illness or disorder not only fail to protect the patient, but are objectionable as excessively legalistic and detrimental to his medical interest.[14] Indeed, some recent mental health legislation, notably in New York[15] and Hawaii,[16] provides instead for commitment on the certificate of two physicians, and makes detailed provision for notice, right to a hearing and the affirmative requirement of periodic review subsequent to actual admission.[17] It is probable that these new laws meet the guidelines laid down in In re Gault[18] and other recent cases,[19] to the effect that any status adjudication will require the "essentials" of procedural due process, and indeed, at least one court has already decided that a hearing subsequent to actual commitment will meet the requirements of due process if the law provides safeguards to prevent the extended detention of any person without a hearing and review.[20]

Commitment on medical certification operates as follows: The spouse, next of kin, or other person authorized by the statute to apply, files an application for commitment with a mental hospital, accompanied by the medical certificates of two physicians who have examined the patient, usually within a few days of the date of the application. The patient is taken to the institution and will be accepted for treatment on the basis of the application and supporting certificates if they meet the requirements of the law. If the institution finds, after examining him, that he is not a proper subject for commitment, he may be released. His commitment under medical certification is normally for a relatively short term, and he has the right to ask for a hearing or for a review either at, or before, the end of the initial term.[21] In New York, for instance, the law also provides for a "Mental Health Information Service" which is in fact a kind of institutional public defender system.[22] It informs patients of the right to a review of their commitments, and helps them to apply for it (or even applies on their behalf).

Commitment on medical certification has gained the support of some psychiatrists and mental health practitioners as preferable to the "barbaric" hearing procedure[23] which often subjected a sick person to considerable indignities without necessarily providing any real protection. It has been asserted, particularly, that most commitment hearings are so routine as to provide the appearance, rather than the reality, of constitutional protections.[24]

A certification procedure places primary reliance in the initial stages on medical expertise. It is supported in part by reasoning that the alcoholic whose commitment is sought is protected from a trial process which may be detrimental to his health and well-being,[25] and in part by reasoning that the required judgments—i.e., that a person is likely to inflict physical harm or is impaired in his judgmental capacity and needs treatment—can be made only by physicians skilled in making balanced evaluations and predictive judgments of a person's mental and psychological condition.

There are, of course, a number of situations—even under statutes that rely primarily on court-ordered commitments—in which reliance is placed almost entirely upon medical certification; for instance, in emergency commitments where there is no opportunity for a hearing, action must be taken on the basis of a medical evaluation alone, subject to further court review at a later time.[26]

It is clear that both commitments based on court order and commitments initially based on medical certification can meet the requirements of due process. In dealing with commitments of alcoholics, medical certification will obviously serve the occasional needs for emergency commitment of an assaultive alcoholic. For longer-term "regular" commitments, either approach may be satisfactory; states will, most likely, follow their established patterns in the development of alcoholism treatment laws. Each of the schemes has its dangers— court hearings for commitment purposes should not degenerate into empty forms, and commitments on medical certification should not go unchecked and unreviewed for any extended period. Whichever scheme is utilized, the soundest protection for the committed alcoholic (as for other committed persons) is frequent mandatory review of the reasons for his continued detention, as well as real opportunities for challenge of the commitment, with assistance of counsel and medical testimony readily available to the patient. There should, of course, be a legal requirement that the patient must be released when the grounds for commitment no longer exist.

PLACE OF COMMITMENT

Most statutes are silent about the place or institution to which the alcoholic will be involuntarily committed. A few provide for commitment to the alcoholism division or other responsible agency,[27] and some provide for confinement at a state hospital, or specifically at a named state hospital;[28] in one state, however, commitment to state mental institutions is expressly prohibited.[29] Some states allow

for placement in any public or private hospital,[30] and in a minority
of states commitment may be to a jail or correctional institution,[31]
while others, on the contrary, specifically prohibit this type of placement.[32]

The underlying problem of whether the courts or another state
agency determines the place of commitment has been referred to
earlier.[33] Its resolution is best made in favor of flexible administration, because only the treatment authorities are equipped to match
the needs of the patient with suitable facilities and treatment programs. The court's primary role is to resolve conflicting evidence and
to determine the existence of legal grounds for commitment, but the
court is not equipped to evaluate treatment programs. The law
should—and, indeed, in a number of states already does—authorize commitment to the department of mental hygiene, the alcoholism
division, or other responsible agency,[33a] which, in turn, should have
the power to place the patient in the most suitable treatment program
under its control and to transfer him from one institution to another,
as the needs of treatment may require. There should, however, be a
specific prohibition against use of any correctional facility for the commitment or treatment of alcoholics who have not been convicted of
a crime.

DURATION OF COMMITMENT

A number of state laws set time limits on alcoholism commitments. Their limits range from 30 days to three years, although
studies of actual practice indicate that the length of stay is usually
less than three months.[34] Other states allow for detention until the
alcoholic is "recovered,"[35] "cured"[36] or "no longer needs treatment."[37]
In a few jurisdictions the law itself provides neither a standard for
release nor a specific time limitation.[38]

In devising provisions for the release of committed alcoholics,
it should be remembered that the objective is not to retain a patient
until he is cured or until his continued abstinence is assured. He can
only be held involuntarily until the grounds for commitment are
no longer present. Thus a person who was committed because
he presented a risk of physical harm to the public should be released
when he no longer presents such a risk. A person in need of treatment, accompanied by judgmental incapacity regarding his need for
care, should be released when his decision-making capacity has been
restored or when treatment is demonstrably no longer doing him any
good, whichever is sooner. If these standards are followed, the decision

to release a committed alcoholic is essentially a medical one and should be delegated to the institutional treatment authorities. Release decisions may, of course, be made subject to review by the courts,[39] but it is unlikely that the committed person or anyone on his behalf will oppose the decision that he be released, and thus provision for court review is unnecessary.

The question as to whether a committed alcoholic is ready to be released should be subject to mandatory review by the court from time to time. When a person has been held for a certain length of time—and in the case of a committed alcoholic a period of one month seems to be reasonable—the matter should be taken back to court and the treatment authorities ought to be charged with the burden of presenting evidence that his continued commitment is necessary. In addition to the periodic review required by statute, the committed person always has the right to test his continued detention by writ of *habeas corpus*.

Some mention has been made of the fact that a number of states commit alcoholics for a legislatively fixed term.[40] Setting a definite term for the release of an alcoholic is questionable because there cannot be any legislative prediction as to whether or not a particular alcoholic will have made such progress in his treatment at the end of the fixed period so as to be ready for release. Such fixed terms do serve a limited purpose when coupled with the authority to recommit, if the length of the term is related to the time that experience has shown to be adequate to get most alcoholics ready for release. Then the initial term set in the commitment is really nothing more than a provision for periodic review, in that it sets the time when the alcoholic's condition must be reviewed by the court in order to continue his detention. In every instance, the review of an alcoholic's condition to determine whether he is ready for release will be meaningful only if the alcoholic has access to counsel and to medical experts of his own to contest the conclusion of the treatment authorities in a meaningful fashion.

INSTITUTIONAL CARE—"RIGHT TO TREATMENT"

At present there are no Constitutional or legal standards for the care and treatment which must be given to a committed person; however, there is increasing interest in "the right to treatment."[41] The proponents of this right contend that if a person has been committed for treatment, he must get adequate treatment or else he should be released. The argument for such a right is more persuasive when the commitment is based on the need for treatment accompanied by judgmental impairment, than when it is based on danger to the public. In commitments based on danger, the right to treatment is more likely to be viewed as secondary to the goal of public protection.

The leading case suggesting a right to treatment arose under a commitment based on the need for care—*Rouse v. Cameron*.[42] In that case the petitioner, who had been involuntarily committed after having been found not guilty by reason of insanity at his criminal trial, attacked his confinement in a *habeas corpus* proceeding because he had received no psychiatric treatment. The crime with which Rouse had been charged, carrying a dangerous weapon, carried a maximum sentence of imprisonment of one year and at the time of his petition he already had been confined for four years. The court recognized the "right to treatment" and remanded the case for further proceedings. The decision relies on the District of Columbia law which expressly provides for "medical and psychiatric care and treatment" for a "person hospitalized in a public hospital."[43] However, it suggests generally that a failure to treat may violate the Constitutional rights of due process and equal protection as well as the prohibition against cruel and unusual punishment.[44]

It is indeed hard to see how a commitment based on the patient's need for treatment can be justified unless treatment is provided, especially since there is no absolute need for confinement as there is in commitments based on danger to the public.[45]

If a right to treatment is to be created by the legislature or recognized by the courts, the limits and extent of the right will have to be defined. The obligation to treat was described in the *Rouse* case as follows:

> The hospital need not show that the treatment will cure or improve him but only that there is a *bona fide* effort to do so.[46]

The court indicated that this effort required making a periodic inquiry into the patient's needs and a review of the treatment program in the light of those needs.[47] The case suggests that the court might actually look into the course of treatment in the light of the patient's diagnosis and other available treatment plans.[48] However, it appears from other cases that a court is likely to find the duty to provide treatment satisfied by a showing that staff and facilities are available,[49] and this may reflect the practical limits of judicial inquiry. If the court finds a languishing patient, who has been committed for reasons other than dangerousness, in circumstances that cannot even be called environmental or "milieu" therapy, it will probably order his release.[50] It is also possible that release may be granted—even if there is evidence of staff and facilities—if it can be convincingly shown that the alleged treatment is not in fact beneficial. However, if a right to treatment is recognized, the burden of proof of denial of the right should be on the patient.[51] It is likely to be a difficult burden to sustain, even if the concept is given full recognition. The "right to treatment" will never achieve reality until adequate resources are devoted to facilities and research.

A statute which provides for involuntary treatment need not, as a practical matter, include a specific right to treatment; given the present state of knowledge it would be impossible to specify how the right could be safisfied. At best, the law may provide that a person who is not dangerous be released when there is no evidence that available treatment is benefiting him. Such a provision, as well as provision for periodic review of the individual case, should adequately protect against institutional neglect.

EMERGENCY COMMITMENT

Emergency commitment is no less a deprivation of liberty than a longer-term commitment, but since its very objective is to provide immediate restraint it must be governed by different procedures.

Full authority to implement the legislative standards must be delegated to the medical profession and other treatment personnel. The emergency itself precludes a prior judicial hearing. The single issue in effecting an emergency commitment is what evidence, if any, should be required. Existing statutes typically require a medical certificate which sets out the facts on which commitment should be based.[52] At least one physician should certify that the person is an alcoholic who has lost control over his drinking and is likely to inflict physical harm. Such a certificate offers at least minimal protection to the person whose commitment is sought.

The application should be made directly to the facility involved; in an emergency situation there is neither the need nor the time to match patient to program. The most important protection against abuse of emergency commitments is effective machinery to govern release. Under existing laws a person may either be held until commitment proceedings get underway[53] or for a specified, limited period.[54] A better solution would be to allow a person to be held for a limited period, but to require earlier release if the emergency has passed, as provided in the Model Alcoholism and Intoxication Treatment Act, §12 (c). However, if the administrator files a petition for commitment and shows that grounds for the emergency commitment continue to exist, he should be allowed to hold the person until the court has acted on the petition, in order to protect the safety of the public.

In summary, involuntary commitment should be allowed in alcoholism treatment legislation only when the person whose commitment is sought is likely to be physically assaultive or is impaired in his capacity to make a judgment about his need for treatment. The procedure for commitment should accord with the essentials of due process by providing for a prior court hearing or for medical certification and court review. In addition there should be rational release standards and provision for mandatory review after a reasonable time; the relevant department should be allowed to place the person subject to commitment in the proper treatment facility. Alcoholism treatment legislation should also provide for short-term emergency commitment without prior judicial approval for persons who are shown to be dangerous on the basis of acts or threats of physical assault.

CHAPTER 7 NOTES

1 *See* ch. 6 *supra,* notes 52-54 and accompanying text; United States *ex rel.* Schuster v. Herold, 410 F.2d 1071 (2d. Cir. 1969).

2 ARK. STAT. ANN. § 83-709 (c) (Supp. 1967); CONN. GEN. STAT. ANN. § 17-155g (Supp. 1969); D.C. CODE ANN. § 24-527 (Supp. II 1969); GA. CODE ANN. § 88-405 (b), (d), (e) (Supp. 1968); IOWA CODE ANN. §§ 229.5, 229.6 (Supp. 1969) (subject present unless "injurious and no advantage"); KAN. GEN. STAT. ANN. § 74-4408 (1964); KY. REV. STAT. §§ 222.140—222.150 (1959); MD. ANN. CODE art. 2c, § 306 (Supp. 1968); MASS. GEN. LAWS ANN. ch. 123, § 51 (1965); MICH. COMP. LAWS ANN. § 330.21 (1967); MINN. STAT. ANN. § 253A.07 (Supp. 1969) (excludes the subject if his presence would be "injurious"; it also provides that no drugs which would hamper subject be administered or if medication is necessary the court be informed; finally, it provides the hearing be conducted as informally as possible); MISS. CODE. ANN. § 436-03 (1956); MONT. REV. CODES ANN. § 38-201 (1961) (includes provision for hearing at "bedside"), and *see* § 80-2404 (Supp. 1967); NEV. REV. STAT. § 433.270 (1967); N.J. STAT. ANN. § 30:19-12.21 (1964); N.C. GEN. STAT. §§ 122-62, 63 (1964) (provides for an informal hearing by clerk); PA. STAT. ANN. tit. 50, § 2105 (Supp. 1969); R.I. GEN. LAWS ANN. §§ 40-12-15, 16 (1956); S.D. COMP. LAWS ANN. § 27-8-1 (1967); TENN. CODE ANN. § 33-810 (Supp. 1968); TEX. REV. CIV. STAT. ANN. art. 5561c, Sec. 9 (c) (Supp. 1968); VT. STAT. ANN. tit. 18, § 7606 (Supp. 1968); VA. CODE ANN. § 37.1-66 (Supp. 1968); W. VA. CODE ANN. §§ 27-6-2, 3 (1966) (presence of subject required only if necessary to protect interest).

3 *E.g.,* HAWAII REV. STAT. § 334-81 (1968); N.Y. MENTAL HYGIENE LAW § 307 (McKinney Supp. 1968); N.C. GEN. STAT. § 122-58 (1964) (an alternative procedure requires a hearing).

4 ILL. ANN. STAT. ch. 91½, § 5-3 (Smith-Hurd 1956) (notice); N.Y. MENTAL HYGIENE LAW §§ 72-74 (McKinney 1964) (certification); HAWAII REV. STAT. §§ 334-53—334-54 (1968) (certification).

4a CAL. WELF. & INST'NS CODE §§ 5000 et seq., §§ 5170 et seq., (West Supp. 1969).

5 387 U.S. 1 (1966).

6 In Baxstrom v. Herold, 383 U.S. 107 (1966), the Court struck down a commitment to a mental institution at the expiration of criminal sentence because the failure to follow New York procedures for civil commitment was a denial of equal protection. In Specht v. Patterson, 386 U.S. 605 (1967), the Court did not allow a sentence under the Colorado Sex Offenders Act without notice and a full hearing since the sentence under the Act required a new finding of fact. The Court said: "These commitment proceedings whether denominated civil or criminal are subject both to the Equal Protection Clause of the Fourteenth Amendment . . . and to the Due Process Clause." Id., at 608. In In re Gault, 387 U.S. 1 (1967), the Court remanded a juvenile delinquency proceeding because of lack of adequate notice, no right to counsel, no right to cross-examination and no right to remain silent. The Court emphasized the deprivation of liberty that is the result of this type of proceeding. Id., at 27.

7 Cf. Romer, Liberty vs. Mental Health—California Examines Compulsory Hospitalization Laws, 24 CALIF. HEALTH 27, 28 (1966), wherein the author states "Court orders in many cases, therefore, are nothing more than a rubber stamp of recommendations of two examining doctors."

8 See Dershowitz, The Psychiatrist's Power in Civil Commitment, PSYCHOLO-GY TODAY, Feb., 1969, at 43, 47, wherein the author discusses the problems of prediction and suggests that physicians' capacity for prediction is limited and that they frequently overpredict. It may be suggested that lay predictions are even less predictable than psychiatric ones.

9 Note, Due Process for All—Constitutional Standards for Involuntary Commitment and Release, 34 U. CHI. L. REV. 633, 654 (1967).

10 But see Note, 76 YALE L. J. 1160, at 1181 (1967).

11 See Note, 79 HARV. L. REV. 1288, 1291 (1966); but see Note, 76 YALE L.J., supra note 10, at 1182, 1183.

12 Note, 79 HARV. L. REV., supra note 11, at 1291. But see Note, The Nascent Right to Treatment, 53 VA. L. REV. 1134, 1142 (1967).

13 ARK. STAT. ANN. § 83-709 (b) (Supp. 1967); KAN. GEN. STAT. ANN. § 74-4408 (1964); KY. REV. STAT. § 222.130 (1959); MISS. CODE ANN. § 436-02 (1956); PA. STAT. ANN. tit. 50, § 2105 (7) (Supp. 1969); TEX. REV. CIV. STAT. ANN. art. 5561c, Sec. 9 (Supp. 1968).

14 Comment, Analysis of Legal and Medical Considerations of Mentally Ill, 56 YALE L.J. 1178, 1193 (1946-47); Kadish, A Case Study in the Signification of Procedural Due Process—Institutionalizing the Mentally Ill, 9 WESTERN POL. Q. 93, 96 (1956).

15 N.Y. MENTAL HYGIENE LAW § 73a (McKinney 1967).

16 HAWAII REV. STAT. §§ 334-81—334-83 (1968).

17 Note 9 supra.

18 Note 5 supra.

19 E.g., Baxstrom v. Herold, supra note 6; Specht v. Patterson, supra note 6.

20 Note, 79 HARV. L. REV., supra note 11, at 1291. But see Note, 53 VA. L. REV., supra note 12, at 1142.

21 Notes 15, 16 supra.

22 N.Y. MENTAL HYGIENE LAW § 88 (McKinney Supp. 1968).

23 Note 10 supra.

24 Note 7 supra.

25 Note 10 *supra.*

26 *See* p. 175 *infra,* notes 52-54 and acompanying text.

27 ARK. STAT. ANN. § 83-709 (Supp. 1967); CONN. GEN. STAT. ANN.
§ 17-155 (e) (Supp. 1969); GA. CODE ANN. § 88-405 (e) (Supp. 1968); KAN.
STAT. ANN. § 74-4408 (1964); N.M. STAT. ANN. § 46-12-7 (Supp. 1967); R.I.
GEN. LAWS ANN. § 40-12-17 (1956); S.D. COMP. LAWS ANN. § 27-8-3 (1967);
TEX. REV. CIV. STAT. ANN. art. 5561c, Sec. 9 (d) (Supp. 1968); VT. STAT.
ANN. tit. 18, § 2951 (b), (d) (Supp. 1968); W. VA. CODE ANN. § 27-1A-11
(1966).

28 *E.g.,* IOWA CODE ANN. § 229.9 (Supp. 1969) (after screening at a local
center); KY. REV. STAT. § 222.150 (1959); MISS. CODE ANN. §§ 436-04, 11
(1956) (allows refusal of a person who willfully and consistently fails to be
rehabilitated unless person pays in advance); MONT. REV. CODES ANN. § 38-208
(1961); NEV. REV. STAT. § 433.280 (1967); N.H. REV. STAT. ANN. § 172:13
(Supp. 1967).

29 TENN. CODE ANN. § 33-811 (Supp. 1968).

30 CONN. GEN. STAT. ANN. § 17-155g (Supp. 1969); OHIO REV. CODE
ANN. § 5122.05 (Baldwin 1964); VT. STAT. ANN. tit. 18, § 8402 (Supp. 1968);
VA. CODE ANN. §§ 37-1-1 (8), 37.1-66, 67 (Supp. 1968).

31 *E.g.,* ARK. STAT. ANN. § 83-709 (d) (Supp. 1967); MASS. GEN. LAWS
ANN. ch. 123, § 62 (1965); WIS. STAT. ANN. § 51.09 (Supp. 1969).

32 *E.g.,* VA. CODE ANN. §§ 37.1-73, 74 (Supp. 1968). (no jail detention
unless specifically authorized).

32a Note 27 *supra.* This follows a recent trend in correctional law and admin-
inistration. *See* MODEL PENAL CODE § 304.1.

33 *See* p. 161-162 *supra.*

34 ARK. STAT. ANN. § 83-705 (1960) (5-90 days); CONN. GEN. STAT.
ANN. § 17-155g (Supp. 1969) (12 mo. max.); D.C. CODE ANN. § 24-525 (Supp.
II 1969) (30 days or 90 for third and subsequent commitments); KAN. STAT.
ANN. § 74-4408 (1964) (30 days-12 mo. or 4 days to 1 year depending on to
whom committed); KY. REV. STAT. §§ 222.150, 222.160 (1959) (6 mo. max.);
MD. ANN. CODE art. 2c, § 306 (Supp. 1968) (30 day maximum); MASS. GEN.
LAWS ANN. ch. 123, § 62 (1965) (2 years maximum); MISS. CODE ANN.
§ 436-03 (1956) (minimum 30 days-maximum 90 days); NEV. REV. STAT.
§433.280 (1967) (maximum 1 year); N. H. REV. STAT. ANN. § 172:13 (Supp.
1967) (minimum 30 days, maximum 90 days); N.J. STAT. ANN § 30:9-12.21
(1964) (maximum 90 days); N.M. STAT. ANN. § 46-12-7 (Supp. 1967) (maximum
30 days); N.Y. MENTAL HYGIENE LAW § 307 (McKinney Supp. 1968) (maximum 6 mo., then new order); N.C. GEN. STAT. § 122-65 (1964) (maximum 180
days); PA. STAT. ANN. tit. 50, § 2107 (1954) (maximum 1 year); R.I. GEN.
LAWS ANN. § 40-12-17 (1956) (60 days minimum-3 year maximum, then new
proceeding); S.D. COMP. LAWS ANN. § 27-8-3 (1967) (maximum 90 days);
TENN. CODE ANN. § 33-810 (Supp. 1968) (4 days minimum-12 mo. maximum);
TEX. REV. CIV. STAT. ANN. art. 5561c, Sec. 9 (d) (Supp. 1968) (15 days to
3 mo.); VT. STAT. ANN. tit. 18, § 8403 (Supp. 1968) (30 days-6 mo.); W. VA.
CODE ANN. § 27-6-4 (1966) (minimum 30 days); for a discussion of actual practice
see Appendix A at 365 ff.

35 *E.g.,* VA. CODE ANN. § 37.1-98 (Supp. 1968) (restored to sanity—improved
or unimproved if not detrimental to public and not necessary for own welfare);
WIS. STAT. ANN. § 51.09 (2) (Supp. 1969) (recovered so that he is able to
care for himself).

36 *E.g.,* IOWA CODE ANN. § 224.3 (Supp. 1969).

37 *E.g.,* CONN. GEN. STAT .ANN. § 17-155 (e) (Supp. 1969).

38 *E.g.,* Louisiana provides no standard for discharge; *see* Appendix B, Chart III.

39 *See* AMERICAN BAR FOUNDATION, THE MENTALLY DISABLED AND
THE LAW 126 (F. Lindman & D. McIntyre, eds., 1961); Katz & Goldstein,
*Dangerousness and Mental Illness, Some Observations on the Decision to Release
Persons Acquitted by Reason of Insanity,* 70 YALE L.J. 225, 231 (1960).

40 *See* p. 170 and note 34 *supra.*

41 *E.g.*, Birnbaum, *The Right to Treatment*, 46 A.B.A.J. 499 (1960); Note, 77 YALE L.J. 87 (1967); Note, 34 U. CHI. L. REV., *supra* note 9, at 633; Note, 53 VA. L. REV., *supra* note 12, at 1134.

42 373 F.2d 451 (D.C. Cir. 1966).

43 D.C. CODE ANN. § 24-301 (d) (1961).

44 373 F.2d at 453; *cf.* United States *ex rel.* Schuster v. Herold, 410 F.2d 1071 (2d Cir. 1969).

45 373 F.2d at 453.

46 *Id.*, at 456.

47 *Id.*

48 *Id.*, at 456-57.

49 *E.g.*, Commonwealth v. Hogan, 341 Mass. 372, 170 N.E.2d 327 (1960); Alexander v. Superintendent of Spring Grove State Hospital, 246 Md. 334, 228 A.2d 236 (1967).

50 *See* Director of Patuxent Institution v. Daniels, 243 Md. 16, 221 A.2d 397 (1966); Note, 77 YALE L.J., *supra* note 41, at 109. But *see* Collins v. Cameron, 377 F.2d 945, 947 (D.C. Cir. 1967), where the court stated that under some circumstances, custodial care standing alone is a form of therapy for some conditions.

51 Note, 34 U. CHI. L. REV., *supra* note 9, at 654 *et seq.* presents a persuasive case for shifting the burden of proof to the state.

52 *E.g.*, CAL. WELF. & INST'NS CODE § 5150 (1967); MASS. ANN. LAWS ch. 123, § 62 (1956); N.Y. MENTAL HYGIENE LAW § 75 (McKinney 1951).

53 *E.g.*, MASS. ANN. LAWS ch. 123, § 62 (1956).

54 *E.g.*, CAL. WELF. & INST'NS CODE § 5150 (1967) (72 hrs.); N.Y. MENTAL HYGIENE LAW § 75 (McKinney 1951) (10 days).

CHAPTER 8
Requisite Facilities

Recent legislation reflects the consensus that a variety of facilities should be available in a comprehensive alcoholism treatment program.[1] In addition, legislation should indicate, to a greater degree than it does at present, the extent to which facilities for the treatment of alcoholism are to be integrated with existing treatment facilities for other problems of health or mental health. The legislative requirement that certain treatment facilities be established, however, without adequate funding for the accomplishment of that goal, will not provide the clinics and the beds that are necessary. Realistically, the implementation of an adequate alcoholism program will require allocations of resources that reflect the acceptance of a fairly high priority for the solution of the social problems posed by alcoholism.

With a single, perhaps minor, exception, the problems of financing alcoholism programs are beyond the scope of this work. However, the recoupment of costs from patients or their families for treatment given can be properly considered in relation to facilities to be established, and will be discussed in the last part of this chapter.

NECESSARY FACILITIES

Most existing alcoholism statutes do not specify the facilities that should be available. Some merely allow inpatient care, a few direct the establishment of an alcoholism center,[2] and a few recognize the need for outpatient clinics or stations and generally set out how such facilities should be maintained.[3] The more recent statutes, in contrast do expressly authorize the kinds of facilities to be established, which include emergency, inpatient, outpatient and intermediate care facilities.[4] This specification is desirable because it sets a proper goal for the program. However, legislation should not, as indicated earlier, endorse any particular treatment method.[5] It is also unnecessary to specify the capacity for each facility or the number of facilities in

102

each category which should be available. Such specificity in legislation is useless in any event, because the size and number of institutions or facilities will depend on available funding, and should be
left flexible to accommodate current needs. The ensuing discussion
of kinds of facilities required is relevant to legal considerations to
the extent that it supports the need for their establishment, and
points to the desirability of integrating them with other care and
treatment services in the state.

Emergency Treatment Facilities

The required treatment for acute intoxication (discussed in
Chapter 2), which involves medical and nursing care, drug therapy
and other medication, is relatively uniform,[6] and can be given either
in a general hospital or in a special facility which is affiliated with
or part of a general hospital, and has access to medical facilities in
cases of emergency.[7] Some of the more recent legislation, notably in
Maryland and the District of Columbia,[8] requires the establishment
of such facilities. Although these laws are too recent for a full
evaluation, special centers for the treatment of intoxication have
already been set up on an experimental basis in several cities and the
programs have proved successful.[9]

However, the new emphasis on treatment for alcoholism should
not be equated with current stress on the establishment of "detoxification centers." Although these facilities meet the emergency needs
of alcoholics and are a means of encouraging them to undergo further
voluntary treatment, they represent only one of several sources of
intake for a broad treatment program. Such a treatment program
must provide for follow-up, and for a broad range of care-giving
and social services, to be afforded through the coordination efforts
of a number of state and local agencies.

Inpatient facilities

Most existing alcoholism programs rely primarily on inpatient
treatment.[10] It is undisputed that some alcoholics do require intensive inpatient care. Alcoholism treatment legislation should insure
that inpatient treatment facilities will be available, but there is a
general consensus that it is not the answer for the majority of alcoholics, nor even necessarily for those who are committed for involuntary treatment. For example, in state hospitals offering psychotherapeutic inpatient care to alcoholics, the average rate of cure one

year after treatment is only 33%.[11] In addition, the overall "cure" rates have been found not to differ significantly between psychotherapeutic inpatient and outpatient programs.[12] Rather than providing routine inpatient care, treatment should be dependent on the needs of the individual patient.[13] It has been suggested, for example, that outpatient clinics may not be adequate for skid row alcoholics for whom inpatient or supportive residential facilities may be necessary.[14] On the other hand, the employed, middle-class father or mother might be more easily treated, and might be more willing to volunteer for treatment on an outpatient basis. For many such patients inpatient care will not be necessary if an adequate range of alternative programs is provided.[15]

Therefore, on the basis of current medical opinion, it would seem unwise for an alcoholism treatment program to rely too heavily on inpatient care. Inpatient care is also substantially more expensive, both in terms of capital outlay and of operating expenses, than other forms of treatment.[16]

The establishment of inpatient facilities would seem to be a less important task than that of insuring that alcoholics who require hospitalization will receive the treatment they require once they are hospitalized. At present, many state mental hospitals offer little or no treatment for alcoholics, and in some, the special treatment is provided by Alcoholics Anonymous or other non-medical personnel. About 10% of the state hospitals do have some special programs, but the average rate of cure is not much higher than in hospitals without programs.[17] In some special programs, however, admission is severely limited to a very small number of selected alcoholics.[18] St. Elizabeth's in Washington, D.C., for example, accepts only 35 carefully selected patients for its program from among 1,500 to 2,000 alcoholic patients.[19] Another problem is that some inpatient programs are located in state prisons or reformatories, giving them an inescapably punitive aspect. Alcoholics who have not been convicted of a crime should not be treated in correctional institutions.[20]

Outpatient Facilities

The legislature should authorize the establishment of facilities for outpatient care, to serve both the function of initial treatment and of follow-up care after inpatient treatment. Florida's 1953 alcoholism law, for example, establishes five regional outpatient clinics; they provide both initial treatment and aftercare for alcoholics who have been treated in a special inpatient treatment facility.[21] The outpatient aftercare is particularly important in view of the high relapse rate of alcoholics. Usually the recovered alcoholic is merely sent back to the community from which he came, and unless given aftercare, he will frequently return to his earlier drinking patterns.[22] Although aftercare can be provided by a variety of lay or residential programs,[23] the basic aftercare facility for most patients will be the outpatient clinic.[24]

In addition, outpatient care is likely to meet the treatment needs of the large number of individuals who do not require intensive inpatient treatment.[25] Outpatient clinics can offer a variety of treatment programs, including group psychotherapy[26] or Antabuse therapy.[27]

Within a legislative system which states a clear preference for voluntary, outpatient treatment for alcoholics, there should be administrative discretion to establish outpatient facilities wherever and whenever a need arises. One clear need is the expansion of available community mental health clinics to treat alcoholics. Increased reliance on outpatient care will require the establishment or expansion of many mental health and other care-giving facilities, because the presently available facilities for the outpatient care for alcoholics have long been inadequate both in terms of quantity and quality of service.

Intermediate Care Facilities

A wide variety of intermediate facilities are needed for alcoholics who do not need intensive inpatient care, but who are not so self-sufficient as to benefit from a regular outpatient program. Such intermediate facilities include halfway houses,[28] foster homes,[29] and special facilities for day or night hospitalization.[30]

Halfway houses are generally small facilities, usually located in residential areas, where alcoholics can live in a controlled environment, hold jobs in the community, and receive some supportive treatment. Although "halfway house" suggests a facility to ease the return of an alcoholic from intensive inpatient care back into society, most residents of halfway houses come directly from the community and not from hospitals or prisons.[31] One source, indeed, has expressed some doubts as to usefulness of halfway houses to alcoholics released from inpatiend and correctional institutions.[32] The establishment of halfway houses should be authorized by the legislature, because they provide an economical way to treat those alcoholics for whom intensive inpatient care is not required, but who lack the motivation or independence to utilize an outpatient clinic.

Residential and Other Supportive Facilities

There is a growing need for facilities for certain older alcoholics for whom complete rehabilitation proves impossible. Only a few residential institutions for this purpose are presently in operation. One such facility is Camp La Guardia, operated by New York City's Department of Social Service in a rural setting and accommodating 1,500 men. Its stated purpose is to provide "an opportunity for older, homeless men to restore health and morale by means of proper rest, wholesome recreation, and work for its therapeutic value." Although medical care is provided, and participation in the program of Alcoholics Anonymous is encouraged, no intensive psychotherapeutic care is offered. The facility is purely voluntary.[33] To give only one example of its permissive atmosphere, the establishment allows the residents of the camp to have beer—a desirable move in view of the fact that it discourages the men from leaving the camp in order to get a drink, while not contributing to troublesome inebriety. Legislation should grant authority for the establishment of such residential institutions so as to permit older alcoholics for whom rehabilitation is unlikely to live in a decent and humane environment.

INTEGRATION OF FACILITIES FOR THE TREATMENT OF ALCOHOLISM WITH OTHER TREATMENT FACILITIES

A considerable increase in facilities and services for the treatment of alcoholics is clearly necessary. It would be undesirable, however, to permit such an expansion of facilities to assume the form of a new and separate "alcoholism establishment." Such a separatist development would lead to undesirable duplication of facilities and administration, and would separate the treatment of alcoholism from the treatment of other socio-medical problems that may be related in terms of causation and social pathology.

To the fullest extent possible, therefore, legislation should direct that other treatment facilities—such as mental hospitals, general hospitals, mental health clinics, etc.—be expanded, wherever necessary, so as to include services for alcoholics. The precise degree of integration of alcoholism treatment services and facilities with other existing facilities will vary from state to state, and will depend to some extent on the nature of the existing facilities, both for the treatment of alcoholism and for other health and mental health treatment in the particular jurisdictions. To bring about the integration of treatment facilities for alcoholics, there will have to be major attitudinal changes among physicians and others that render treatment in hospitals, mental institutions and clinics. Too many hospitals and clinics presently turn away alcoholics, because they are disinterested in treating them and consider them poor treatment risks. Full integration of treatment facilities will therefore require some reeducation of the medical and mental health establishments. Social services in hospitals need to be enhanced; at present most hospitals administer only medical care and are not equipped to render emergency social services or to provide appropriate referrals.[34] In the past, many general hospitals have been reluctant to admit intoxicated persons, particularly if they were indigent.[35] At the very least, legislation should require that emergency facilities for the treatment of alcoholism have access to back-up emergency medical facilities in a hospital whenever necessary.

Outpatient treatment centers should whenever possible be integrated with existing outpatient facilities. Indeed, wherever a community mental health center is established, it should make special provision for the inclusion of alcoholics in its treatment services. As a practical matter, there is no reason why legislation should not direct the integration of all public outpatient facilities, because at present there are no more than 135 specialized alcoholism outpatient clinics in the entire United States,[36] some operating only part-time.[37] Thus the problem of combining existing facilities would be relatively minor. Yet to bring alcoholics within existing health and mental health facilities will require substantial effort since existing general psychiatric clinics and community health centers tend to give alcoholics low priority.[38] Usually alcoholics are "screened out" because clinic staffs consider them hopeless.[39]

In many states inpatient facilities for alcoholics are already integrated with other facilities; most inpatient treatment is provided in state mental hospitals.[40] Although inpatient treatment in community-based facilities is more desirable, it is probable that the state hospital will continue to be an important inpatient treatment facility for some time. Inpatient facilities should in any event provide adequate care and alcoholism treatment programs even though special alcoholism facilities are unnecessary. Intermediate care facilities, on the other hand, may properly be operated either separately or in conjunction with facilities for persons with similar social-medical problems.

Finally, with the continuing need for experimentation in the field of treatment, the alcoholism division or other treatment agency should be authorized to engage in demonstration projects which need not initially form a part of existing services. In sum, whenever possible, both existing and new help-giving facilities should be utilized so as to prevent unnecessary duplication and fragmentation of services in the treatment of alcoholics.

CHAPTER 8 NOTES

[1] D.C. CODE ANN. § 24-523 (Supp. II, 1969); MD. ANN. CODE art. 2c, § 302 (Supp. 1968).

[2] FLA. STAT. ANN. § 396.031 (Supp. 1969); S.C. CODE ANN. § 32.895 (Supp. 1968); VA. CODE ANN. § 32-371 (1964).

[3] *E.g.,* ALA. CODE tit. 55, § 373 (13a) (Supp. 1967); ARK. STAT. ANN. § 83-701 (1960); GA. CODE ANN. § 88-403 (Supp. 1968); ILL. ANN. STAT. ch. 91½, § 100-10 (Smith-Hurd 1963); KY. REV. STAT. § 222.035 (1) (1962); LA. REV. STAT. ANN. § 40.2008.3 (1965).

[4] D.C. CODE ANN. § 24-523 (Supp. II, 1969); MD. ANN. CODE art. 2c, § 302 (Supp. 1968); *see Proposed: An Act Establishing a Comprehensive Intoxication and Alcoholism Control Plan and Program* 6 (Mass. 1969 legislative session).

[5] Ch. 4 *supra.*

[6] A description of the physical effects of chronic alcoholism and of acute intoxication can be found in JELLINEK, THE DISEASE CONCEPT OF ALCOHOLISM 82-110 (1960). *See* PRESIDENT'S COMM'N ON LAW ENFORCEMENT & ADMINISTRATION OF JUSTICE, TASK FORCE REPORT: DRUNKENNESS 53-54 (1967); NATIONAL INSTITUTE OF MENTAL HEALTH, ALCOHOL AND ALCOHOLISM 31-33 (Public Health Service Pub. No. 1640, 1968); McNichol, *et al., Management of Withdrawal from Alcohol (including Delirium Tremens)*, 60 SO. MED. J., J. SO. MED. ASS'N 7-12 (1967).

[7] *See* TASK FORCE REPORT: DRUNKENNESS, *supra* note 6, at 5, 61; R. GLASSCOTE, T. PLAUT, D. HAMMERSLEY, F. O'NEILL, M. CHAFETZ, E. CUMMING, THE TREATMENT OF ALCOHOLISM 20 (1967) (hereinafter cited as GLASSCOTE).

[8] D.C. CODE ANN. § 24-523 (Supp. II, 1969); MD. ANN. CODE art. 2c, § 302 (Supp. 1968).

[9] TASK FORCE REPORT: DRUNKENNESS, *supra* note 6, at 5, 50-55, 61. There are few such centers operated on a state-wide basis; most limit their activities to a particular locality whitin the state. *See* Appendix C, Chart VI.

[10] *See* Appendix C, Chart. I.

[11] Moore & Buchanan, *State Hospitals and Alcoholism*, 27 Q.J. STUD. ALCOHOL 459, 463 (1966).

[12] Edwards & Guthrie, *A Controlled Trial of In-patient and Out-patient Treatment of Alcohol Dependency*, 1 LANCET 555 (1967).

[13] *See* Lisansky, *The Woman Alcoholic*, 315 ANNALS 73, 79 (1958).

[14] Rubington, *The Chronic Drunkenness Offender*, 315 ANNALS 65, 70-71 (1958). *See* Weil & Price, *Alcoholism in a Metropolis*, 9 CRIME & DELINQUENCY 60, 66 (1963) (stating that outpatients tend to be more stable, economically secure, and middle class than inpatients).

[15] GLASSCOTE, *supra* note 7, at 29.

[16] HARRISON TREATMENT & REHABILITATION CENTER, COLLEGE OF OSTEOPATHIC MEDICINE; DES MOINES, IOWA, PROGRESS REPORT SEPT. 2, 1967 - DEC. 31, 1961, UPDATED MAY 15, 1968, 10, 22 (1968).

[17] GLASSCOTE, *supra* note 7, at 18; T. PLAUT, ALCOHOL PROBLEMS 65 (1967); Moore & Buchanan, *supra* note 11, at 463. *See* Appendix C, Chart I.

[18] PLAUT, *supra* note 17, at 67.

[19] VISITING COMM. OF THE WASHINGTON, D.C., AREA COUNCIL ON ALCOHOLISM, FIRST REPORT ON THE CURRENT STATUS OF ALCO-HOLISM PROGRAMS AND FACILITIES 2 (1967) (hereinafter cited as WACA).

[20] *See* p. 26 *supra.*

[21] GLASSCOTE, *supra* note 7, at 56-61, 65.

[22] Meyerson & Mayer, *Origins, Treatment and Destiny of Skid Row Alcoholic Men,* 19 S.C.L. REV. 332, 338 (1967); GLASSCOTE, *supra* note 7, at 140.

[23] Occoquan Reformatory has a day work-release program for involuntary alco-holic inpatients; WACA, *supra* note 19, at 31. The Long Island Program of the Boston City Hospital has a similar program for voluntary patients; Weil & Price, *supra* note 14, at 67. Halfway houses and foster homes are also used; *id. See* TASK FORCE REPORT: DRUNKENNESS, *supra* note 6, at 19.

[24] For example, in Florida's comprehensive alcoholism program outpatient clinics are used to provide follow-up care for patients released from the inpatient facility; GLASSCOTE, *supra* note 7, at 62.

[25] GLASSCOTE, *supra* note 7, at 29.

[26] Group therapy is most commonly chosen for treatment of alcoholics. *E.g.,* Vogel, *Psychiatric Treatment of Alcoholism,* 315 ANNALS 99, 106 (1958); GLASS-COTE, *supra* note 7, at 15. "Group counselling is a practical and economical method of treating a large number of persons;" Soden, *Constructive Coercion and Group Counselling in the Rehabilitation of Alcoholics,* 30 FED. PROBATION (No. 3) 56, 60 (1966). Group therapy has been found particularly useful in treating skid row alcoholics. Rubington, *supra* note 14, at 66-69.

[27] 75% of state mental hospitals use some form of psychochemotherapy in treating alcoholics, and 22% of state mental hospitals use Antabuse in treating alcoholics; Moore & Buchanan, *supra* note 11, at 461.

[28] *E.g.,* WACA, *supra* note 19, at 32-37; Rubington, *supra* note 14, at 70, 71.

[29] *See* note 23 *supra.*

[30] *Id.; see* WACA, *supra* note 19, at 31.

[31] Plaut, *Alcoholism and Community Caretakers: Programs and Policies,* 12 SOCIAL WORK (No. 3) 42, 47 (1967). Halfway houses are used for follow-up treatment in some states, however; *see* Appendix C, Charts III, V. *Hearings on H.R. 6143 before the Subcomm. of the House Comm. on the District of Columbia,* 90th Cong., 1st Sess. 24, 32 (1967).

[32] *Hearings on H.R. 6143 before the Subcomm. of the House Comm. on the District of Columbia, supra* note 31, at 27, 28.

[33] DEPARTMENT OF SOCIAL SERVICES, CITY OF N.Y., AN INTRODUC-TION TO CAMP LAGUARDIA (undated).

[34] PLAUT, *supra* note 17, at 57-58; *see* Appendix C, Chart VIII. But some hospitals, such as Massachusetts General Hospital Boston, have attempted follow-up programs; GLASSCOTE, *supra* note 7, at 83, 84.

[35] For example, only four of Washington, D.C.'s private hospitals will treat alcoholics; WACA, *supra* note 19, at 23. *See* GLASSCOTE, *supra* note 7, at 20; PLAUT, *supra* note 17, at 57, 58.

[36] Plaut, *supra* note 31, at 42, 43. But a figure of 125 such clinics in 1967 is given in GLASSCOTE, *supra* 7, at 19. Outpatient clinics are used for follow-up treatment in some states; Appendix C, Charts III, V.

[37] GLASSCOTE, *supra* note 7, at 19; *Hearings on H.R. 6143 before the Sub-comm. of the House Comm. on the District of Columbia, supra* note 31, at 26.

[38] Plaut, *supra* note 31, at 45; GLASSCOTE, *supra* note 7, at 21. General Psychiatric Clinics do tend to neglect alcoholics, giving them fewer interviews than other patients, and having a generally lower success rate (27%) than special alcoholism clinics (51%); Bahn *et al., Out-patient Psychiatric Clinic Services to Alcoholics,* 1959, 24 Q.J. STUD. ALCOHOL 213, 217-218 (1963).

[39] Plaut, *supra* note 31, at 45. It used to be the stated policy of many social welfare agencies to refuse alcoholics; Sapia, *Social Work and Alcoholism,* 315 ANNALS 125 (1958).

[40] Plaut, *supra* note 31, at 42. *See* Appendix C, Chart I.

CHAPTER 9

The Administrative Structure Of An Alcoholism Program

The main outlines of the administrative structure of a jurisdiction's alcoholism program are commonly reflected in the legislation that establishes the program. The development of such a program involves questions of public policy, public administration and law. The choices that must be resolved are commonly choices between legally permissible alternatives, both with respect to the administrative structure of the agency that deals with alcoholism itself, and with respect to its functions, powers and duties. The purpose of a sound structure is to aid in effective administration, as well as to obtain recognition within the state government for the importance of a long-neglected problem.

THE NATURE AND PLACE OF THE AGENCY

Alcoholism and the problems of the alcoholic are—and should be—the concern of a number of state agencies, including those having responsibilities for institutional care, social care, social welfare, labor and employment, education, police and correction. Each of these departments or agencies, as well as a number of others, have responsibility for providing certain kinds of care, services or control that may be required by alcoholics in varying situations and circumstances. An agency charged with responsibility for the problems of alcoholism clearly could not assume the variety of tasks that other care-giving agencies and departments should continue to carry out. On the other hand, alcoholism as a major social problem of state and nation-wide concern has been long neglected. An agency is therefore needed in all of the states that will carry primary responsibility for education, research and treatment, and that will coordinate the activities of other care-giving agencies that relate to problems of alcoholism in order that there may be a consistent and rational plan of attack.

111

Existing statutory provisions usually place alcoholism programs within a specified department,[1] and provide that a bureau or division be charged with specific administrative responsibility.[2] Usually alcoholism statutes establish an unpaid advisory committee, responsible either to the department head or the governor.[3] Instead of creating a special bureau or division, the law may provide solely for an independent commission,[4] composed of non-government personnel[5] or of heads of various agencies,[6] serving *ex officio,* to study, and make policy for, the treatment of alcoholism, and sometimes to administer an actual program.

The creation of an independent commission may offer a few limited advantages—it is not bound by the procedures of any existing department, and it can go directly to the legislature with program and funding requests.[7] It will clearly have a single focus, and will not give low priority to alcoholism services as may happen if they are placed within an existing agency framework. The composition of such a commission is a matter of considerable significance—if it is composed, as in Alabama,[8] of heads of various executive agencies serving *ex officio,* it may well receive very limited attention from each. If it is served by interested but uncompensated laymen, on the other hand, as it is in Arkansas,[9] it may lack in professional approach and in adequate coordination with other state agencies.

On balance, placement of the alcoholism program within an existing department is preferable. Such placement is likely to result in a wider range of resources without unnecessary duplication of services, and thus is likely to be more economical.[10] Moreover, since it is evident that an effective alcoholism program requires coordination with other help-giving services,[11] placement of the program within an appropriate department should avoid fragmentation and improve overall planning.[12] The special problems of alcoholism can then be assigned to an alcoholism division within the department. Finally, establishing such a division, rather than a separate agency or commission, is less likely to create a self-perpetuating "alcoholism establishment."

DEPARTMENTAL RESPONSIBILITY

A wide variety of departments are charged by law with responsibility for alcoholism programs. Programs are located in the departments of health,[13] mental health,[14] health and welfare,[15] social welfare,[16] vocation and rehabilitation,[17] institutions and hospitals.[18] Placement of responsibility for alcoholism programs depends on both the particular state structure and the willingness of the department to accept the task. In general, it is likely that a hospital or institutions department will place major emphasis on long-term inpatient care, possibly with inhibitory consequences for the program as a whole. Whether an alcoholism program should be placed in a department of public health or mental health is a more difficult choice. A mental health department seems more appropriate since it is widely agreed that for most alcoholics excessive drinking begins as a false solution to other personality problems rather than as a problem in itself.[19] Moreover, if alcoholism is viewed as a behavioral or social disorder primarily responsive to psychiatric, psychological and related therapies, its treatment seems clearly to be the concern of a department of mental health.

Practical experience and practical considerations, too, argue strongly for the inclusion of alcoholism treatment services as part of mental health services generally. Mental health has an established administrative system and system of facilities in most states—though admittedly, it too suffers from inadequacies. To build a major separate system for the treatment of alcoholism, particularly in view of the expanding scope of the treatment effort under discussion, would be wasteful and would harm both existing mental health programs and incipient alcoholism programs. The point has been well made by one expert, Dr. Thomas F. A. Plaut, who has expressed the view that the development of specialized services will discourage general mental health facilities and general hospitals from treating alcoholics altogether. He cites three major reasons for treating alcoholism through existing mental health and other services:

> (1) Drinking problems are of such magnitude that sufficient funds and manpower cannot be mobilized for a special network except by "robbing" other network programs. (2) These problems do not exist in isolation from other social, psychological and health problems. It is inconceivable that any system of specialized facilities could be established to deal adequately with all three associated problems. (3) Large numbers of problem drinkers are already known to major caregiving agencies and often are obtaining some kind of help from them. The separation of this type of help from assistance for the drinking problem would be unfortunate and even disastrous.[20]

This view gains support, too, when the precise nature of the disease or disorder of alcoholism is still under definition. The notion that it is a single, distinct disease entity has been replaced in the minds of many specialists by the acceptance of the idea that alcoholism may be as much a symptom of other disorders as a disorder itself.[21] To take alcoholism out of the mental health field might thus be a disservice to the advancement of both.

On the other hand, cogent reasons may be advanced for placing the responsibility for alcoholism within a department of public health. It has been said that such a department is more likely to have an open mind to *any* treatment approach, not limited to that of mental health, and that treatment of alcoholism as a "disease" within the department of public health relieves it of the purported stigma of a "mental illness" which is feared to be implicit in treatment efforts by a department of mental health.[22] It is said that keeping treatment for alcoholism out of the department of mental health avoids the stigma and makes it more likely that alcoholics will seek treatment voluntarily.[23] While the growing public awareness of and interest in mental health, as well as the rapid advances in the treatment of mental illness, might make the arguments against mental health jurisdiction less persuasive now than in earlier times, it is clear that the department's name—public health or mental health—is of far less importance than its basic orientation.

QUALIFICATIONS OF THE DIRECTOR

The qualifications of the chief administrator of the program need statutory specification. At present, typical statutory qualifications are interest in the subject and administrative ability.[24] A few states require that the administrator be a physician;[25] this is not too relevant a qualification, unless there is a further requirement of special training in the treatment of alcoholism. One state requires that the administrator be an "arrested" alcoholic, that is, someone who no longer drinks and is an active member of Alcoholics Anonymous.[26] Exclusive reliance on Alcoholics Anonymous is hardly a sound basis for an alcoholism program,[27] and though an "arrested" alcoholic may serve useful functions within a program, there is no ground to assume that his prior condition will produce the expertise necessary for a chief program administrator. Directors of tuberculosis programs are not generally required to suffer from arrested tuberculosis. Until special training in the treatment of alcoholism becomes more widely available, the requisite qualifications must be broad enough to allow the appointment of a variety of persons who have expertise or training that is relevant, even if the experience or training is not specifically in the field of alcoholism, but relate to the treatment of behavioral disorders generally.

ADVISORY COMMITTEES

A number of states provide for some type of advisory committee as part of the administrative structure.[28] The use of unpaid advisory committees to generate public support and legislative interest is desirable, but such committees cannot be expected to perform technical tasks of evaluation and development. This view in turn suggests that the committee be responsible to the agency, rather than the governor, in spite of the greater prestige this would give the members. It also suggests that committee members should be informed and interested citizens—though diversity of professional backgrounds is desirable, the requirement that the committee consist of at least "2 physicians, 1 lawyer, 2 reformed alcoholics, etc.," frequently found in existing statutes,[29] is unnecessarily cumbersome and pretentious. The same is true of a statutory requirement of geographical representation, which now prevails in some states.[30] A general statement requiring that members of the committee have an interest in or experience with the treatment of alcohol problems allows the governor sufficient flexibility to make representative appointments. The functions of the advisory committee should be limited in scope; there should be no attempt to have the committee perform tasks of a technical nature that require a professional staff. The citizens' committee or council should be available as a sounding board to advise the agency or division, and as a link in communications with the general public, to generate interest in and support for alcoholism programs.

COORDINATION OF ACTIVITIES

The point has been made earlier that the alcoholism division or other similar agency ought to provide leadership in research, education and treatment, but that it cannot by itself provide all of the services that may become necessary in the rehabilitation of alcoholics and in the operation of an alcoholism program generally. Consequently there is a great need for coordination of the activities of all public care-giving agencies, both state and local, in so far as their activities serve alcoholics. Since public facilities are presently inadequate to meet all treatment needs, coordination between public and private agencies in the field is also necessary. A third area of coordination that must also be considered is coordination and cooperation across state lines.

To meet the need for interdepartmental coordination—and possibly also for state and local coordination—the newer state laws,[31] including some proposed state laws,[32] have required the establishment of a coordinating council or committee. Commonly, the proposals call for a committee consisting of the heads of departments that are likely to provide services to alcoholics—public health, mental health, hospitals, education, welfare, public safety, occupational rehabilitation, etc. Coordinating committees are intended to establish rules for interdepartmental cooperation in the field of alcoholism, to coordinate their alcoholism programs, and to assist in the development of a comprehensive state plan for the management of alcohol-related problems, usually as part of the state's comprehensive health plan required by Federal law.[33] A coordinating committee composed *ex officio* of department heads will undoubtedly stengthen interdepartmental coordination if the members devote time and attention to it. Unfortunately, experience with *ex officio* boards of this kind has not always been impressive, mainly because too often department heads who have a primary concern with running their own departments find it burdensome to give attention to matters they consider outside their own sphere of interest, and give short shrift to activities that appear extraneous. To avoid the difficulty as far as possible, there ought to be a provision to allow department heads to send deputies to committee meetings, even though this often has the practical consequence of delaying decisions until they can be cleared at a higher level. In addition, the division of alcoholism ought to be empowered to coordinate its efforts with other public and private agencies independently of the coordinating committee—the coordinating committee should advance efforts at cooperation, but it should not be in a position to prevent them by its inaction.

Coordination and cooperation with private groups and agencies should be fully authorized, and the division should be empowered to contract with such groups or agencies for research as well as treatment services, as well as to make grants for specific purposes when appropriate. Industrial programs for the detection and treatment of alcoholism have been particularly effective,[34] and there should, therefore, be express authorization in the law—as there is under the Maryland alcoholism statute[35]—to cooperate with business and industry in alcoholism programs.

The power to cooperate and coordinate activities should expressly include the power to make cooperative arrangements across state lines. Since jurisdictional lines often cut across metropolitan areas, facilities for treatment should be operated on a cooperative inter-jurisdictional basis, through contract or cost reimbursement arrangements, wherever necessary. So too, in sparsely populated areas, two or more states may find it more advantageous to combine in operating a single institution effectively and economically than for each to try a small operation on an inadequate scale. Most such arrangements will be possible without the formal machinery of an interstate compact (which may require Congressional consent) but they will require special authorization by law.

POWERS AND DUTIES OF DIVISION OF ALCOHOLISM

In enumerating the powers and duties of the agency charged with the administration of an alcoholism program, legislation tends to be very general. Indeed, this is necessary because appropriations for alcoholism programs have long been inadequate, and to impose specific duties with inadequate resources for their accomplishment would give rise to great difficulties. It has long been true that the real basis for an effective program is to be found in appropriation bills to at least as great an extent as in the powers and duties section of the substantive law.

In addition to its function in relation to treatment discussed in previous chapters, the division of alcoholism should be directed with some specificity to perform educational functions and to engage in or encourage research. Moreover, the division's responsibility for treatment facilities should be defined and some attention should be given to protection of patients who utilize the facilities.

Research

Most state laws give the division of alcoholism or similar agency power to carry out and support relevant research in very general terms. In one state there is specific provision for an alcoholism research center to be operated in cooperation with the state medical school[36] and another state establishes a special bureau to study chronic police cases,[37] but such special directives are rare. While special circumstances may justify special authorizations, a general mandate is entirely sufficient.[38]

The important point is that the law encourage research into the causes, nature and treatment of alcoholism. A particular problem which relates to research needs is the lack of reliable statistics on the various state programs in the treatment of alcoholics. The questionnaire survey conducted in connection with this study which is summarized in Appendix C[39] demonstrates the paucity of good statistical data. Thus it is well to include in the legislation a specific direction to collect relevant statistics and to suggest the major areas on which the collection of data should focus.

Education

Most existing laws require the division of alcoholism to carry out some educational functions, usually in very general terms. Some statutes emphasize the education of children[40] and some emphasize the provision of actual materials.[41] The educational functions of the division of alcoholism should be legislatively defined in general terms so that educational efforts may place emphasis on the methods and techniques that experience shows to be most effective.

Primary and secondary school education about alcohol and alcoholism presents a special problem. Most states do require schools to provide some alcoholism education—there are indications, however, that this instruction is often remote from the alcoholism program, may be based on inadequate factual background and may contradict the program's philosophy.[42] It would be unworkable in many jurisdictions to place total responsibility for alcoholism education in the schools on the division of alcoholism, but the division should be empowered to assist in the school program in some fashion—if help is offered by the alcoholism division to the education department in the form of up-to-date teaching materials and information, it is likely that the division's expertise will be utilized.

Functions Relating to Treatment Facilities

The subject of the relationship of the division of alcoholism to treatment and care-giving services generally has been referred to earlier.[43] It is clear that the division will not be in charge of all of the institutions in the state in which alcoholics are treated. Thus, patterns of coordination with local and private treatment facilities need to be established. This is a subject that has received no attention at all in past alcoholism legislation. No supervisory or even licensing pattern has as yet been proposed, and such developments await the future direction of the field. To the extent that contractual relations or grantor-grantee relations exist between state and local, or state and private facilities, the grant or contract has built-in supervisory aspects.

As the field expands, and as treatment facilities are established in greater numbers, the possibility of greater and more systematic state supervision will have to be considered.

Protection of Patients' Right of Privacy

Patients who are institutionalized should be assured that certain rights will be protected, most notably the right of confidentiality of their records and, for patients in inpatient facilities, the right of free and confidential communication. Only a few states specify such protections, and some distinguish between involuntary and voluntary patients.[44] There is no apparent necessity for the distinction.

As long as alcoholism carries with it a stigma which does not attach to other diseases, patients should receive legislative protection against social disgrace from publicity. Only a few states presently meet the problem in their legislation.[45] Those that do either limit the protection to voluntary patients[46] or, in a few instances, to involuntary patients.[47] No valid reason for a distinction has ever been supplied. Some of these statutes provide for disclosure only on a court order,[48] or only for medical purposes;[49] other statutes provide only for disclosure on consent.[50] The more recent statutes in the District of Columbia and Maryland give a qualified protection only to detoxification unit records.[51]

A patient's records must of course be available when they are relevant to his treatment, and should be available, subject to court order, when a socially useful purpose will be served. For example, it may be important in a child custody proceeding for the court to be fully apprised of the diagnosis and prognosis of an alcoholic father, or it may be important in a claim for wrongful detention at a detoxification unit for a court to be informed of a person's medical condition at the time of detention. In situations such as these, the need for the information should be weighed by the court against the possible harm of disclosure.

There is a need, too, to have treatment records available for purposes of research, and provisions should be made for the disclosure of records to established professional researchers engaged in serious alcoholism studies; such disclosures for research purposes should be made only, however, if the privacy of the patient will be safeguarded. The confidentiality provisions of the mental health laws in New York and California furnish examples of desirable patterns of legislation.[52]

The right of communication is exercised by a patient in an inpatient facility in two ways: through visitation and through correspondence with those outside. Although some states provide for a limited right to communicate with public officials or a central hospital agency,[53] few have provided for an absolute right[54] on the theory that the patient ought to be protected from certain correspondence which may impede his recovery.[55] Yet it is clear that the right to challenge a commitment through appeal and *habeas corpus* is likely to be meaningful only if a patient is able to obtain advice and guidance freely. There should be an absolute rule preserving the confidentiality of communication and specially protecting the right to communicate with counsel.

Visitation rights should be and often are protected,[56] but for administrative reasons these rights cannot be absolute. The hospital must be able to regulate the modes and frequency of visits in the light of administrative needs and the patients' welfare although there should be a general right to see visitors. The right to visit with counsel, however, should be subject to minimal limitations only —such as visits during day time—but should not be circumscribed in any other way.

CHAPTER 9 NOTES

1 ALASKA STAT. § 47.30.470 (1966); ARIZ. REV. STAT. ANN. § 36-141 (Supp. 1969); CAL. HEALTH & SAFETY CODE § 427.1 (West Supp. 1968); COLO. REV. STAT. ANN. § 66-1-7 (23) (1963); CONN. GEN. STAT. ANN. § 17-155a (Supp. 1969); FLA. STAT. ANN. § 396.021 (1960); GA. CODE ANN. § 88-403 (Supp. 1968); IDAHO CODE ANN. § 67-3110 (Supp. 1967); ILL. ANN. STAT. ch. 91½, § 100-10 (Smith-Hurd 1963); IND. ANN. STAT. § 22-1504 (1964); IOWA CODE ANN. § 123A.2 (Supp. 1969); KY. REV. STAT. § 222.035 (1962); LA. REV. STAT. ANN. § 40.2008.3 (1965); ME. REV. STAT. ANN. tit. 22, § 1351 (1961); MD. ANN. CODE art. 2c, § 301 (Supp. 1968); MASS. GEN. LAWS ANN. ch. 111, § 4a (1967); MICH. COMP. LAWS ANN. § 35.702 (1968); MINN. STAT. ANN. § 144.831 (Supp. 1969); NEB. REV. STAT. § 83-159 (1968); NEV. REV. STAT. § 458.010 (1967); N.H. REV. STAT. ANN. § 172:1 (1964); N.J. STAT. ANN. § 26:2B-1 (1964); N.Y. MENTAL HYGIENE LAW §§ 302, 303 (McKinney Supp. 1968); N.C. GEN. STAT. § 122-7.1 (1964); OHIO REV. CODE ANN. § 3701.142 (Baldwin 1964); ORE. REV. STAT. § 430.080 (1967); PA. STAT. ANN. tit. 50, § 2101 (1954); R. I. GEN. LAWS ANN. § 40-12-3 (1956); S.C. CODE ANN. § 32-895.1 (Supp. 1968); TENN. CODE ANN. § 33-804 (Supp. 1968); UTAH CODE ANN. § 55-13-1 (Supp. 1967); VA. CODE ANN. § 32-365 (1969); WASH. REV. CODE ANN. § 70.96.040 (1963); W. VA. CODE ANN. § 27-1A-11 (1966); see Appendix B, Chart I.

2 CAL. HEALTH & SAFETY CODE § 427.1 (West Supp. 1968); CONN. GEN. STAT. ANN. § 17-155a (1961); COLO. REV. STAT. ANN § 66-1-7 (23c) (1963); IND. ANN. STAT. § 22-1504 (1964); IOWA CODE ANN. § 123A.2 (Supp. 1969); KY. REV. STAT. ANN. § 222.020 (Supp. 1968); LA. REV. STAT. ANN. § 40.2008.3 (1965); MD. ANN. CODE art. 2c, § 301 (Supp. 1968); NEB. REV. STAT. § 83-159 (1968); NEV. REV. STAT. § 458.010 (1967); N.Y. MENTAL HYGIENE LAW §§ 302, 303 (McKinney Supp. 1968); PA. STAT. ANN. tit. 50, § 2101 (1954); R.I. GEN. LAWS ANN. § 40-12-3 (1956); VA. CODE ANN. § 32-365 (1969); W. VA. CODE ANN. § 27-1A-11 (1966); see Appendix B, Chart I.

3 *E.g.,* ALASKA STAT. § 44.29.030 (1967) ; CAL. HEALTH & SAFETY CODE § 427.9 (West Supp. 1968) ; CONN. GEN. STAT. ANN. § 17-155 (d) (1961) ; IND. ANN. STAT. § 22-1505 (1964) ; LA. REV. STAT. ANN. §§ 40.2008, 40.2008.1 (1965) ; MINN. STAT. ANN. § 144.81 (Supp. 1969) ; NEB. REV. STAT. § 83-160 (1968) ; NEV. REV. STAT. § 458.120-45 (1960) ; N.Y. MENTAL HYGIENE LAW § 320 (McKinney Supp. 1968) ; R.I. GEN. LAWS ANN. § 40-12-5 (1956) ; S.C. CODE ANN. § 32-896 (Supp. 1968). *See* Appendix B, Chart I.

4 ALA. CODE tit. 55, § 373 (11) (Supp. 1967) ; ARK. STAT. ANN. § 83-704 (1960) ; KAN. GEN. STAT. ANN. § 74-4402 (1964) ; N.M. STAT. ANN. § 46-12-1 (1966) ; N.D. CENT. CODE § 54-38-02 (1960) ; OKLA. STAT. ANN. tit. 63, § 2102 (Supp. 1968) ; TEX. REV. CIV. STAT. ANN. art. 5561c (Supp. 1968) ; VT. STAT. ANN. tit. 18, § 2943 (1968).

5 ARK. STAT. ANN. § 83-704 (1960) ; KAN. GEN. STAT. ANN. § 74-4402 (1964) ; N.M. STAT. ANN. § 46-12-1 (1966) ; OKLA. STAT. ANN. tit. 63, § 2102 (Supp. 1968) ; TEX. REV. CIV. STAT. ANN. art. 5561c, Sec. 3 (Supp. 1968).

6 ALA. CODE tit. 55, § 373 (11) (Supp. 1967) ; N.D. CENT. CODE § 54-38-02 (1960).

7 W. Meyers, Jr., State Alcoholism Programs: Purposes and Administration, January 21, 1965, 41-43 (unpublished thesis in Columbia Law School Library).

8 ALA. CODE tit. 55, § 373 (11) (Supp. 1967).

9 ARK. STAT. ANN. § 83-703 (1960).

10 Meyers, *supra* note 7, at 45-47.

11 T. PLAUT, ALCOHOL PROBLEMS 177-178 (1967), suggests that even separate divisions within existing departments be viewed as a transitional measure.

12 Meyers, *supra* note 7, at 45-47.

13 *E.g.,* CAL. HEALTH & SAFETY CODE § 427.1 (West Supp. 1968) ; COLO. REV. STAT. ANN. § 56-1-7 (23) (1963) ; GA. CODE ANN. § 88-403 (Supp. 1968) ; IDAHO CODE ANN. § 67-3110 (Supp. 1967) ; IOWA CODE ANN. § 123.A.2 (Supp. 1968) ; KY. REV. STAT. ANN. § 222.035 (1962) ; MASS. GEN. LAWS ANN. ch. 111, § 4A (1967) ; N.J. STAT. ANN. § 26:2B-1 (1964) ; PA. STAT. ANN. tit. 50, § 2101 (1954) ; OHIO REV. CODE ANN. § 3701.142 (Baldwin 1964) ; VA. CODE ANN. § 32-365 (1969) ; WASH. REV. CODE ANN. § 70.96.020 (1962). *See* Appendix B, Chart I.

14 *E.g.,* CONN. GEN. STAT. ANN. § 17-155a (1961) ; ILL. ANN. STAT. ch. 91½, § 100-10 (Smith-Hurd 1963) ; IND. ANN. STAT. § 22-1504 (1964) ; MD. ANN. CODE art. 2c, §§ 103 (a), 301 (Supp. 1968) ; N.Y. MENTAL HYGIENE LAW (McKinney Supp. 1968) ; N.C. GEN. STAT. § 122-7.2 (1964) ; ORE. REV. STAT. § 430.080 (1967) ; TENN. CODE ANN. § 33-804 (Supp. 1968) ; W. VA. CODE ANN. § 27-1A-11 (1966). *See* Appendix B, Chart I.

15 ALASKA STAT. § 47.30.500 (1) (1966) ; ME. REV. STAT. ANN. tit. 22, § 1351 (1961) ; NEV. REV. STAT. § 458.010 (1963) ; N.H. REV. STAT. ANN. § 172:1 (1964) ; *see* Appendix B, Chart I.

16 R.I. GEN. LAWS ANN. § 40-12-3 (1956) ; *see* Appendix B, Chart I.

17 S.C. CODE ANN. § 32-895.1 (Supp. 1968) ; *see* Appendix B, Chart I.

18 *E.g.,* FLA. STAT. ANN. § 396.011 (1960) ; LA. REV. STAT. ANN. § 40.2008.3 (1965) ; NEB. REV. STAT. § 83-159 (1968). *See* Appendix B, Chart. I.

19 PLAUT, *supra* note 11, at 145.

20 Plaut, *Alcoholism and Community Caretakers: Programs and Policies,* 12 SOCIAL WORK (No. 3) 42, 49 (1967). *See* McGee & Scher, *Integration of Alcoholism and Mental Health Services,* 18 Q.J. STUD. ALCOHOL 658, 659 (1957).

21 One researcher has given the following description of alcoholism: "Alcoholism is not a single entity, but rather a cluster of disorders, which have a common feature in pathological drinking, but which also exhibit many differences." Bailey, Haberman & Sheinberg, "Distinctive Characteristics of the Alcoholic Family," Report of the Health Research Council of the City of New York, 13 (1965). *See* Chafetz, *Note,* 25 Q.J. STUD. ALCOHOL 358 (1964) ; Michigan's response to this study's questionnaire, Appendix C, Introduction n. 3.

22 Meyers, *supra* note 7, at 41-55.

23 *Id.,* at 53, 54.

24 *E.g.,* R.I. GEN. LAWS ANN. § 40-12-4 (1956); TENN. CODE ANN. § 33-804 (5) (Supp. 1968); VA. CODE ANN. § 32-366 (1964).

25 *E.g.,* IND. ANN. STAT. § 22-1504 (1964); PA. STAT. ANN. tit. 50, § 2102 (1954).

26 NEV. REV. STAT. § 458.040 (1963); *see* N.M. STAT. ANN. § 46-12-6 (1966).

27 Trice, *Alcoholics Anonymous,* 315 ANNALS 108, 113 (1958).

28 *See* note 3 *supra* and Appendix B, Chart I.

29 *E.g.,* IND. ANN. STAT. § 22-1505 (1964); LA. REV. STAT. ANN. § 40.2008 (1965); MINN. STAT. ANN. § 144.831 (Supp. 1969); R.I. GEN. LAWS ANN. § 40-12-5 (Supp. 1968). *See* Appendix B, Chart I.

30 S.C. CODE ANN. § 32-846 (1966); TENN. CODE ANN. § 33-801 (1963).

31 CAL. HEALTH & SAFETY CODE § 427.8 (West Supp. 1968); D.C. CODE ANN. § 24-523 (Supp. II, 1969); IOWA CODE ANN. §§ 123A.1-8, 224.1, 229.42 (Supp. 1969); OHIO REV. CODE ANN. §§ 3701.141, 142 (Baldwin 1964).

32 Comprehensive Alcoholism Treatment and Rehabilitation Bill § 4 (Proposal to Mass. legis. 1969).

33 *Id.*

34 Maurer, "The Beginning of Wisdom About Alcoholism," FORTUNE, May, 1968, at 176.

35 MD. ANN. CODE art. 2c, § 301 (11) (Supp. 1968).

36 VA. CODE ANN. §§ 32-371, 32-378.1 (1969).

37 CONN. GEN. STAT. ANN. § 17-155c (1961).

38 In spite of considerable emphasis on research, there are many areas of incomplete knowledge about alcoholism. For instance, the question as to whether alcoholism is physiologically addictive needs exploration; *see,* JELLINEK, THE DISEASE CONCEPT OF ALCOHOLISM 82-110, 149 (1960); Williams, *Identifying and Treating Potential Alcoholics,* 49 J. CRIM. L.C. & P.S. 218 (1958). Note that a substance to which alcohol reacts specifically has been found to be more common in alcoholics than non-alcoholics; Armstrong, *The Search for the Alcoholic Personality,* 315 ANNALS 40, 46 (1958). Further study relating to the claim of success of such organizations as Alcoholics Anonymous is needed; *see* Trice, *Alcoholics Anonymous, supra* note 27, at 111. It is claimed that AA has cured 400,000 alcoholics; Maurer, *supra* note 34, at 211.

39 *See* Appendix C.

40 *E.g.,* IND. ANN. STAT. § 22-1507 (c) (1964).

41 *E.g.,* MD. ANN. CODE art. 2c, § 301 (4) (Supp. 1968).

42 PLAUT, *supra* note 11, at 8-9.

43 *See* pp. 202-203 *supra.*

44 *E.g.,* KAN. STAT. ANN. § 74-4410 (1963) provides confidentiality for records of only voluntary patients. *Cf.* ARK. STAT. ANN. § 83-716 (1960), which provides confidentiality for records of only involuntary patients.

45 *E.g.,* ARK. STAT. ANN. § 83-716 (1960); GA. CODE ANN. § 88-411 (Supp. 1968); N.H. REV. STAT. ANN. § 172:13 (1964); R.I. GEN. LAWS ANN. § 40-12-22 (1956).

46 *E.g.,* KAN. STAT. ANN. § 74-4410 (1963); N.H. REV. STAT. ANN. § 172:13 (1964); N.M. STAT. ANN. § 46-12-9 (1953).

47 *E.g.,* ARK. STAT. ANN. § 83-716 (1960); GA. CODE ANN. § 88-411 (Supp. 1968).

48 ARK. STAT. ANN. § 83-716 (1960); GA. CODE ANN. § 88-411 (Supp. 1968); KAN. STAT. ANN. § 74-4410 (1963); N.M. STAT. ANN. § 46-12-9 (1953).

[49] N.H. REV. STAT. ANN § 172:13 (1964).

[50] *E.g.,* R.I. GEN. LAWS ANN. § 40-12-22 (1956).

[51] D.C. CODE ANN. § 24-524 (c) (Supp. II, 1969); MD. ANN. CODE art. 2c, § 316 (Supp. 1968).

[52] CAL. WELF. & INST'NS CODE § 5328 (West Supp. 1968); N.Y. MENTAL HYGIENE LAW § 20 (McKinney Supp. 1968).

[53] *See* Appendix B, Chart II.

[54] *E.g.,* HAWAII REV. STAT. § 334.57 (1968); MINN. STAT. ANN. § 253A.05 (Supp. 1969).

[55] *E.g.,* NEB. REV. STAT. § 83-314 (1966), which provides a person may write and be provided with writing materials and letter shall be mailed unless obscene, threatening or improper; OHIO REV. CODE § 5122.29 (Baldwin 1968), which provides for visitation and communication rights subject to general rules and determinations of head of hospital and assures communications with physician, family, attorney, and department of mental hygiene.

[56] *E.g.,* CAL. WELF. & INST'NS CODE § 5326 (West Supp. 1968).

PART III

THE ALCOHOLIC OFFENDER:
CRIMINAL RESPONSIBILITY;
TREATMENT

CHAPTER 10

Criminal Responsibility Of Alcoholics And Intoxicated Persons

In the initial chapter, we had occasion to review and appraise the relationship between intoxication and crime and the handling and control of publicly intoxicated persons through the processes of the criminal law. It was noted that arrest and prosecution for so-called drunkenness offenses most frequently are aimed at alcoholics, and we had occasion to comment briefly on the fact that recent legislative developments for treatment legislation were precipitated by the concern that criminal prosecution of alcoholics—and consequently, their routine arrests in police street-sweeping operations—were likely to run into constitutional objections. Thus, the practical impact of legal theories of responsibility on the treatment or correctional alternatives for alcoholics is apparent. The extent to which alcoholics may be held responsible for their crimes will next be examined. This examination will include an inquiry into the criminal responsibility for the drunkenness offenses, public intoxication, drunk and disorderly conduct, etc. previously discussed, as well as for criminal offenses that do not involve intoxication as part of the charge.

In the chapter following, treatment and correctional alternatives will be explored, both for alcoholics convicted of crime, and for alcoholics acquitted because of alcoholism, by reason of lack of responsibility.

ALTERNATIVES TO CORRECTIONAL TREATMENT

Modern criminal law works primarily on the principle of deterrence—namely that the imposition of criminal penalties or sanctions is reasonable only if it is capable of deterring the offender who is being tried as well as others who are likely to commit similar offenses. A person who, through no fault of his own, has no conscious

127

knowledge of what he is doing or a person who lacks power of self-control, or persons who have no understanding of the nature of punishment are, in consequence of any of these defects, incapable of being deterred. Such persons are treated as lacking in "responsibility," and hence cannot be convicted of a crime. This does not mean that a person who has no appreciation of the nature of his acts, or who lacks control over them will escape all consequences, for such a person may well be more dangerous than one who knowingly commits crimes. A person who lacks responsibility who has committed dangerous acts that would otherwise be criminal is a proper subject for treatment rather than correction. Thus, a judgment must be made whether particular offenders—or particular classes of offenders, such as drug addicts, sex offenders or alcoholics—have the requisite responsibility for their acts. If they do not, then treatment in care-giving institutions may be more appropriate than correction in penal institutions. The determination of criminal responsibility has become a necessary one in the case of drug addicts, alcoholics or sex offenders, whose offenses are likely to result from certain behavioral or socio-medical disorders, and these categories of offenders insistently compel a choice "between the use of public agencies and public force to condemn the offender by conviction, with the resultant sanction in which there is inescapably a punitive ingredient—and modes of disposition in which the ingredient is absent. . ."[1]

At present, alcoholics are not regarded as lacking criminal responsibility and evidence that a defendant is an alcoholic will not relieve him from criminal prosecution or punishment. There are indications, however, that the law of responsibility with respect to alcoholics may soon undergo significant changes. Consideration of an alcoholic's criminal responsibility is of special importance to the majority of states which retain laws prohibiting drunkenness, but it is also relevant to states which remove such prohibitions. This chapter examines existing law and the prospects for new developments.

PREVAILING LAW

In its doctrines of responsibility or culpability, criminal law presently gives no separate recognition to alcoholism. It does, however, recognize the effects of intoxication, and it does allow an alcoholic to invoke the defense of insanity if he can prove that his condition meets the particular state's definition of irresponsibility.

Intoxication as a Defense

The general—and ancient—rule in most jurisdictions, either by statute or judicial decision, is that "voluntary" intoxication is no defense to a criminal charge based on acts committed while intoxicated.[2] The law does not ignore the medical fact that intoxication diminishes perception and judgment,[3] but rather proceeds on the notion that a person is free to choose whether or not to drink. If he voluntarily chooses to become intoxicated, he has wilfully increased the risk of harm to others by reducing his capacity for evaluating danger and controlling his actions.[4] As one court put it with righteous indignation almost 100 years ago:

> He must be held to have purposely blinded his moral perceptions, and set his will free from the control of reason—to have suppressed the guards and invited the mutiny; and should therefore be held responsible as well for the vicious excesses of the will thus set free, as for the acts done by its prompting.[5]

The law does, however, make a theoretical exception for "involuntary" intoxication. However, in actual fact there has never been a case in which a court excused a crime on the grounds of involuntary intoxication, even though cases have been reported in which drunkenness was not entirely self-induced.[6] The Model Penal Code gives content to the concept by calling involuntary intoxication intoxication which is "not self-induced," and by defining the term as including ingestion pursuant to medical advice or under duress.[7]

Moreover, in many, but not all jurisdictions, evidence of intoxication may be used to reduce the severity or degree of the crime in most cases where "specific intent" to commit a particular crime must be shown.[8] The usual statement of the rule is that evidence of intoxication is admissible when relevant to disprove a specific intent which is an element of the crime charged, but not disprove "general intent" when that is the required element.[9] The distinction between specific and general intent is a highly technical one; for present purposes it will suffice to say that specific intent usually implies a preconceived, planned and deliberate criminal purpose, while general intent implies less deliberation. The result of the rule of partial exculpation is that crimes such as burglary, larceny, robbery and assault with intent to rape have been reduced to crimes of a lesser degree when committeed by intoxicated persons.[10] Moreover, if the crime charged is murder in the first degree which requires premeditation and deliberation, the proof of intoxication which destroys the capacity for specific intent may reduce the conviction to that of murder in the second degree which is said to require only a "general intent."[11] The underlying rationale for allowing the reduction in the degree of crimes of specific intent to crimes of a lesser degree by reason of intoxication is that such crimes, if done with the actor's requisite intent and knowledge, present a special and greater cause of danger to society than if done without such knowledge or intent.[12] However, offenses such as public intoxication or drunk and disorderly conduct, which involve drink-related behavior, may well be unaffected by the specific intent exception since they may be viewed as "absolute" crimes, *i.e.*, crimes in which intent or knowledge is not a necessary element.[13] (In the case of an absolute crime, the act itself is prohibited, regardless of the perpetrator's intent; many minor and a few more important offenses fall into this category—parking and other traffic offenses, littering, failing to curb one's dog, as well as a host of regulations for housing, health and safety.)

It is quite clear that under existing law the intoxicated alcoholic is treated no differently from other inebriates. Moreover, the crimes he is most likely to commit are not generally the serious crimes in which the law recognizes the effects of intoxication by reducing the charge. Of course, the basic issue that has increasingly concerned the courts in the recent past is whether or not the alcoholic drinks because he wants to, or because he cannot help drinking.[14] There is persuasive evidence that the alcoholic does not purposely "blind his moral perceptions, and set his will free from the control of reason."[15]

Alcoholism and Its Relation to the Defense of Insanity

"Insanity" is a defense to a criminal charge, but alcoholism has never been recognized as a form of "insanity" for this purpose. It is generally agreed that if an alcoholic shows the symptoms of mental disease—typically of delirium tremens—or if he is afflicted by a mental disease which is independent of alcoholism, then he may claim insanity as a defense to a criminal charge under the applicable rule of the jurisdiction.[16] Under existing law, it is unlikely that most alcoholics can assert the defense of insanity.[17]

The most widely applied test of criminal responsibility is the *M'Naughten* rule.[18] Under that rule, a person is excused from criminal responsibility if as a result of mental disease he does not know the difference between right and wrong. Thus, the defendant must establish a total impairment of cognition in order to be excused.[19] The other tests of criminal responsibility are less restrictive. A minority of jurisdictions have modified the M'Naughten rule by allowing in addition to the "right from wrong test" a defense of insanity based on "irresistible impulse," *i.e.*, a *sudden* and *total* impairment of the capacity for self-control.[20] The *"Durham"* test[21] adopted fifteen years ago in the District of Columbia requires that the criminal act be a product of a mental disease or defect, so that it recognizes volitional and cognitive impairment.[22] Finally, the rule of responsibility proposed in the American Law Institute's Model Penal Code, which has been accepted by many Federal courts since it was proposed in 1962, also requires: "either a substantial impairment of cognition or volition."[23]

While these rules may lead to divergent results in similar cases, none of them is likely to help the alcoholic who stands accused of a crime. The initial requirement for exculpation under every one of the rules is proof of mental illness, and most alcoholics do not meet that test. Haggard and Jellinek suggest that alcoholic psychosis is not a common occurence in alcoholics, and that while certain personality changes do occur which result in a deterioration of conduct, they cannot be properly called "insanity."[24] On the other hand, it has been suggested that alcoholics are likely to show other manifestations of mental abnormality upon searching, and probably time-consuming, diagnosis by a competent and thorough psychiatrist.[25] Even if this minority view is correct, necessary psychiatric evaluation is likely to be both expensive and difficult to obtain. Moreover, it may not be desirable to classify alcoholism as a mental disease. The practical consequence of such a classification is likely to be acquittal on the criminal charge, followed, however, by a long-term commitment to a mental institution that may make no special provisions for the treatment of alcoholics.[26]

RECENT DECISIONS ON THE ALCOHOLIC'S CRIMINAL RESPONSIBILITY FOR THE CRIME OF PUBLIC INTOXICATION

In an earlier chapter, in discussing the usual mode of dealing with persons found in public in an intoxicated condition through the criminal law, mention was made of the fact that recent developments in the direction of more treatment-oriented legislation had been precipitated by a number of cases which had put in doubt the constitutionality of convicting alcoholics of the crime of public intoxication. These cases were, of course, mainly concerned with the problem of an alcoholic's criminal responsibility. Thus, the following discussion of cases emphasizes the wholly practical consequences of questions of responsibility, theoretical and jurisprudential though they may seem.

From Robinson v. California to Powell v. Texas

In 1962 defendant Robinson was convicted in California under a statute which made it unlawful to be "addicted to narcotics."[27] In reviewing the conviction the U.S. Supreme Court found that narcotic addiction was an illness and held that to punish an addict for his illness violates the prohibition of the Eighth Amendment against cruel and unusual punishment.[28] *Robinson* thus concerns itself with the nature of criminal acts, rather than with the circumstances under which criminal activity should be excused. However, subsequent cases involving narcotics addicts raised the issue whether prosecution of an addict not for his addicted condition, but for *acts* he must engage in to carry on his addiction was also banned, in view of the fact that addiction itself was no longer punishable as a crime. Courts generally responded by limiting *Robinson* to a prohibition of "crimes of status," *i.e.*, the alleged crime of "being" an addict. Consequently, they allowed punishment of narcotic addicts for such "acts" as use,[29] being under the influence,[30] possession[31] and larceny.[32] The courts also allowed the punishment of homosexuals for deviant conduct. For example, the court in *Perkins v. N. Carolina* stated:

> Imprisoning Perkins for his homosexual conduct is not un-like putting a person in jail for being addicted to the use of narcotics. . . but it is important to note that the statute has been interpreted to condemn the status of narcotic addiction as a criminal offense. Perkins was convicted of an overt act—a distinction more important to law than medicine—but a legally valid distinction.[33]

It was not long before the new prohibition on prosecution for "status crimes" was applied to the case of prosecution of alcoholics. When Joe B. Driver, who had been convicted of public intoxication at least 200 times, appealed his most recent convictions to the Fourth Circuit in 1965, a new view of the scope of the Eighth Amendment prohibition emerged.[34] The Fourth Circuit agreed that defendant was a "chronic alcoholic,"[35] and classified alcoholism as a disease.[36] Relying on *Robinson*, the court held that it was constitutionally barred from convicting Driver as a criminal for behavior, *i.e.*, public intoxication, which was "compulsive as symptomatic of the disease."[37] The court reversed Driver's conviction, and in so doing stated that:

> . . . the alcoholic's presence in public is not his act for he did not will it. It may be likened to the movements of an imbecile or a person in a delirium of fever.[38]

Shortly after Driver was freed, a similar case arose in Washington, D.C. There the conviction of Dewitt Easter for public intoxication was reversed by the District of Columbia Circuit upon proof that he, too, was a chronic alcoholic. In the *Easter* case the court relied on the decision in *Driver*, and in addition, the court drew support for its decision from an earlier though largely unused District of Columbia statute which had the stated purpose of substituting treatment for jailing of "chronic alcoholics."[39]

Thus, in two cases the courts found that criminal prosecution was barred, not because of any finding of insanity, but because the alleged criminal conduct was found to be a symptom of the defendant's illness.[40] A few other cases showed some acceptance of this doctrine, but it was neither adopted on a large scale nor was it much clarified or expanded.[41] In one case it was suggested that proof of debilitating alcoholism could defeat a criminal prosecution for non-support[42] and in another it was suggested, without benefit of expert opinion, that "no one can contend that robbery is compulsive as symptomatic of the disease of alcoholism."[43]

The doctrine that relieved alcoholics from prosecution for public drunkenness had far-reaching consequences in stimulating legislative activity to supply treatment substitutes for the revolving door process of the criminal law.[44] The doctrine was short-lived, however, because in June 1968, in the case of *Powell v. Texas*[45] the Supreme Court refused to follow the *Driver* and *Easter* cases and affirmed the conviction of Leroy Powell on a charge of public intoxication. Leroy Powell was an alcoholic. Yet in spite of the result of the case, future developments are far from foreclosed. The *Powell* case was decided by a closely divided court—both the prevailing opinion[46] and the dissent[47] were subscribed to by four justices; one crucial concurring opinion (there were two)[48] adopts in large measure the reasoning of the dissent but disagrees with the dissent's interpretation of the underlying facts. Because of its crucial position in the law of alcoholism, the case and its four separate opinions need careful consideration.

Powell v. Texas

THE PREVAILING OPINION

The prevailing opinion of Mr. Justice Marshall does not disagree with the view advanced in *Robinson* (*i.e.* that a person cannot be punished merely for being in a condition of illness) but limits the doctrine to crimes of "mere status."[49] It holds that *Robinson* does not suggest that conduct cannot be punished merely because it is involuntary or occasioned by compulsion.[50] Moreover, it states that a reading of the Eighth Amendment requested by appellant Powell would result in a constitutionally required test of responsibility,[51] and would thus turn certain evidentiary requirements into constitutional ones—the Court, in other words, is unwilling to make a constitutional issue out of every defense of lack of responsibility growing out of such behavioral disorders as addiction or alcoholism.

The opinion carefully reviews the evidence and finds that there is no proof to substantiate the findings of the lower court, particularly with respect to the inner compulsion which drove Powell to appear in public while intoxicated. The Court also attempts to assess the deterrent effect of making public intoxication a crime. The opinion states:

> We are unable to conclude, on the state of the record or on the current state of medical knowledge, that chronic alcoholics in general, and Leroy Powell in particular, suffer from such an irresistible compulsion to drink and to get drunk in public that they are utterly unable to control their performance of either or both of these acts and thus cannot be deterred at all from public intoxication.[52]

The prevailing opinion, in addition to upholding the criminal responsibility of alcoholics also indicates the Court's concern as to the consequences that would follow the invalidation of prosecutions —and arrests—for public intoxication. The Court points to the need for alternative treatment devices both to protect the public and to protect the inebriate, who, no longer subject to arrest, might well be worse off than before. There is considerable evidence in the prevailing opinion that the lack of available treatment facilities had a strongly inhibiting effect on the Court's inclination to invalidate the criminal prosecution of persons who are found drunk in public.

Concurring Opinion—Mr. Justice Black (Subscribed To By Mr. Justice Harlan)

Justice Black's concurring opinion limits the scope of the *Robinson* holding even more sharply than the prevailing opinion. It specifically limits the scope of the Eighth Amendment prohibition pronounced in *Robinson* to crimes of status, *i.e.* the crime of "being" an addict, where there is no act of any kind involved.[53] It states that there is no constitutional requirement that human behavior should be immune from punishment because it is involuntary or the result of compulsion,[54] and suggests that finding a *constitutional* requirement that only voluntary acts may provide grounds for criminal conviction would not be desirable.[55] This concurrence rejects the test of criminal responsibility which would result from acceptance of the dissent's view, because to accept that view would require all jurisdictions to determine prior to conviction if the accused is "morally blameworthy."[56]

CONCURRING OPINION—MR. JUSTICE WHITE

The concurring opinion of Mr. Justice White is actually much closer to the dissent than to the prevailing opinion, because Justice White concurs only in the result of the affirmance of Powell's conviction and not in the reasoning of the other judges who reached that result. Mr. Justice White agrees with the dissenters—and with the *Easter* and *Driver* cases—to the extent of finding that alcoholism is a disease and that Powell had no control over his drinking.

The central difference between Justice White's opinion and the dissent is that Mr. Justice White found that the proof failed to show that appellant had a compulsion to frequent public places when intoxicated.[57] The opinion is not particularly clear about the dimensions of the Eighth Amendment prohibition. However, the opinion suggests that no person can be punished for compulsive behavior, *i.e.* for behavior subject to conditions which deprive him of his mental or physical powers and thus cannot be controlled.[58] It is probable that had there been convincing evidence that Powell was "powerless to choose" whether or not to appear in public while intoxicated, Justice White would have joined the four-man minority—thereby turning it into a majority.

THE DISSENT

The dissenting opinion joined in by four justices, is closest in point of view to the *Driver* and *Easter* decisions.[59] The dissent adopted findings of fact of the lower court and read them as showing that appellant—who had had 100 prior convictions for public intoxication—was powerless to avoid drinking, that he had an uncontrollable compulsion to drink and that once intoxicated he could not prevent himself from appearing in a public place.[60] The dissent found that appellant could not be convicted because under the prohibition against cruel and unusual punishment of the Eighth Amendment there can be no criminal conviction

> if the condition essential to constitute the defined crime is part of the pattern of the disease and is occasioned by a compulsion symptomatic of the disease.[61]

More generally, the dissent articulates the view that penalties may not be inflicted upon a person for being "in a condition he is powerless to change"[62] or a "condition he has no capacity to avoid."[63] There is an attempt to draw a distinction between status or condition (*i.e.* being in a state of intoxication) on the one hand and act (*i.e.* appearing in public) on the other, but this is not made fully explicit.[64] The dissenting opinion *does state* that the defense of chronic alcoholism would not apply to such crimes as driving a car while intoxicated, assault, theft, or robbery, since such crimes are not the result of the disease;[65] but these conclusionary statements are not fully supported by the rationale of the opinion. The opinion in effect leaves open the possibility, in future cases, of proving a connection between crimes other than drunkenness offenses and the disease of alcoholism.

Broadly read, the dissenting opinion suggests that the Eighth Amendment prohibits punishment, and thus requires excuse from responsibility, if the defendant suffers from a disease (which need not be a disease of the mind or mental illness) which causes him ". . .to be powerless to choose not to violate the law."[66]

Powell v. Texas—Options for the Future

The *Powell* case shows that any change in the law with respect to the criminal responsibility of alcoholics will first require a change in the way an alcoholic's drinking conduct is viewed. The clear implication of the prevailing opinion is that there will be a change in the law only if absolutely convincing evidence can be presented of the compulsive nature of an alcoholic's drinking *and* of his appearance in public.[67] Evidence, too, of reliable treatment methods and available treatment facilities would clearly prove persuasive to the Court that criminal prosecution of alcoholics for drunkenness offenses could be abandoned without risk to the public and to the intoxicated persons themselves.[68]

In view of the decision by a deeply divided court in *Powell v. Texas,* there is no assurance that the decision will remain the law for long. The new directions the law may take must therefore be explored on alternative assumptions that the prevailing opinions will remain the law or that the dissent will eventually have the last word.

OPTIONS UNDER THE PREVAILING OPINION

If the prevailing opinion in the *Powell* case remains the law, there will be no constitutionally required test of criminal responsibility, and the alcoholic will not be protected against prosecution by any doctrine of constitutional law.

However, even without such constitutional protections it is possible that some drunken behavior by alcoholics may be excused under general doctrines of criminal law. The argument would rest on the assumption that the conduct (or certain specified conduct) of an alcoholic while intoxicated is, using the standards for criminal responsibility established by the Model Penal Code,[69] "involuntary." It would be necessary to prove that intoxication incapacitates judgment— which has already been accepted, at least tentatively[70]—and, most crucially, that the alcoholic's becoming intoxicated is beyond his control.[71] The language of *Driver*, quoted also in *Easter*, strongly suggests this development in the law in likening an alcoholic's appearance in public to that of "an imbecile or a person in a delirium of fever."[72] Of course, the prevailing opinion in *Powell* would probably reject this analogy. On the other hand, a recent Minnesota case, *Stake v. Fearon*,[73] adopted this view by finding that the appearance of chronic alcoholics in public while drunk was not voluntary, as required for conviction by the state's statute.

There is no reason to assume that the defense of "involuntary" conduct, if acceptable, would necessarily have to be limited to a public intoxication charge.[74] Whenever it could be shown that the defendant's intoxication was so incapacitating that he did not know what he was doing or could not control his actions, and that the state of intoxication was involuntary because he was an alcoholic, he could be excused under a defense analogous to that of insanity or automatism.[75]

An even more difficult question is posed by criminal conduct of an alcoholic while sober. One commentator, in describing the stages through which an alcoholic moves, relates the following:

> Mr. J. has manifested changes, socially unacceptable changes in areas other than those related to drinking. Dishonesty, excessive rationalization, avoidance and other deviations. . . Accidents, job losses, family quarrels. . . may take place not just when he is under the influence of alcohol, but even when he is not.[76]

A sober alcoholic thus may undergo many personality changes, but it is probable that his criminal conduct would not be considered involuntary so as to support a judicial finding of lack of criminal responsibility. The lacking element is some acute form of unconsciousness or unawareness which, in some courts' view, can be satisfied by a response which is like one in a "delirium of fever" but not by apparently sober behavior.[77] While "delirium of fever" may be a firm standard to measure the alcoholic's lack of control in an intoxicated state, his behavior when sober would not be characterized by a lack of responsibility.[78] Medical expertise is necessary to make such judgments of responsibility, but available descriptions of the sober alcoholic give a sense of deviant but controllable behavior.[79]

OPTIONS UNDER THE DISSENT

If the dissenting view eventually prevails, it may be read to require a constitutional test of criminal responsibility, which would affect existing law in two important ways. First, proof of mental illness would no longer be necessary to establish lack of responsibility, and second, it would require courts to accept as an alternative to *cognitive* impairment, evidence of *volitional* impairment which—unlike "irresistible impulse"—is not necessarily sudden or immediate.[80] The resulting change in the law of criminal responsibility would be quite considerable. Such a change might, in the long run, affect not only the criminal responsibility of alcoholics but also the responsibility of other addicted and behaviorally disordered persons.[81]

The most widely used *M'Naughten* test of criminal responsibility —knowledge of right from wrong—does not include any recognition of loss of control,[82] and the "irresistible impulse" modification of the *M'Naughten* rule considers loss of control to be exculpating only if the impairment is sudden and total.[83] Moreover, the dissenting opinion's recognition of purely volitional impairment eliminates the need to present evidence of mental disease—and this would change even the more liberal tests of responsibility of the *Durham* rule, and the rule suggested by the Model Penal Code,[84] since there would no longer be a need to relate the volitional impairment to mental disease or disorder, a requirement that is difficult to meet in borderline situations.[85]

If the constitutional test of responsibility suggested by the minority in *Powell* prevails, moreover, logic will soon compel its unlimited application, not only to drunkenness offenses, but to any criminal offense committed by an alcoholic while intoxicated, upon a showing that the defendant was powerless to choose not to obey the law.[86] As a matter of logic, moreover, such a constitutional rule cannot long be limited to alcoholics—any behaviorally disordered person who lacks control over his conduct is likely to be excused from punishment. A recent concurring opinion,[87] which discusses the problem of alcoholism and criminal responsibility reflects this logic; the opinion suggests that the *Durham* rule be expanded to excuse from criminal responsibility any conduct of an alcoholic which is not the result of an exercise of free will.[88]

The rationale of the dissent in *Powell,* as well as that of the earlier *Driver* and *Easter* decisions tend inevitably in the direction of a general rule of responsibility in spite of the evident aim to fashion a test limited to drunkenness offenses only—a test which, under the Eighth Amendment, will excuse alcoholics from responsibility for "drinking" offenses, such as public intoxication or vagrancy, but which will not have the effect of excusing alcoholics from responsibility for other criminal conduct, because this would, in effect, impose a general *constitutional* test of responsibility. As will be demonstrated, a test of such limited scope is not possible, although the dissenting opinion in *Powell* tries to accomplish this by the following distinction:

> A person may not be punished if the condition essential to constitute the defined crime is part of the pattern of his disease and is occasioned by a compulsion symptomatic of the disease.[89]

This means, in effect, that only behavior which is clearly related to the "disease"cannot be punished. Under this rule, for example, the narcotic addict would not be punished for use of narcotics, the kleptomaniac would not be convicted for theft, the sex-offender would not be punished for crimes of exhibition and perversion, nor would the pyromaniac be punished for arson.[90] Yet, returning to the underlying rationale, it is clear that the reason for the view that such conduct should not be punished is that the behavior is compulsive, *i.e.* results from (or is a "product of") the disease, and thus cannot be avoided. The peculiar nature of alcoholism highlights the futility of the distinction articulated by the *Powell* dissent because it fails to apply the basic rationale of excluding compulsive behavior from criminal responsibility. The only compulsive symptom of alcoholism, if there is any, is the need to drink or to continue drinking—and drinking itself is not a prohibited activity. But the result of excessive drinking is intoxication, which in turn leads to a loss of judgment, perception and control. However, any prohibited behavior which occurs after intoxication, be it public drunkenness and drunk and disorderly conduct, or such other crimes as assault, robbery or burglary, is not demonstrably or necessarily the consequence of the direct compulsions of the illness. Thus, appearing drunk in public is not necessarily any more "symptomatic" of the disease of alcoholism than is a burglary committed by an alcoholic—the former is merely more frequent. If the Eighth Amendment prohibition under *Robinson* is truly limited to what is a compulsive symptom of the disease, it is hard to see how it affects the criminal responsibility of the alcoholic at all—whether his offense be his appearing in public *or* the commission of a burglary.

Another Opinion—Legislation

The law on the criminal responsibility of alcoholics presently fails to meet the special problem, and both the approach of the prevailing opinion and of the dissent resolve some of the issues but create new ones. The prevailing opinion in the *Powell* case leaves the law in its present unsatisfactory state, because it fails to recognize the compulsive, non-volitional nature of the alcoholic's drinking pattern—and it also has had the effect of slowing the movement for more effective treatment-oriented laws for alcoholics. The dissenting opinion would, of course, create an immediate need for the establishment of shelter and treatment facilities for severely intoxicated persons and for the treatment of alcoholics generally, to take the place of the procedures of the criminal law and of the local drunk tank. In so doing, however, the dissenting opinion would open up the entire issue of the criminal responsibility of alcoholics and other persons with behavioral disorders for crimes that are not directly connected with, or symptomatic of, their disease. As was previously noted, the reluctance of the Court in the *Powell* case to find that alcoholics lack responsibility for the offense of public drunkenness may be attributed in major part to their reluctance to relieve alcoholics of responsibility for other, more serious offenses.

It is not unlikely that the laws of criminal responsibility will eventually move in a direction more favorable to alcoholics and other persons suffering from behavioral disorders. But sound treatment laws for alcoholics need not await that eventuality, for the means are at hand to deal with the problem legislatively, in advance of constitutional and other decisions made in particular cases. Legislation should more generally be adopted, similar to the recent Maryland law, to abolish drunkenness offenses—such as public intoxication, drunk and disorderly conduct, etc.—and to substitute a system of treatment facilities for acutely intoxicated persons and legal machinery for protective detention of persons who are so drunk as to require it. Such legislation would not only be desirable as a rational response to the problems of intoxication and alcoholism, but would also relieve the courts of the necessity of resolving the very difficult problems of criminal responsibility that must inevitably be faced when trying to resolve the criminal liability of alcoholics under public intoxication statutes. It should be stressed that nothing contained in the prevailing opinion in the *Powell* case stands in the way of resolving the problem of the intoxicated alcoholic legislatively—the Court merely held that, as a constitutional matter, it is permissible to treat intoxicated alcoholics as criminal offenders. This holding leaves the legislatures entirely free to determine that alcoholics should *not* be treated as criminals, but rather as persons in need of help.

CHAPTER 10 NOTES

[1] MODEL PENAL CODE § 4.01, Comment (Tent. Draft No. 4, 1955).

[2] *E.g.,* Roberts v. People, 19 Mich. 408 (1870); GA. CODE ANN. § 26-403 (1953).

[3] *E.g.,* Thomas v. State, 105 Ga. App. 754, 125 S.E.2d 679 (1962); Commonwealth v. Farrell, 322 Mass. 606, 78 N.E.2d 697 (1948).

[4] *Id.*

[5] Roberts v. People, *supra* note 2, 19 Mich. at 419.

[6] HALL, GENERAL PRINCIPLES OF CRIMINAL LAW 539 (2d ed. 1960).

[7] MODEL PENAL CODE § 2.08(4) (5) (Proposed Official Draft, 1962).

[8] *E.g.,* Wheatley v. United States, 159 F.2d 599 (4th Cir. 1946); People v. Ford, 60 Cal. 2d 772, 36 Cal. Rptr. 620 (1964), Annot., 8 A.L.R. 3d 1236 (1966).

[9] *Id.*

[10] Womack v. United States, 336 F.2d 959 (D.C. Cir. 1964) (robbery); Moran v. State, 34 Ala. App. 238, 39 So. 2d 419, *cert. denied,* 252 Ala. 60, 39 So. 2d 421 (1949) (assault with intent to commit rape); Johnson v. State, 32 Ala. App. 217, 24 So. 2d 328 (1945) (larceny); People v. Soynowski, 22 Ill. App. 540, 177 N.E.2d 146 (1961) (burglary, rev'd on other grounds). *See* HALL, *supra* note 6 at 545; Paulsen, *Intoxication as a Defense to Crime,* 1961 U. ILL. L. F. 1, 9-11 (1961); MODEL PENAL CODE § 2.08, Comment (Tent. Draft No. 9, 1959).

[11] United States v. Dye, 221 F.2d 763 (3d Cir.), *cert. denied,* 350 U.S. 875 (1955); HALL, *supra* note 6, at 545 n. 11.

[12] Paulsen, *supra* note 10, at 11.

[13] People v. Hoy, 3 Mich. App. 666, 143 N.W.2d 577 (1966). *See* note 80 and accompanying text *infra.*

[14] Powell v. Texas, 392 U.S. 514 (1968); Driver v. Hinant, 356 F.2d 761 (4th Cir. 1966); Easter v. District of Columbia, 361 F.2d 50 (D.C. Cir. 1966).

[15] *Supra* note 5.

[16] McIntyne v. Alaska, 379 P.2d 615 (Alas. 1963); Paulsen, *supra* note 10, at 21.

[17] *See* HAGGARD & JELLINEK, ALCOHOL EXPLORED 220, 223 (1954).

18 M'Naghten's Case, 10 Cl. & F. 200, 8 Eng. Rep. 718 (1843), cited in HALL, *supra* note 6, at 472.

19 *Id., see* Wechsler, *The Criteria of Criminal Responsibility,* 22 U. CHI. L. REV. 367, 371 (1953).

20 United States v. Freeman, 357 F.2d 606, 620 (2d Cir. 1966).

21 Durham v. United States, 214 F.2d 862 (D.C. Cir. 1954).

22 *Id.,* 214 F.2d, at 874.

23 MODEL PENAL CODE § 4.01 (Proposed Official Draft, 1962). The responsibility test is: "A person is not responsible for criminal conduct if at the time of such conduct as a result of mental disease or defect he lacks substantial capacity either to appreciate the criminality [wrongfulness] of his conduct or to conform his conduct to the requirements of law." *Id.,* § 4.01 (1). This responsibility test has achieved "wide acceptance" including the 2d, 7th and 8th circuits which have applied it in full and the 3d and 10th which have applied it in part; United States v. Chandler, 393 F.2d 920, 928 (4th Cir. 1968).

24 HAGGARD & JELLINEK, *supra* note 17.

25 Diamond, *From M'Naghten to Currens, and Beyond,* 50 CALIF. L. REV. 189, 194 (1962).

26 *Cf.* Lynch v. Overholser, 369 U.S. 705 (1962).

27 *See* Robinson v. California, 370 U.S. 660 (1962).

28 *Id.*

29 *E.g.,* Browne v. State, 24 Wis. 2d 491, 129 N.W.2d 175 (1964); *In re* Beceira, 218 Cal. App. 2d 746, 32 Cal. Rptr. 910 (1963).

30 State v. Dennis, 80 N.J. Super. 411, 194 A.2d 3 (1963); Salas v. State, 365 S.W.2d 174 (Tex. 1963).

31 Loyd v. United States, 343 F.2d 242 (D.C. Cir. 1964); People v. Zapata, 220 Cal. App. 905, 34 Cal. Rptr. 171 (1962); State v. Da Vila, 150 Conn. 1, 183 A.2d 852 (1962).

32 People v. Borrero, 19 N.Y.2d 332, 227 N.E.2d 18 (1967); *see also* De Vongas v. State, 29 Wis. 2d 489, 139 N.W.2d 17 (1966).

33 234 F. Supp. 333, 337 (W.D.N.C. 1964).

34 Driver v. Hinant, *supra* note 14.

35 *Id.,* 356 F.2d, at 763.

36 *Id.,* 356 F.2d, at 764.

37 *Id.*

38 *Id.*

39 Easter v. District of Columbia, *supra* note 14.

40 *Id.,* Driver v. Hinant, *supra* note 14.

41 *E.g.,* Fultz v. United States, 365 F.2d 404 (6th Cir. 1966); Dobs v. State, 2 Md. App. 524, 235 A.2d 764 (1967); Prather v. Warden, Maryland State Penitentiary, 1 Md. App. 478, 231 A.2d 726 (1967); State v. Freiberg, 35 Wis. 2d 480, 151 N.W.2d 1 (1967).

42 State v. Freiberg, *supra* note 41.

43 Dobs v. State, *supra* note 41; Prather v. Warden, Maryland State Penitentiary, *supra* note 41.

44 D.C. CODE ANN. §§ 24-521—24-535 (Supp. II 1969); MD. ANN. CODE art. 2c, § 307 (Supp. 1968); N.C. GEN. STAT. §§ 122-65.6—122-65.9 (Supp. 1967).

45 Powell v. Texas, 392 U.S. 514 (1968).

46 *Id.,* at 514.

47 *Id.,* at 554.

48 *Id.,* at 548.

49 *Id.,* at 532.

50 *Id.,* at 533.

[51] *Id.*

[52] Id., at 535.

[53] *Id.,* at 542.

[54] *Id.,* at 540.

[55] *Id.,* at 541.

[56] *Id.,* at 544.

[57] *Id.,* at 549.

[58] *Id.,* at 552.

[59] *Id.,* at 554.

[60] *Id.,* at 568.

[61] *Id.,* at 569.

[62] *Id.,* at 567.

[63] *Id.,* at 568.

[64] *Cf.* Comment, 82 HARV. L. REV. 63, 108-110 (1968).

[65] Powell v. Texas, *supra* note 45, at 559 n. 2.

[66] *Id.,* at 567.

[67] Burger v. State, 118 Ga. App. 328, 163 S.E.2d 333 (1968), which upheld a drunkenness conviction emphasized these aspects.

[68] *Id.* This case mentions the absence of facilities and suggests that incarceration serves to remove intoxicated persons from the street.

[69] MODEL PENAL CODE § 2.01 (2) (Proposed Official Draft 1962). The involuntary acts as defined therein range from simple reflex actions to post-hypnotic suggestion.

[70] *See supra* (text accompanying footnotes 8-12) where it is generally agreed that intoxication may be so incapacitating as to render a person incapable of forming the requisite intent.

[71] This is, in view of some, a characteristic of alcoholism. *See generally* Powell v. Texas, *supra* note 45; Driver v. Hinant, *supra* note 14; Easter v. District of Col., *supra* note 14.

[72] Driver v. Hinant, *supra* note 14, at 764.

[73] 283 Minn. 90, 166 N.W.2d 720 (1969).

[74] However, a finding that an alcoholic is not responsible for crimes committed while intoxicated would not affect the law on criminal responsibility of other behaviorally disordered persons. It is improbable that the "intoxication" of narcotic addicts will be found to relieve them of responsibility, even if the actual condition of intoxication is determined to be involuntary. Paulsen, *supra* note 10, at 23, 24. For other disorders it is unlikely that the impulse leading to the wrongful conduct will be found to be sufficiently "unconscious" to sustain a defense based on lack of responsibility; the wrongful acts of a kleptomaniac and a pyromaniac are typically those of which the actor is aware, even if they cannot be controlled; they are not movements that can be analogized to a person in a "delirium of fever." *Cf.* HALL, GENERAL PRINCIPLES OF CRIMINAL LAW 488 (2d ed. 1960).

[75] The concept of automatism is new and its dimensions are not entirely clear. Its usual element is an act which is both involuntary and unconscious. *E.g.,* Edwards, *Automatism and Social Defense,* 8 CRIM. L.Q. 258, 270 (1966) ; Howard, *Automatism and Insanity,* 4 SYD. L. REV. 36 (1964). The defense has never been attempted in a case involving compulsive criminality since the party is conscious but subject to an irresistible impulse. WILLIAMS, CRIMINAL LAW: THE GENERAL PART 14 (1953). *But cf.* Starrs, *The Disease Concept of Alcoholism and Traditional Criminal Law Theory,* 19 S.C.L. REV. 349, 367 (1967), which states: "The sum total of the cases leads to the conclusion that automatism . . . would be a most available defense to alcoholics who are charged with criminal

conduct." "The essence of automatism is that the person who committed the crime is not the same person before this court." BRETT, AN INQUIRY INTO CRIMINAL GUILT 196 (1963).

76 Bacon, *Alcoholics Do Not Drink,* 315 ANNALS 55, 63 (1958). *See also* HAGGARD & JELLINEK, ALCOHOL EXPLORED 223-227 (1954).

77 *See* note 75 *supra* and accompanying text.

78 *See, e.g.,* Roberts v. State, 164 N.W.2d 525 (Wis. 1969), in which the dissent indicated a willingness to consider alcoholism a defense in a murder case but found that since defendant was not intoxicated at the time of the crime, the defense of alcoholism would not apply.

79 *See* note 76 *supra* and accompanying text.

80 Moreover, a curious result is possible though not probable. It may be that the drink-related crimes will be classified as public welfare offenses so that an insanity plea could be deemed irrelevant. *See, e.g.,* People v. Hoy, 3 Mich. App. 666, 143 N.W.2d 577 (1966) ; *cf.* Sayre, *Public Welfare Offenses,* 33 COLUM. L. REV. 55 (1933), which suggests that insanity is not a defense to strict liability offenses. *Id.,* at 78. However, he identifies the strict liability offenses as crimes that do not single out the individual wrongdoer for punishment or correction and those in which there are no prison sentences. *Id.,* at 72. Under these criteria it does not seem that drink-related offenses should be so classified, since they are typically characterized by prison sentences, either conjunctive to or as an alternative to monetary fines. *E.g., supra* Appendix A.

81 It is likely to affect the responsibility of narcotics addicts, sex-offenders, kleptomaniacs, and pyromaniacs, for whom the insanity defense has seldom proved useful, since a major problem is the propriety of classifying such persons as mentally ill. *E.g.,* Walder, *Psychiatry and the Problem of Criminal Responsibility,* 101 U. PA. L. REV. 378 (1952). *Compare* Heard v. United States, 348 F.2d 43 (D.C. Cir. 1965), which held ". . . a mere showing of narcotic addiction, without more, does not constitute 'some evidence' of mental disease or 'insanity' so as to raise the issue of criminal responsibility" *id.,* at 44 with Hansford v. United States, 365 F.2d 920 (D.C. Cir. 1966), which stated "Current medical knowledge indicates that use of narcotics often produces a psychological and physiological reaction known as acute brain syndrome which is a basic mental condition." *Id.,* at 922.

82 *Supra* p. 31.

83 *Supra* p. 232.

84 *Id.*

85 The classification problem is admittedly a difficult one. *Supra* note 81. *See also* Diamond, *supra* note 25, at 195, 196 (1962) ; Weihofen, *The Flowering of New Hampshire,* 22 U. CHI. L. REV. 356, 358 (1955) ; Guttmacher, *The Psychiatrist as an Expert Witness,* 22 U. CHI. L. REV. 324, 327 (1955). A dramatic illustration is the "weekend" decision made by St. Elizabeth's Hospital in the District of Columbia where in the middle of a trial doctors decided that "henceforth the hospital would consider that patients diagnosed as Sociopathic Personality Disturbance would be considered to have a 'mental disease' in terms of the Durham Decision." Cavanagh, *Problems of a Psychiatrist in Operating Under the M'Naghten, Durham and Model Penal Code Rules,* 45 MARQ. L. REV. 478, 488 (1962).

86 Powell v. Texas, *supra* note 45.

87 Salzman v. United States, 405 F.2d 358, 364 (D.C. Cir. 1968) (concurring opinion of Wright, J.) .

88 *Id.*

89 Powell v. Texas, *supra* note 45, at 569 (1968).

90 *E.g., id.,* 392 U.S. at 549, where Mr. Justice White suggests that existing law prohibits punishment of a narcotic addict for use.

CHAPTER 11

Treatment For The Alcoholic Criminal Offender

The previous chapter addressed itself to the issue of whether an alcoholic may, constitutionally or legally, be held responsible for the commission of crimes, both drunkenness offenses and other major offenses not directly connected with his drinking behavior. The problem to be explored now is that of the treatment to be afforded to the alcoholic—either after conviction, or in the event that he is relieved from criminal responsibility by reason of his disorder.

The treatment of alcoholics convicted of crime will usually be left, at least in the first instance, to the correctional authorities, and should therefore be reflected primarily in the state correction law rather than in its alcoholism treatment law. But this does not mean that correctional control and treatment for alcoholism can be separated entirely, for the two may at times be closely related: if a person who has been convicted of crime or who has been excused from criminal responsibility is *selected* for treatment by the court or the correctional authorities, he may come under the jurisdiction of the alcoholism division.[1] Moreover, determinations in individual cases about the appropriateness of civil commitment will, as a practical matter, need to draw on the expertise of the alcoholism division. Finally, any commitment of a convicted or acquitted offender must closely parallel the usual procedure for civil commitment, as a matter of constitutional due process.[2]

In discussing the issues that relate to the procedures following acquittals based on a defense of alcoholism, as well as to the procedures that provide an alternative to imprisonment for alcoholics convicted of crime, reliance will be placed on recent decisions and writings on similar problems of mentally ill offenders.[3] It should be stressed that much of the discussion that relates to civil commitment procedures following acquittal for crime by reason of alcoholism is

145

speculative and prospective. As the previous chapter has shown, acquittals for alcoholism are rare—in fact, they are limited to the few jurisdictions that acquit alcoholics of drunkenness offenses, and the few instances when an alcoholic is acquitted of a more serious crime because he has deteriorated to such an extent that an insanity defense has become appropriate. Aside from its relevance for the small number of cases mentioned, the discussion looks to the future when rules of responsibility may well change. The discussion of alternatives to imprisonment is less prospective—a number of states do provide in some fashion for commitment in lieu of jail[4]—but the discussion is nonetheless speculative since it must draw on the few recent cases which rather than dealing with alcoholics, relate to transfers and commitments of mentally ill persons, drug addicts and sexual psychopaths.

PROCEDURES AFTER ACQUITTAL OR DISMISSAL OF CHARGE FOR LACK OF CRIMINAL RESPONSIBILITY

When a defendant is acquitted, or the charge is dismissed because he lacks responsibility for his criminal conduct, two courses are open —either to release him outright, or to provide for compulsory treatment for the disorder on which his acquittal is based. Simple release does not serve the goals of rehabilitation, deterrence, or incapacitation, nor does it in any manner allay public fears (which are entirely justified, particularly in cases of serious and compulsive offenders). A recent decision suggests the problems that would be faced if the only alternative to punishment were release:

> For society, the alternative is unhappy, and frequently it is so for the defendant. A man like M'Naughten ought not to be released with its great risks that he would again resort to violence upon those whom he fancied his persecutors. Nor should he be left untended in the misery of his oppressive delusions, if institutional care with psychiatric and psychological services may assist him.[5]

Yet compulsory treatment which will protect society while it affords therapy to the patient raises complex questions of constitutional law as well as public policy.

PROPRIETY OF CIVIL COMMITMENT AFTER ACQUITTAL

Many states provide by law for either automatic or discretionary commitment to mental institutions whenever a defendant is held to lack criminal responsibility and is acquitted because of a successful "insanity" defense;[6] such provisions have been consistently upheld over challenge.[7] For example, a Kansas court in rejecting a constitutional challenge to its commitment statute by one who had been accused of murder stated:

> The purposes of the statute are highly beneficient. It gives protection to the public against repetitions of homicides, or other acts of irresponsible frenzy or distraction, and affords to the unfortunate persons so committed safe seclusion and humane treatment which it is the province of the state to give in the exercise of its parental power.[8]

Moreover, the concept of confinement for treatment purposes upon acquittal is endorsed by the Model Penal Code,[9] the relevant comments in the Code suggest that such a provision may also work to the advantage of the defendant because the insanity defense is likely to be more acceptable to a judge and jury[10] who know that acquittal need not lead to outright release. Recent decisions have recognized, too, that the safety of both the public and the defendant supply a valid basis for civil commitment after a successful insanity plea, although they note that such acquittal is based on a finding of insanity at the time of the commission of the crime and not at the time of acquittal.

The underlying rationale of these post-acquittal commitment statutes is, of course, protection of the public from danger. Since the acquittal implies that the defendant is a person who by reason of insanity cannot be deterred by criminal sanctions, the proper way to satisfy the goal of public protection is through incapacitation by civil commitment, and through attempted rehabilitation in a treatment setting, rather than in a correctional one.

Recent decisions have already indicated, however, that the interests of the defendant or patient may not be sacrificed to the public desire for protection. The facts that he has been acquitted of a crime and that he is the recipient of treatment instead of correction, do not lessen the need for Constitutional protections in the course of commitment procedures; more particularly, these procedures must meet the requirements of due process and equal protection. Moreover, the commitment should not be only a means of incapacitative detention, but should also assure adequate treatment during confinement and prompt release when treatment has been successful—otherwise civil commitment would become a mere subterfuge for imprisonment.[11]

The procedures that must be followed to meet constitutional requirements have been made explicit in recent decisions. In sum, they suggest that a person acquitted because of lack of responsibility may be civilly confined without a hearing, but only for as long as is necessary for an adequate examination of his condition. Then if the acquitted person is found to be a proper subject for treatment, he must be afforded a full hearing with substantially the same protections—such as rights to counsel and cross-examination—as would be afforded a person in any other civil commitment hearings in the jurisdiction.[12] Moreover, once a person acquitted for lack of criminal responsibility has been committed, his rights should closely parallel those of other patients who have been civilly committed; for example, he should have the same right to periodic review of the need for further confinement.

Recent decisions also suggest that the grounds for commitment of an acquitted person must parallel those required in any other involuntary civil commitment.[13] This may raise difficulties in the future. If the laws of criminal responsibility were to be changed, an alcoholic who was found impaired in his decision-making capacity might be excused from criminal responsibility for crimes such as larceny, forgery, or disorderly conduct, and yet he might not meet the grounds for civil commitment—"unable to take care of his own affairs," "dangerous to himself or others," etc. This problem will have to be resolved by appropriate legislation if rules of responsibility are changed—it would, of course, be resolved by the more limited grounds for commitment under the Model Alcoholism and Intoxication Treatment Act.

Finally, a North Carolina statute,[14] adopted in response to the *Driver* decision, which deals with persons who are excused from responsibility for the crime of public intoxication by reason of alcoholism, allows for a range of solutions. The relevant part of the statute authorizes the court to make alternative dispositions of the acquitted defendant. It may order the commencement of commitment proceedings under the state's mental health laws, or it may permit appropriate arrangements—under court supervision—by the alcoholic or his family for treatment in private or local facilities, for outpatient or inpatient care.[15] The court retains jurisdiction for two years, and it has authority to change its initial disposition, and to cause the transfer of the patient from one facility to another, so that inappropriate determinations can be corrected. Thus, it would be possible for the court to allow the alcoholic to make arrangements for outpatient treatment, and yet retain the authority to order inpatient commitment when necessary. This authority is likely to encourage the alcoholic to cooperate, and it will also protect the public if he gets into a condition where he is likely to cause physical harm.

When, under existing laws, or more appropriately, under newly developed ones, a defendant is acquitted because he lacks criminal responsibility by reason of alcoholism, some mode of compulsory treatment will have to be considered so as to provide both for the protection of the public and for the rehabilitation of the alcoholic. What treatment alternatives are chosen will depend in part on the characteristics of the defendant and in part on the nature of the offense of which he was acquitted. In some instances commitment to the state department of mental hygiene for treatment in a state mental institution may be appropriate but alternatives to inpatient treatment should be considered. Outpatient treatment, including privately arranged treatment, and other modes, should be available, and should be preferred choices over confinement to a state institution, unless the protection of the public requires it. An order to commit for compulsory treatment should only be made, however, in a proceeding that is separate from the criminal presentation in which the defendant was acquitted, and upon grounds and procedures that would be sufficient for other civil commitments.

TREATMENT ALTERNATIVES TO IMPRISONMENT

Under present rules of responsibility, alcoholism is not generally a defense, and alcoholics are indeed convicted of crimes. Even though they are found sufficiently responsible to be convicted, they still should be treated. There are a number of choices for treatment, either after conviction, or in lieu of conviction and correctional sentence. After conviction, alcoholics may be treated under appropriate programs inside correctional institutions, or they may be assigned or committed to treatment facilities, rather than correctional institutions. An alcoholic charged with crime may also be committed prior to conviction, for treatment in lieu of criminal prosecution and sentence. Finally, alcoholics convicted of crime may, following conviction, be permitted to volunteer or apply for treatment in lieu of imprisonment.

Post-Conviction Treatment

Only a few states have responded in any fashion to the problem. In some—Georgia, for example—the solution has been to make treatment provisions only for those whose offense is causally connected with alcoholism.[16] The workability of such a provision is extremely doubtful—there is simply no firm evidence upon which to make precise determinations of causality. At least two states, Texas and Arkansas, permit treatment only if special facilities are available for alcoholics convicted of crime.[17] The special facilities are not described, but it appears that the purpose is to prohibit a mixing of "criminal" and non-criminal alcoholics. Although the separation of very serious offenders may have some merit, a strict policy of separating *all* criminal offenders for treatment purposes may lead to an expensive duplication of facilities and programs. It is apparent that treatment for alcoholism within correctional institutions may raise administrative, and probably therapeutic, difficulties but, on the whole, it does not raise any substantial legal ones.

Commitment to a treatment institution after conviction, however, has a number of consequences that give rise to constitutional and legal issues. A person who is convicted and sentenced normally has a sentence with a determinable maximum term, and at the end of that term he must be released. Moreover, he is eligible to be considered for release on parole after a certain portion of that term has been served. He also has a number of fairly well-established privileges not accorded to those in treatment facilities while imprisoned.[18] When he is committed to a treatment institution, however, he commonly may be held for a wholly indefinite term—*i.e., until* "cured"; he has no right, even, to be considered for parole release at any time—such release would be wholly at the discretion of the treatment authorities. In fact many persons committed for treatment after conviction have remained in institutions far, far longer than the term of their original criminal sentence. In the light of the potentially serious consequences of commitment to treatment institutions after criminal conviction, recent decisions have held that the subject must be afforded substantially the same protections given to a person subject to civil commitment. A recent case, in discussing the validity of a transfer to a hospital for the criminally insane, held that the prisoner

> . . . must be afforded substantially the same procedural safeguards as are provided in civil commitment proceedings, including proper examination, a hearing upon notice, periodic review of the need for commitment, and trial by jury.[19]

The court also suggests that the same grounds for commitment must be proved as in civil commitments. The decision rests on the premise that transfer to a treatment institution effectively eliminates the possibility of parole, increases restraints, and may expose the person to hardships, indignities and frustrations that exceed the rigors of life in a prison.

From recent decisions it would appear that a person convicted of a crime has the right to be held in a correctional institution. If he is to be transferred to any other kind of institutional setting, however well-motivated such a transfer may be, he is entitled to the same procedural protection as a person subjected to civil commitment.

Finally, it appears that the removal of a convict to a treatment institution carries with it an obligation to provide treatment. The failure to provide treatment destroys the main reason for differentiating civil commitment from criminal conviction.[20] Unless treatment is afforded to the alcoholic offender, for instance, there is no reason why he should be committed to a so-called treatment institution, rather than sentenced to imprisonment. The standard to measure the adequacy of treatment is likely to be the same as in the case of a non-criminal patient committed for treatment—i.e., an attempt to determine if there is at least a genuine effort to treat.[21] If there is no such effort, the person should either be remanded to the correctional institution, or, if the period of actual commitment equals or has exceeded the term of the sentence for the offense, he should be released.

Commitment Prior to Conviction

When an alcoholic is charged with the commission of a crime, one of the available alternatives is to terminate or hold in abeyance the criminal prosecution, and to substitute for it a proceeding for his involuntary commitment for purposes of treatment. The procedure of substituting such a commitment for prosecution is authorized in a number of jurisdictions for drug addicts[22] and sex offenders,[23] as well as for alcoholics. Recent alcoholism treatment laws in California,[24] the District of Columbia[25] and Maryland[26] provide for this option. The rationale for the alternative commitment procedure is that in the cases of certain behaviorally disordered persons and certain compulsive offenders, the use of criminal procedures and imprisonment will not serve the major purposes of the criminal law—to deter the offender in the future, and to deter others from engaging in similar conduct;[27] but the state does have the right to protect society against future anti-social conduct by persons suffering from particular disorders by committing them for treatment. This serves both to make it temporarily impossible for them to commit other offenses, and to rehabilitate them so as to lessen the likelihood of offenses in the future.

Substitution of procedures leading to commitment to treatment facilities for criminal prosecution has been authorized in a number of states for some time.[28] In the recent case of *Specht v. Patterson*,[29] decided by the United States Supreme Court in 1967, which involved a due process challenge to the special sentencing procedure under the Colorado sexual psychopathy law, there were indications that such procedures will be upheld as long as the commitment is based on full procedural protection, which must include a hearing and right of counsel. It is possible that such pre-conviction commitments may also be challenged on the ground that the criminal charge against an alcoholic is not an adequate basis for selecting him for compulsory treatment as against any number of other alcoholics not similarly selected. Such a challenge—based on a claim of an improper classification that violates Constitutional guarantees of the equal protection of the laws—would probably fail. A more serious challenge, one which would have to be based on the circumstances of a particular case, would be a claim of denial of due process, asserting that the arrest and criminal charge were not genuine, but were arranged only to force the defendant to undergo treatment. As in the case of post-conviction commitment for treatment, such a commitment made prior to conviction must be based on grounds and procedures similar to those in other civil commitments, and treatment must actually be provided.

A final option, thus far available in only a couple of jurisdictions,[30] is that of permitting the alcoholic who is charged with a crime to accept treatment voluntarily, in place of criminal prosecution and sentence. Voluntary treatment prior to trial has advantages, even though the person cannot be allowed the guest status in institutions accorded to a true voluntary patient. The alcoholic need not face the rigors of trial or the stigma of conviction, and he may improve his lot by treatment, rather than merely serving time in a penal institution. Yet the availability of this option may raise due process issues. It may be viewed as a coercive device to lure a defendant from his day in court, by offering him what may be represented to him as a lesser penalty. The issue of due process would be raised by suggesting that the element of free choice is lacking, in that a person who is innocent of the charge yet fearful of the outcome of a trial would be likely to "volunteer" for treatment as the lesser risk. Legislation that offers the defendant the option of treatment in lieu of prosecution must, therefore, be very carefully drawn so as to assure that the defendant's choice is free of coercion, whether subtle or overt.

In sum, whether treatment options are made available before or after trial, whether they are available at the option of the court or of the alcoholc or other behaviorally disordered defendant, the law now recognizes that procedural protection must be afforded the offender whether he is to be sent to prison or to a treatment institution. In spite of the benign purposes of treatment laws, the courts have come to recognize that indefinite commitment to a treatment facility may be as burdensome as correctional confinement, and may often involve even greater deprivation of liberties. In the shaping of treatment legislation, therefore, detailed attention must be given to procedural protections, for mere reliance on a declaration of benign treatment purposes will no longer carry the day.

CHAPTER 11 NOTES

[1] For an examination of this process in New York, *see* SPECIAL COMMITTEE ON THE STUDY OF COMMITMENT PROCEDURES & THE LAW RELATING TO INCOMPETENTS OF THE ASSOC. OF THE BAR OF THE CITY OF N.Y., MENTAL ILLNESS, DUE PROCESS AND THE CRIMINAL DEFENDANT (Fordham University Press 1968).

[2] The United States Supreme Court in 1966 struck down a commitment to a mental institution at the expiration of criminal sentence, holding that failure to follow New York procedures for civil commitment was a denial of equal protection. Baxstrom v. Herold, 383 U.S. 108 (1966). A recent Court of Appeals case to the same effect is United States *ex rel.* Schuster v. Herold, 410 F.2d 1071 (2d Cir. 1969). *See also* Specht v. Patterson, 386 U.S. 605 (1967); Cameron v. Mullin, 387 F.2d 193 (D.C. Cir. 1967); People v. Lally, 19 N.Y.2d 27, 224 N.E.2d 87, 277 N.Y.S.2d 654 (1966).

[3] *Id.* In addition *see, e.g.,* Lynch v. Overholser, 369 U.S. 705 (1962); Bolton v. Harris, 395 F.2d 642 (D.C. Cir. 1968); People v. Fuller, 24 N.Y.2d 292, 300 N.Y.S.2d 102 (1969).

[4] Rhode Island provides in its criminal statutes that a court may commit vagrants and common drunkards to treatment facilities after examination and recommendation by the division of alcoholism; R.I. GEN. LAWS ANN. § 11-45-1 (Supp. 1967). In Arkansas and Texas a defendant convicted of a misdemeanor resulting from his use of alcohol may be committed to treatment facilities if they are available, and Georgia has a similar provision dependent upon the willingness of the Department of Alcoholism to take custody; ARK. STAT. ANN. § 83-712 (1960); TEX. REV. CIV. STAT. ANN. art. 5561c, Sec. 12 (Supp. 1968); GA. CODE ANN. § 88-814a (1963). In Hawaii the officer of a correctional institution may file with the director of health an application for transfer of any resident of the institution to a state hospital; if approved, the resident may be kept in the institution for the duration of his maximum term (after which new proceedings must be initiated or he must be released); HAWAII REV. STATS. § 334-74 (1968). In New Jersey a judge who is satisfied that a defendant suffers from acute alcoholism may order that all or part of his sentence be served in treatment facilities; N.J. STAT. ANN. § 30:9-12.20 (1964). The District of Columbia provides that a chronic alcoholic convicted of public intoxication who constitutes a continuing danger, or any defendant acquitted of public intoxication on the ground of chronic alcoholism, may be committed to an inpatient center if adequate and appropriate treatment is available; D.C. CODE ANN. § 24-527 (Supp. II 1969). *Cf.* CAL. WELF. & INST'NS CODE §§ 5225-5230 (West Supp. 1968) (dangerous or gravely disabled defendants who are chronic

alcoholics may, upon court order, gain evaluation that might result in detention for treatment); MD. ANN. CODE art. 2c, § 307 (Supp. 1968) (reference to general law of probation, parole or other criminal disposition); N.M. STAT. ANN. § 46-12-7 (Supp. 1967) (commitment to treatment facilities of those convicted five times of intoxication); VT. STAT. ANN. tit. 18, § 8459 (1968) (a judge may commit a defendant to the custody of the alcoholism board if he has three times been sentenced for drunkenness, if adequate facilities and personnel are available).

5 United States v. Chandler, 393 F.2d 920, 927 (4th Cir. 1968).

6 For a comprehensive summary, see Lynch v. Overholser, supra note 3, 369 U.S. at 725, 726 & nn. 4-7 (Clark dissenting).

7.In re Clark, 80 Kan. 539, 121 P. 492 (1912); In re Beebe, 92 Kan. 1026, 142 P. 269 (1914); Hodison v. Rogers, 37 Kan. 950, 22 P.2d 491 (1933); State v. Burris, 169 La. 520, 125 So. 580 (1929); Bailey v. State, 210 Ga. 52, 77 S.E.2d 511 (1953); In re Brown, 39 Wash. 160, 81 P. 552 (1905).

8 In re Clark, supra note 7, 56 Kan. at 553, 121 P. at 498.

9 MODEL PENAL CODE § 4.08 (Proposed Official Draft 1962).

10 MODEL PENAL CODE § 4.08, Comment (Tent. Draft No. 4, 1955).

11 See People v. Lally, supra note 2; Bolton v. Harris, supra note 3.

12 Id.

13 Cameron v. Mullin, supra note 2. See also cases cited notes 11, 12 supra.

14 N.C. GEN. STAT. §§ 122-65.7, 65.8 (Supp. 1967).

15 Id.

16 GA. CODE ANN. § 88-814a (1963).

17 ARK. STAT. ANN. § 83-712 (1960); TEX. REV. CIV. STAT. ANN. art. 5561c Sec. 12 (Supp. 1968). Cf. D.C. CODE ANN. § 24-527 (Supp. II 1969); VT. STAT. ANN. tit. 18, § 8459 (1968).

18 In this connection, see also United States ex rel. Schuster v. Herold, supra note 2 (appendix to the opinion of the Court).

19 United States ex rel. Schuster v. Herold, supra note 2, 410 F.2d at 1073.

20 Millard v. Cameron, 373 F.2d 468, 471, 472 (D.C. Cir. 1966).

21 See, e.g., Commonwealth v. Hogan, 341 Mass. 372, 170 N.E.2d 327 (1960).

22 E.g., N.Y. MENTAL HYGIENE LAW § 210 (McKinney Supp. 1968). The federal statute is to similar effect; 18 U.S.C. §§ 4251-4255, 28 U.S.C. § 2904 (Supp. III 1967) (the latter section is in the chapter on the judiciary and states that a commitment does not constitute a conviction; this would seem somewhat superfluous, and, indeed, New York repealed a nearly identical provision in 1967; LAWS 1966, ch. 192, § 19). See also MASS. GEN. LAWS ANN. ch. 111a, § 6 (1967).

23 E.g., ALA. CODE tit. 15, §§ 436 (Supp. 1967), 440, 441 (1959); ILL. ANN. STAT. ch. 38, § 105-3 (Smith-Hurd 1964); MO. ANN. STAT. §§ 202.710, 202.740 (1959); N.H. REV. STAT. ANN. §§ 173:3, 173:13 (1964). See also, NEB. REV. STAT. § 29-2906 (1964); WASH. REV. CODE ANN. §§ 71.06.20, 71.06.60, 71.06.90 (1962).

24 CAL. WELF. & INST'NS CODE §§ 5225-5230 (West Supp. 1968).

25 D.C. CODE ANN. § 24-524 (Supp. II 1969).

26 MD. ANN. CODE art. 2c, § 307 (Supp. 1968).

27 See, e.g., Wechsler, The Criteria of Criminal Responsibility, 22 U. CHI. L. REV. 367 (1955).

28 E.g., N.M. STAT. ANN. § 46-12-7 (Supp. 1967); R.I. GEN. LAWS ANN. § 11-45-1 (Supp. 1967); VT. STAT. ANN. tit. 18, § 8459 (1968).

29 386 U.S. 605 (1967).

30 D.C. CODE ANN. § 24-525 (Supp. II 1969). *Cf.* CAL. WELF. & INST'NS CODE § 5226 (West Supp. 1968), under which a defendant may expressly insist upon *criminal* proceedings despite recommendations otherwise (and it may be that due process requires this to be a part of all these statutes by implication). *See also* the procedures used at the St. Louis Detoxification Center, where an arrested patient who refuses to remain at treatment facilities is prosecuted for criminal drunkenness: *Hearings on H.R. 6143 Before Subcomm. No. 3 of the House Comm. on the District of Columbia*, 90th Cong., 1st Sess., at 17 (1967); PRESIDENT'S COMM'N ON LAW ENFORCEMENT & ADMINISTRATION OF JUSTICE, TASK FORCE REPORT: DRUNKENNESS 50-57 (1967).

BIBLIOGRAPHY

Bibliography

BOOKS:

AMERICAN BAR FOUNDATION, THE MENTALLY DISABLED AND THE LAW (Lindman & McIntyre, eds., 1961).

AMERICAN LAW INSTITUTE, MODEL PENAL CODE, PROPOSED OFFICIAL DRAFT (1962).

AMERICAN LAW INSTITUTE, MODEL PENAL CODE, TENTATIVE DRAFT NO. 4 (1955).

ASSOCIATION OF THE BAR OF THE CITY OF N.Y., MENTAL ILLNESS, DUE PROCESS AND THE CRIMINAL DEFENDANT (1968).

P. BRETT, AN INQUIRY INTO CRIMINAL GUILT (1963).

A. DEUTSCH, THE MENTALLY ILL IN AMERICA (2d ed. 1949).

R. DONIGAN, CHEMICAL TESTS AND THE LAW (1957).

DORLAND'S ILLUSTRATED MEDICAL DICTIONARY (23d ed. 1957).

E. FISCHER, VEHICLE TRAFFIC LAW (1961).

T. FLINT, EMERGENCY TREATMENT AND MANAGEMENT (3d ed. 1964).

D. GLASER & U. O'LEARY, THE ALCOHOLIC OFFENDER (1961).

R. GLASSCOTE, T. PLAUT, D. HAMMERSLEY, F. O'NEILL, M. CHAFETZ & E. CUMMING, THE TREATMENT OF ALCOHOLISM—A STUDY OF PROGRAMS AND PROBLEMS (1967).

J. GOLDFARB, ROADBLOCKS TO PROGRESS IN THE TREATMENT OF THE CHRONIC INEBRIATE, SELECTED PAPERS (North American Ass'n of Alcoholism Programs 1967).

F. GRAD, PUBLIC HEALTH LAW MANUAL (1965).

H. HAGGARD & E. JELLINEK, ALCOHOL EXPLORED (1954).

J. HALL, GENERAL PRINCIPLES OF CRIMINAL LAW (2d ed. 1960).

HARRISON TREATMENT AND REHABILITATION CENTER PROGRESS REPORT, COLLEGE OF OSTEOPATHIC MEDICINE, DES MOINES, IOWA (1968).

E. JELLINEK, THE DISEASE CONCEPT OF ALCOHOLISM (1960).

NEW YORK DEPT. OF CIVIL SERVICE, DEPT. OF MENTAL HYGIENE, SUPERVISORS GUIDE TO ALCOHOLISM (N.Y.C. Dept. of Social Services, An Introduction to Camp La Guardia, 1968).

OHIO DEPT. OF HEALTH, ALCOHOLISM UNIT, SOCIAL AND PSYCHOLOGICAL AND DEMOGRAPHIC CHARACTERISTICS OF ARRESTED DRUNK OFFENDERS (1967).

D. PITTMAN & W. GORDON, THE REVOLVING DOOR, A STUDY OF THE CHRONIC POLICE CASE INEBRIATE (1958).

D. PITTMAN & C. SNYDER, eds. SOCIETY CULTURE AND DRINKING PATTERNS (1962).

T. PLAUT, ALCOHOL PROBLEMS (A Report to the Nation by the Cooperative Comm'n on the Study of Alcoholism, 1967).

PRESIDENT'S COMM'N ON LAW ENFORCEMENT & ADMINISTRATION OF JUSTICE, TASK FORCE REPORT: DRUNKENNESS (1967).

W. PROSSER, THE LAW OF TORTS (3d ed. 1964).

UNITED STATES DEPT. OF TRANSPORTATION, ALCOHOL AND HIGHWAY SAFETY (A Report to the Congress, 1968).

VERA FOUNDATION, MANHATTAN BOWERY PROJECT, 1ST ANNUAL REPORT (1969).

VISITING COMMITTEE OF THE WASHINGTON, D.C. AREA COUNCIL ON ALCOHOLISM, FIRST REPORT ON THE CURRENT STATUS OF ALCOHOLISM PROGRAMS AND FACILITIES (1967).

G. WILLIAMS, CRIMINAL LAW: THE GENERAL PART (2d ed. 1961).

ARTICLES:

Androes & Whitehead, The "Buddy System" in Hospital Treatment of Alcoholics, 27 Q.J. STUD. ALCOHOL 524 (1966).

Armstrong, The Search for Alcoholic Personality, 315 ANNALS 40 (1958).

Aronwitz, *Civil Commitment of Narcotics Addicts,* 67 COLUM. L. REV. 405 (1967).

Bacon, *Alcoholics Do Not Drink,* 315 ANNALS 55 (1958).

Bahn *et al., Out-patient Psychiatric Clinic Services to Alcoholics* 1959, 24 Q.J. STUD. ALCOHOL 213 (1963).

Bailey, *Some Issues in Epidemiologic Surveys of Alcoholism,* 57 AM. J. PUBLIC HEALTH 987 (1967).

Bailey *et al., The Epidemiology of Alcoholism in an Urban Residential Area,* 26 Q.J. STUD. ALCOHOL 27 (1965).

Bailey, Haberman & Steinberg, *Distinctive Characteristics of the Alcoholic Family,* REPORT OF THE HEALTH RESEARCH COUNCIL OF THE CITY OF NEW YORK (1965).

Bailey & Stewart, *Normal Drinking by Persons Reporting Previous Problem Drinking,* 28 Q.J. STUD. ALCOHOL 305 (1967).

Bartholomew, *A Long-Acting Phenotheazine in the Treatment of Alcoholics in an Out-patient Clinic,* 27 Q.J. STUD. ALCOHOL 510 (1966).

Bauer, *Experimental Observations on Motorists Under the Influence of Alcohol,* 29 DEUT. ZTSCHR. F.D. GES GERICHLICHE MED. 193 (1938).

Birnbaum, *The Right to Treatment,* 46 A.B.A.J. 499 (1960).

Blane *et al., Social Factors in the Diagnosis of Alcoholism,* 24 Q.J. STUD. ALCOHOL 640 (1963).

Blum, *Mind-Altering Drugs and Dangerous Behavior: Alcohol,* PRESIDENT'S COMM'N ON LAW ENFORCEMENT & ADMINISTRATION OF JUSTICE, TASK FORCE REPORT: DRUNKENNESS 29 (1967).

Blumberg *et al., The Development, Major Goals and Strategies of a Skid Row Program: Philadelphia,* 27 Q.J. STUD. ALCOHOL 242 (1966).

Bourne *et al., Treatment of Skid Row Alcoholics with Disulfiram,* 27 Q.J. STUD. ALCOHOL 42 (1966).

Bowden, *Driving Under the Influence of Alcohol,* 11 J. FORENSIC MEDICINE 6 (1964).

Brown, *An Aftercare Program for Alcoholics,* 9 CRIME & DELINQUENCY 77 (1963).

Bruun, *Outcome of Different Types of Treatment of Alcoholics,* 24 Q.J. STUD. ALCOHOL 280 (1963).

Cavanagh, *Problems of a Psychiatrist in Operating Under the M'Naghten, Durham and Model Penal Code Rules,* 45 MARQ. L. REV. 478 (1962).

Chafetz, *Note,* 25 Q.J. STUD. ALCOHOL 358 (1964).

Chafetz et al., *Establishing Treatment Relations with Alcoholics,* 134 J. NERVOUS & MENTAL DISEASE 395 (1962).

Chambliss, *Types of Deviance and the Effectiveness of Legal Sanctions,* 1967 WIS. L. REV. 703.

Charnoff, Kissin & Reed, *An Evaluation of Various Psychotherapeutic Agents in the Long-Term Treatment of Chronic Alcoholism: Results of a Double Blind Study,* 246 AM. J. MED. SCI. 172 (1963).

Chwast, *A Small Goal Is Big Enough,* 9 CRIME & DELINQUENCY 158 (1963).

Cohen, *Administration of the Criminal Sexual Psychopath Statute in Indiana,* 32 IND. L.J. 450 (1957).

Coopersmith, *Adaptive Reactions of Alcoholics and Nonalcoholics,* 25 Q.J. STUD. ALCOHOL 262 (1964).

Corotto, *An Exploratory Study of the Personality Characteristics of Alcoholic Patients Who Volunteer for Continued Treatment,* 24 Q.J. STUD. ALCOHOL 432 (1963).

Couger, *Perception, Learning and Emotion: The Role of Alcohol,* 315 ANNALS 31 (1958).

Cowen, *A Six-Year Follow-Up of a Series of Committed Alcoholics,* 15 Q.J. STUD. ALCOHOL 413 (1954).

Cramton, *The Problem of the Drinking Driver,* 54 A.B.A.J. 945 (1968).

Cressey, *The Differential Association Theory and Compulsive Crimes,* 45 J. CRIM. L.C. & P.S. 29 (1954).

Curran, *Hospitalization of the Mentally Ill,* 31 N.C.L. REV. 274 (1953).

David & Ditman, *The Effects of Court Referral and Disulfurim on Motivation of Alcoholics,* 24 Q.J. STUD. ALCOHOL 276 (1963).

Davis, *Mental Hygiene and the Class Structure,* 4 PSYCHIATRY 55 (1938).

Demone, *Experiments in Referral to Alcoholism Clinics,* 24 Q.J. STUD. ALCOHOL 495 (1963).

Dershowitz, *The Psychiatrist's Power in Civil Commitment,* PSYCHOLOGY TODAY, Feb. 1969, at 43.

Diamond, *From M'Naghten to Currens, And Beyond,* 50 CALIF. L. REV. 189 (1962).

Edwards, *Automatism and Social Defense,* 8 CRIM. L.Q. 258 (1966).

Edwards & Guthrie, *A Controlled Trial of In-patient and Out-patient Treatment of Alcohol Dependency,* 1 LANCET 555 (1967).

Foote, *Vagrancy-Type Law and Its Administration,* 104 U. PA. L. REV. 613 (1956).

Greenberg, *Intoxication and Alcoholism: Physiological Factors,* 315 ANNALS 22 (1958).

Gross, *Management of Acute Alcoholic Withdrawal,* 28 Q.J. STUD. ALCOHOL 665 (1967).

Guttmacher, *The Psychiatrist as an Expert Witness,* 22 U. CHI. L. REV. 324 (1955).

Haberman, *Childhood Symptoms in Children of Alcoholics and Comparison Group Parents,* 28 J. MARRIAGE & FAMILY 152 (1966).

Hacker & Frym, *The Sexual Psychopath Act in Practice: A Critical Discussion,* 43 CALIF. L. REV. 766 (1955).

Harger, *Debunking the Drunkometer,* 40 J. CRIM. L. & CRIMINOLOGY 497 (1949).

Heise & Halporn, *Medico-Legal Aspects of Drunkenness,* 36 PA. MED. J. 190 (1932).

Hill & Banc, *Evaluation of Psychotherapy with Alcoholics; A Critical Review,* 28 Q.J. STUD. ALCOHOL 76 (1967).

Hoff, *Comprehensive Rehabilitation Program for Alcoholics,* 7 ARCH. ENVIRON'L HEALTH 40 (1963).

Howard, *Automatism and Insanity,* 4 SYD. L. REV. 36 (1964).

Hunter, *Alcoholism and the Family Agency,* 24 Q.J. STUD. ALCOHOL 61 (1963).

Jackson, *Alcoholism and the Family,* 315 ANNALS 90 (1958).

Jackson, Fagan & Burr, *The Seattle Police Department Rehabilitation Project for Chronic Alcoholics,* 22 FED. PROBATION (No. 2) 36 (1958).

Jetter, *The Diagnosis of Acute Alcoholic Intoxication by a Correlation of Clinical and Chemical Findings,* 196 AM. J. MED. SCI. 475 (1938).

Kadish, *A Case Study in the Signification of Procedural Due Process— Institutionalizing the Mentally Ill,* 9 W. POL. Q. 93 (1956).

Kalant, *Some Recent Physiological and Biochemical Investigations on Alcohol and Alcoholism, A Review,* 23 Q.J. STUD. ALCOHOL 52 (1962).

Katz, *The Salvation Army Men's Social Service Center,* 25 Q.J. STUD. ALCOHOL 324 (1964).

Katz & Goldstein, *Dangerousness and Mental Illness, Some Observations on the Decision to Release Persons Acquitted by Reason of Insanity,* 70 YALE L.J. 225 (1960).

Keller, *Definition of Alcoholism,* 21 Q.J. STUD. ALCOHOL 125 (1960).

Keller & Efron, *Alcoholism,* 1 ENCYCLOPEDIA AMERICANA 348 (1956).

Kendall, *Normal Drinking in Former Alcohol Addicts,* 26 Q.J. STUD. ALCOHOL 247 (1965).

King, *The Role of the Court in Treatment of the Addicted or Mentally Ill,* 52 AM. JUDICATURE SOCIETY 71 (1968).

Kittie, *Compulsory Mental Treatment and the Requirements of "Due Process,"* 21 OHIO ST. L.J. 28 (1960).

Krimmel & Falkey, *Short-Term Treatment of Alcoholics,* 7 SOCIAL WORK 102 (1962).

Krystal & Moore, *Who Is Qualified to Treat the Alcoholic? A Discussion,* 24 Q.J. STUD. ALCOHOL 705 (1963).

Lacey, *Vagrancy and Other Crimes of Personal Condition,* 66 HARV. L. REV. 1224 (1953).

Ladd & Gibson, *Legal Medical Aspects of Blood Tests,* 29 VA. L. REV. 749 (1943).

Ladd & Gibson, *The Medico-Legal Aspects of the Blood Test to Determine Intoxication,* 24 IOWA L. REV. 191 (1938).

Lefourneau, *Legal Aspects of the Hospital Emergency Room,* 16 CLEV.-MAR. L. REV. 50 (1967).

Lemere, *What Happens to Alcoholics,* 109 AM. J. PSYCHIATRY 674 (1953).

Lemere & Voetglin, *An Evaluation of the Aversion Treatment of Alcoholism,* 11 Q.J. STUD. ALCOHOL 199 (1950).

Lemert, *Dependency in Married Alcoholics,* 23 Q.J. STUD. ALCOHOL 590 (1962).

Lisansky, *The Woman Alcoholic,* 315 ANNALS 73 (1958).

MacCormick, *Correctional Views on Alcohol, Alcoholism and Crime,* 9 CRIME & DELINQUENCY 15 (1963).

Mackay, *Problem Drinking Among Juvenile Delinquents,* 9 CRIME & DELINQUENCY 29 (1963).

Margolis, Krystal & Siegel *Psychotherapy with Alcoholic Offenders,* 25 Q.J. STUD. ALCOHOL 85 (1964).

Martinson, *The California Recovery House: A Sanctuary for Alcoholics,* 48 MENTAL HYGIENE 432 (1964).

Maurer, *The Beginning of Wisdom About Alcoholism,* FORTUNE 176 (May 1968).

Maxwell, *Alcoholics Anonymous: An Interpretation,* in SOCIETY, CULTURE AND DRINKING PATTERNS 577 (D. Pittman & C. Snyder, eds. 1962).

Mayer, Needham & Myerson, *Contact and Initial Appearance at an Alcoholism Clinic,* 26 Q.J. STUD. ALCOHOL 480 (1965).

McGee & Scher, *Integration of Alcoholism and Mental Health Services,* 18 Q.J. STUD. ALCOHOL 658 (1957).

McNichol *et al., Management of Withdrawal from Alcohol (Including Delirium Tremens),* 60 SO. MED. J. 1 (1967).

Meyerson & Meyer, *Origins, Treatment, and Destiny of Skid Row Alcoholic Men,* 19 S.C.L. REV. 332 (1967).

Mills & Hetrick, *Treating the Unmotivated Alcoholic,* 9 CRIME & DELINQUENCY 46 (1963).

Moore & Buchanan, *State Hospitals and Alcoholism: A Nationwide Survey of Treatment Techniques and Results,* 27 Q.J. STUD. ALCOHOL 459 (1966).

Moore & Murphy, *Denial of Alcoholism as an Obstacle to Recovery,* 22 Q.J. STUD. ALCOHOL 597 (1961).

Nason, *A Safe Method of Detoxicating the Acutely Ill Alcoholic,* 8 Q.J. STUD. ALCOHOL 43 (1947).

Newman, *Proof of Alcoholic Intoxication,* 34 KY. L.J. 250 (1946).

O'Reilly & Funk, *LSD in Chronic Alcoholism,* 9 CANAD. PSYCHIAT. ASS'N J. 258 (1964).

Palola *et al., Alcoholism and Suicidal Behavior,* in SOCIETY CULTURE AND DRINKING PATTERNS 511 (Pittman & Snyder eds. 1962).

Pattison, *A Critique of Alcoholism Treatment Concepts,* 27 Q.J. STUD. ALCOHOL 49 (1966).

Paulsen, *Intoxication as a Defense to Crime*, 1961 U. ILL. L.F. 1.

Perkins, *The Vagrancy Concept*, 9 HASTINGS L.J. 237 (1958).

Pinardi, *The Chronic Drunkenness Offender: What One City Is Doing About the Revolving Door*, 12 CRIME & DELIN-QUENCY 339 (1966).

Pittman, *Public Intoxication and the Alcoholic Offender in American Society*, in PRESIDENT'S COMM'N ON LAW ENFORCE-MENT & ADMINISTRATION OF JUSTICE, TASK FORCE REPORT: DRUNKENNESS 7 (1967).

Plaut, *Alcoholism and Community Caretakers: Programs and Policies*, 12 SOCIAL WORK (No. 3) 42 (1967).

Plunkert, *Skid Row Can Be Eliminated*, 26 FED. PROBATION (No. 2) 41 (1961).

Powell, *Consent to Operative Procedures*, 21 MD. L. REV. 189 (1961).

Robson, Paulus & Clarke, *An Evaluation of the Effect of a Clinical Treatment Program on the Rehabilitation of Alcoholic Patients*, 26 Q.J. STUD. ALCOHOL 264 (1965).

Romer, *Liberty vs. Mental Health—California Examines Compulsory Hospitalization Laws*, 24 CALIF. HEALTH 27 (1966).

Ross, *Commitment of the Mentally Ill: Problems of Law and Policy*, 57 MICH. L. REV. 945 (1959).

Rubington, *The Chronic Drunkenness Offender*, 315 ANNALS 66 (1950).

Saenger & Wile, *The Abstinent Alcoholic*, 6 ARCH. GEN. PSYCHIA-TRY 83 (1962).

Sanderson *et al.*, *An Investigation of a New Aversive Conditioning Treatment for Alcoholism*, 24 Q.J. STUD. ALCOHOL 261 (1963).

Sapia, *Social Work and Alcoholism*, 315 ANNALS 125 (1958).

Sarett, Cheek & Osmond, *Reports of Wives of Alcoholics of Effects of LSD-25 Treatment of Their Husbands*, 14 ARCH. GEN. PSYCHIAT. 171 (1966).

Sayre, *Public Welfare Offenses*, 33 COLUM. L. REV. 55 (1933).

Shupe, *Alcohol and Crime, A Study of Urine-Alcohol Concentrations Found in 882 Persons Arrested During or Immediately After the Commission of a Felony*, 44 J. CRIM. L.C. & P.S. 662 (1954).

Slough & Wilson, *Alcohol and the Motorist*, 44 MINN. L. REV. 673 (1960).

Smilde, *Risks and Unexpected Reactions in Disulfram Therapy of Alcoholism*, 24 Q.J. STUD. ALCOHOL 489 (1963).

Soden, *Constructive Coercion and Group Counselling in the Rehabilitation of Alcoholics*, 30 FED. PROBATION (No. 3) 56 (1966).

Stark, *A Substitute for Institutionalization of Serious Delinquents*, 9 CRIME & DELINQUENCY 242 (1963).

Starrs, *The Disease Concept of Alcoholism and Traditional Criminal Law Theory*, 19 S.C.L. REV. 349 (1967).

Sterne & Pittman, *The Concept of Motivation: A Source of Institutional and Professional Blockage in the Treatment of Alcoholics*, 26 Q.J. STUD. ALCOHOL 41 (1965).

Straus, Robert & McCarthy, *Non-Addictive Pathological Drinking Patterns of Homeless Men*, 12 Q.J. STUD. ALCOHOL 601 (1951).

Strayer, *The Social Worker's Role in Handling the Resistances of the Alcoholic*, 9 CRIME & DELINQUENCY 39 (1963).

Swartz, *Compulsory Legal Measures and the Concept of Illness*, 19 S.C.L. REV. 372 (1967).

Szasz, *Alcoholism: A Socio-Ethical Perspective*, 6 WASH. L.J. 225 (1967).

Thompson, *Understanding Alcoholism*, 315 ANNALS 40 (1968).

Trice, *Alcoholics Anonymous*, 315 ANNALS 108 (1958).

Trice, *The Job Behavior of Problem Drinkers*, in SOCIETY CULTURE AND DRINKING PATTERNS (D. Pittman & C. Snyder, eds. 1962).

Van Dusen et al., *Treatment of Alcoholism with Lysergide*, 28 Q.J. STUD. ALCOHOL 295 (1967).

Vogel, *Psychiatric Treatment of Alcoholics*, 315 ANNALS 99 (1958).

Waelder, *Psychiatry and the Problem of Criminal Responsibility*, 101 U. PA. L. REV. 375 (1952).

Watts, *Some Observations on Police Administered Tests for Intoxication*, 45 N.C.L. REV. 34 (1966).

Wechsler, *The Criteria of Criminal Responsibility*, 22 U. CHI. L. REV. 367 (1955).

Wedel, *Involving Alcoholics in Treatment*, 26 Q.J. STUD. ALCOHOL 468 (1965).

Weihofen, *The Flowering of New Hampshire*, 22 U. CHI. L. REV. 356 (1955).

Weil & Price, *Alcoholism in a Metropolis,* 9 CRIME & DELIN-
QUENCY 60 (1963).

Wellman, Maxwell & O'Hollaren, *Private Hospital Alcoholic Patients
and the Changing Conception of the "Typical Alcoholic,"* 18
Q.J. STUD. ALCOHOL 401 (1957).

Whitmore, *Comments on a Draft Act for the Hospitalization of the
Mentally Ill,* 19 GEO. WASH. L. REV. 512 (1950).

Williams, *Identifying and Treating Potential Alcoholics,* 49 J. CRIM.
L.C. & P.S. 218 (1958).

Winick, *Narcotic Addiction and Its Treatment,* 22 LAW & CON-
TEMP. PROB. 9 (1957).

Wooten, *The Law, The Doctor and the Deviant,* 2 BRIT. MED.
J. 197 (1963).

Wooten, *Sickness or Sin,* 159 TWENTIETH CENTURY 43 (1956).

Comment, *Analysis of Legal and Medical Considerations in Commitment of the Mentally Ill,* 56 YALE L.J. 1178 (1947).

Note, *Civil Commitment of the Mentally Ill: Theories and Procedures,* 79 HARV. L. REV. 1288 (1966).

Note, *Legal Status of the Alcoholic,* 51 IOWA L. REV. 492 (1966).

Note, *Alcohol and Safe Driving,* 110 J. AM. MED. ASS'N 1617
(1938).

Note, *Mental Illness and Contracts,* 57 MICH. L. REV. 1021 (1959).

Note, *The Plight of the Sexual Psychopath: A Legislative Blunder
and Judicial Acquiescence,* 41 N.D.L. REV. 527 (1966).

Note, *The Vagrancy Concept Reconsidered: Problems and Abuses
of Status Criminality,* 37 N.Y.U.L. REV. 102 (1962).

Note, *Vagrancy: A Constitutional Battle,* 16 SYR. L. REV. 646
(1965).

Note, *Due Process for All—Constitutional Standards for Involuntary
Civil Commitment and Release,* 34 U. CHI. L. REV. 633
(1967).

Note, *Civil Commitment of Narcotic Drug Addict Held Constitutional,* 8 UTAH L. REV. 367 (1964).

Note, *The Nascent Right to Treatment,* 53 VA. L. REV. 1134
(1967).

Note, *Civil Restraint, Mental Illness, And the Right to Treatment,*
77 YALE L.J. 87 (1967).

Note, *Civil Commitment of Narcotics Addicts*, 76 YALE L.J. 1160 (1967).

Baltimore Sun, Sept. 16, 1968, at B 10, col. 4.

Hearings on H.R. 6143 Before Subcommittee No. 3 of the House Committee on the District of Columbia, 1st Sess., 90th Cong.

Ingraham, *Test Class for Drunken Drivers Making the Grade in Phoenix*, N.Y. Times, Sept. 28, 1968, at 65, col. 2.

Lyons, *Genetic Abnormality Is Linked to Crime*, N.Y. Times, Apr. 21, 1968, at 1 col. 3.

W. Meyers, Jr. *State Alcoholism Programs—Purposes and Administration* (Unpublished Thesis, Colum. L.S. Library, 1965).

Nelson, *A Shocking Treatment for Alcoholics*, N.Y. Post, Sept. 24, 1968, at 37, col. 2.

New York Times, Oct. 27, 1968 (City ed.), at 31, col. 3.

Otten, *Politics and People, Iowa's Outspoken Governor Harold Hughes*, Wall St. J., July 19, 1965, at 8, col. 3.

Alcoholism And Intoxication Treatment Act

SECTION 1. SHORT TITLE.

This act shall be known and may be cited as the Alcoholism and Intoxication Treatment Act.

SECTION 2. LEGISLATIVE FINDING AND DECLARATION OF PURPOSES.

(a) The legislature finds that alcoholism is a medical-social problem which cannot be dealt with effectively under the provisions of criminal law. The legislature further finds that the criminal law is ineffective to deter public intoxication and that drinking to intoxication is a matter of personal conduct that (except in specified instances such as drunken driving) should not be subjected to the strictures of criminal law, but that should be dealt with by the instrumentalities of education, public health and mental health. Accordingly, the repeal of laws that treat as criminal offenses such conduct as public intoxication and other conduct in which intoxication forms one of the component elements, such as vagrancy, or drunk and disorderly behavior, is both justified and desirable, but such a course requires that alternative modes of treatment for alcoholics and for intoxicated persons who are in need of care or medical attention must be found. As a medical-social problem, alcoholism is best dealt with within the framework of the state's system for the protection and advancement of mental and public health, with appropriate assistance from other care-giving instrumentalities, including the state's mental health, public health and social welfare systems. It is found that voluntary treatment is more appropriate than involuntary treatment, and that involuntary treatment, including civil commitment, is best employed only in limited situations, appropriately defined.

(b) The purpose of this Act is to establish a comprehensive program for the prevention of alcoholism and the rehabilitation of alcoholics; to provide for medical, psychiatric and other treatment of alcoholics so as to assure that every such person who is in need of treatment and who seeks the same is afforded full opportunity for such care as may be necessary to restore him to adequate functioning; to establish methods of handling intoxicated persons that will be beneficial to them and will more fully protect them and the public; to promote research activities on the risks of intoxication and the dangers of alcoholism, and to disseminate information on alcohol-related problems in programs of public education.

SECTION 3. DEFINITIONS.

For purposes of this Act

1) "Alcoholic" means any person who chronically, habitually or periodically uses alcoholic beverages to the extent that they injure his health or substantially interfere with his social or economic functioning.

2) "Department" means the state department of [mental] [public] health.

3) "Commissioner" means the commissioner of the state department of [mental] [public] health.

4) "Division" means the division of alcoholism within the department, established under section five of this Act.

5) "Director" means the director of the division of alcoholism.

6) "Emergency service patrol" means the patrol established pursuant to section 16 of this Act.

7) "To lose the power of self-control with respect to the use of alcoholic beverages" means to lose the power to abstain from alcoholic beverages, or to lose the power to refrain from drinking to intoxication whenever drinking an alcoholic beverage.

SECTION 4. REPEAL OF INTOXICATION AND PUBLIC DRINKING OFENSES; AMENDMENT OF OFFENSES OF DISORDERLY CONDUCT.

a) Section —— of the Penal Code defining the crime of public intoxication is hereby repealed.

b) Section —— of the Penal Code defining the crime of public drinking is hereby repealed.

c) Section —— of the Penal Code defining the crime of being drunk and disorderly is hereby repealed.

d) Section —— of the Penal Code which defines vagrancy in terms of being a common or habitual drunkard or being found in certain places in an intoxicated condition is hereby repealed.

e) Section —— of the Penal Code which defines the offense of disorderly conduct is [amended to provide that an intoxicated person who is in need of help or incapacitated, and who is liable to arrest for disorderly conduct for other than assaultive behavior, shall be treated under the provisions of section 10 of the Alcoholism and Intoxication Treatment Act, rather than prosecuted for disorderly conduct.]

f) No county, municipality or other political subdivision of this state shall adopt any local law, ordinance, resolution or regulation having the force of law rendering public intoxication, public drinking, drunk and disorderly conduct, or vagrancy or other behavior that includes as one of its elements either drinking in public or being a common drunkard or being found in enumerated places in an intoxicated condition, an offense, a violation or the subject of criminal or civil penalties or sanctions of any kind. Nothing herein contained shall affect any laws, ordinances, resolutions or regulations against drunken driving, driving under the influence of alcohol, or other similar offenses that involve the operation of motor vehicles, machinery or other hazardous equipment.

SECTION 5. DIVISION OF ALCOHOLISM.

(a) There is established within the department a division of alcoholism. The division shall be headed by a qualified director, appointed by the commissioner. The director shall be a physician with special training or experience in the treatment of behavioral disorders or medical-social problems, or a qualified professional with training or experience in the treatment of behavioral disorders or medical-social problems, or in the organization or administration of treatment services for persons suffering from such behavioral disorders or medical-social problems.

(b) The division, subject to the general program and policies of the department, shall assist the department in the management and operation of all state facilities or parts of such facilities for the treatment and rehabilitation of alcoholics and for the emergency medical and other treatment and care of persons who are intoxicated and in need of assistance.

(c) The division shall sponsor and encourage research into the causes, nature and treatment of alcoholism, and shall serve as the state's clearing house for information relating to alcoholism. It shall collect and make available relevant statistical information, including but not limited to number of persons treated, frequency of admissions and readmissions to inpatient facilities, length of stay at inpatient facilities and length of treatment under other programs.

(d) The division, with the advice and cooperation of the inter-departmental coordinating committee, shall develop, encourage and support statewide, regional and local plans and programs in the field of alcoholism and shall provide technical assistance and consultation to all political subdivisions of the state with respect to programs for the prevention and treatment of alcoholism and the rehabilitation of al-coholics. It shall stimulate more effective use of existing resources and available services for the prevention and treatment of alcoholism, and to that purpose it shall seek to achieve the most effective methods of coordinating the efforts of all public and private agencies within the state to deal with the problem, and shall enlist the assistance of public and private health, education, welfare and rehabilitation agencies in a concerted effort. The division may make grants to, and enter into contractual arrangements with public and private agencies in order to increase the effectiveness of existing resources and available services.

(e) The division shall advise the governor in the preparation of a comprehensive plan for the treatment of alcoholism for inclusion in the state's comprehensive health plan to be sumitted for federal fund-ing pursuant to Comprehensive Health Planning and Public Health Services of Amendments of 1966 and shall advise the governor in the preparation of any other plans or compilation of data which he may request in order to fulfill the requirements of federal legislation.

(f) The division shall prepare, publish and disseminate educa-tional materials dealing with the prevention and treatment of al-coholism and the rehabilitation of alcoholics. It shall make the materials available to public and private educational institutions in the state, and shall assist in the preparation of information on alcohol-related problems for use in public and private elementary and high schools and institutions of higher learning. It shall initiate and participate in training programs to prepare persons for work in education or research in alcoholism, or in the treatment of alcoholics.

(g) The division shall encourage and cooperate with alcoholism rehabilitation programs in businesses and industries in the state.

(h) The division shall encourage, and assist in the development of, alcoholism rehabilitation programs for state and local government employees.

(i) The division [subject to applicable provisions of law] may coordinate its activities and cooperate with alcoholism programs in other states. The division may enter into contracts and other joint or cooperative arrangements with state, local or private agencies in other states for the treatment and rehabilitation of alcoholics and for the common advancement of alcoholism programs.

SECTION 6.   INTERDEPARTMENTAL COORDINATING COMMITTEE.

(a) There shall be an interdepartmental coordinating committee, composed of the [commissioners] of public health, mental health, education, public welfare, correction, vocational rehabilitation [add other appropriate agencies] and the director of the division. The coordinating committee shall meet at least twice annually, at the call of the commissioner, who shall be its chairman. The committee shall provide for the coordination of all programs relating to alcoholism, and shall act as a permanent liaison between the various departments engaged in activities affecting alcoholics and intoxicated persons. The committee shall arrange for the exchange of information on relevant programs between the departments, and shall correlate different departmental activities so as to serve the common purpose of education, prevention, treatment and rehabilitation. The committee shall also assist the commissioner and the director in formulating a comprehensive plan for the prevention of alcoholism and for the provision of rehabilitation services for alcoholics.

(b) In exercising its coordinating functions, the committee shall insure (1) that the appropriate state agencies provide all necessary medical, social, rehabilitative and educational services for alcoholics and for the prevention of alcoholism without unnecessary duplication of services; (2) that the various state agencies cooperate in the use of facilities and in the treatment of alcoholics; and (3) that all state agencies follow similar policies and adopt consistent attitudes in the treatment and rehabilitation of alcoholics and the prevention of alcoholism.

SECTION 7. CITIZENS ADVISORY COUNCIL ON ALCOHOLISM.

(a) The governor shall appoint a citizens advisory council on alcoholism, composed of [not less than 7 nor more than 25] members. The members shall serve for overlapping terms of three years each; one-third of the members first appointed, as near as may be practicable, shall be appointed for one, two, and three-year terms respectively. Members shall have professional, research or personal experience with or interest in alcohol problems. The council shall meet at least once every [three] months, and shall report on its activities and make recommendations to the director at least once a year.

(b) The advisory council shall advise the director on broad policies and goals of the alcoholism program and on such other matters as the director may from time to time refer to it, and shall encourage public understanding and support of the alcoholism program.

(c) Members of the advisory council shall serve without compensation, but shall receive reimbursement for travel and other necessary expenses actually incurred in the performance of their duties.

SECTION 8. TREATMENT AND REHABILITATION FACILITIES AND PROGRAMS.

(a) The division shall employ a variety of treatment methods and shall provide or arrange for a variety of treatment facilities in order that the needs of persons afflicted with alcoholism and of persons who are intoxicated and in need of emergency medical and other care may be fully and expeditiously met. To the fullest extent possible the division shall utilize the facilities and coordinate its programs with the programs of community mental health centers presently existing or hereafter to be established. Treatment services and facilities shall include but need not be limited to the following:

(1) Emergency medical-social services and facilities. Facilities and services to render emergency medical care, including detoxification, and emergency social services shall be open 24 hours every day, and shall be located conveniently near population centers so as to be quickly and easily accessible to patients. Such facilities and services shall provide for the immediate physical and social needs, including

the needs for medication and shelter, of intoxicated persons, and shall also provide for initial examination, diagnosis and referral. Each facility or service shall be affiliated with or constitute a part of the general medical service of a [general] hospital or other medical facility, but need not be physically a part of such [general] hospital or facility.

(2) Outpatient facilities, including, but not limited to clinics, vocational rehabilitation services and community mental health centers. The outpatient care facilities, to the fullest extent possible, shall be part of existing care-giving services provided by facilities of the department, or of other state or local departments or agencies.

(3) Intermediate care services, including but not limited to partial hospitalization and supportive residential facilities, such as community mental health centers, foster home placement, hostels and half-way houses. The intermediate care facilities may be operated by, or may be jointly operated with, state or local departments of social welfare or social service.

(4) Inpatient short term or extended care facilities for diagnostic study, intensive study, treatment and rehabilitation of alcoholics. The facilities may be part of general hospitals, mental hospitals or community mental health centers but shall not be part of any correctional institution.

(b) The division (subject to applicable provision of law) may arrange for the use of local and private treatment facilities on a cooperative basis, by contractual, cost-sharing or other method of joint or shared support, whenever the director, subject to the policies of the department, considers this to be the most effective and economical course to follow.

SECTION 9.   ACCEPTANCE FOR TREATMENT; REGULATIONS.

The division shall adopt and from time to time modify and promulgate rules and regulations for the acceptance of persons into the treatment program, in light of the available treatment resources and facilities, with a view to the early and effective provision of care and treament for all alcoholics who seek it. In establishing such rules and regulations the division shall be guided by the following standards:

(1) A patient shall be initially assigned to, or transferred to, outpatient or intermediate rather than inpatient care, unless he is

found to require inpatient care for medical reasons, or unless he is found to be likely to inflict physical harm on others if not admitted.

(2) Whenever possible, a patient shall be treated on a voluntary, rather than an involuntary basis.

(3) No person shall be denied treatment solely because he has withdrawn from an inpatient or outpatient facility against medical advice on one or more prior occasions, or because he has relapsed one or more times after earlier treatment.

SECTION 10. TREATMENT AND SERVICES FOR INTOXICATED PERSONS.

(a) Any intoxicated person may voluntarily come to an emergency service or facility for emergency medical care or social service. Any person who is intoxicated in a public place and who appears in need of help, if he consents to the proffered help, may be assisted to his home or to an emergency service or facility, whether public or private, by the police or by the emergency service patrol. Any person who is intoxicated in a public place and appears to be incapacitated shall be taken by the police or by such emergency service patrol to an emergency service or facility. A person shall be deemed incapacitated when he appears to be in immediate need of emergency medical attention, or when he appears to be unable to make a rational decision about his need for care.

(b) In detaining an intoxicated person and in taking him to a faciltiy or service for emergency care, the police or the emergency service patrol shall proceed whenever possible with the consent of the intoxicated person. If the person appears to be incapacitated and refuses his consent, he shall be detained and shall be taken for emergency care against his will, but force which is likely to inflict physical injury upon the intoxicated person shall not be used.

(c) Any person who voluntarily comes or is brought to an emergency service or facility shall be examined by a licensed physician as soon as possible. The physician in charge of the emergency service or facility may admit a person as a patient or refer him to another facility or service for emergency care, the police or the emergency service another facility, the referring emergency service or facility shall arrange for his transportation. The emergency service or facility may provide emergency help to a person who is not admitted as a patient.

(d) Any person who at the time of admission to an emergency service or facility is incapacitated shall remain at the service or facility until he is no longer incapacitated, but not longer than 48 hours after his admission as a patient. Any person admitted to an emergency service or facility who is not incapacitated at the time of admission, or any person who is no longer incapacitated, may consent to remain at the emergency service or facility for as long as the medical officer believes warranted, but any patient who is not incapacitated shall be free to leave the emergency service or facility at any time.

(e) Any person who is not admitted to an emergency service or facility or who is not referred to another facility and who has no funds may be taken to his home, if he has one. If he has no home, the emergency service or facility shall assist him in obtaining shelter and in getting there.

(f) When a patient is admitted to an emergency service or facility for treatment, his family or next of kin shall be notified as promptly as possible. If a patient who is not incapacitated requests that there be no notification, his request shall be respected.

(g) The police or the emergency service patrol, in detaining an intoxicated person and in taking him to an emergency service or facility, shall be deemed to be taking him into protective custody and shall make every reasonable effort to protect his health and safety. A taking into protective custody under this section shall not be considered an arrest for any purpose and no entry or other record shall be made to indicate that he has been arrested or has been charged with a crime.

(h) The police or members of the emergency service patrol who act under this section shall be considered as acting in the conduct of their official duty and shall not be held criminally or civilly liable for false arrest or false imprisonment.

(i) If the physician in charge of the emergency service or facility determines that such a course is for the patient's benefit, a patient in an emergency service or facility shall be encouraged to agree to further diagnosis and to voluntary treatment at suitable inpatient, outpatient, or intermediate care facilities.

SECTION 11. VOLUNTARY TREATMENT OF ALCOHOLICS.

(a) Any person may voluntarily apply for treatment for alcoholism directly to any public inpatient, outpatient, or intermediate care facility which provides such treatment. If the patient is a minor or an incompetent, application for voluntary inpatient, intermediate or outpatient treatment, and the request for discharge from an inpatient institution shall be made by his parent, legal guardian or other legal representative.

(b) The administrator in charge of any public inpatient, outpatient, or intermediate facility, subject to the rules and regulations established by the director, may determine who shall be admitted for treatment. If a person is refused admission to a facility, the administrator in charge, subject to the rules and regulations established by the director, shall refer the person to another facility for treatment whenever possible.

(c) Upon his discharge from, or upon leaving a public treatment facility, a patient shall be encouraged to consent to appropriate outpatient, intermediate care, or other aftercare treatment. If it appears to the administrator in charge of the treatment facility that the patient is an alcoholic who requires such help, the division shall arrange for assistance in obtaining supportive services and residential facilities, such as maintenance in a hostel or halfway house operated by the department or by any other state or private agency.

(d) When a patient checks out of a public inpatient facility, whether with or against the advice of the administrator in charge of the facility, the division shall assure that reasonable provisions for his transportation to his home have been made. If he has no home, he shall be assisted in obtaining shelter and in getting there.

SECTION 12.   EMERGENCY COMMITMENT OF ALCOHOLICS.

(a) A person may be admitted to a treatment facility for emergency care and treatment upon application accompanied by the certificate of one licensed physician. The application may be made by any one of the following: the certifying physician, the patient's spouse or guardian, any relative of the patient, or any other responsible person. The application shall state facts to support the need for immediate commitment, including factual allegations showing that the person to be committed has threatened, attempted, or actually inflicted physical harm upon another. The physician's certificate shall state that he has examined the person within two days of the certificate date and shall set out the facts to support the physician's conclusion that the person is an alcoholic who has lost the power of self-control with respect to the use of alcoholic beverages and that unless immediately committed he is likely to inflict physical harm on another.

(b) The administrator in charge of a facility may refuse an application if in his opinion the application and certificate fail to sustain the grounds for commitment. Upon acceptance of the application by the administrator in charge of the facility, the person shall be transported to the facility by a peace officer, health officer, the emergency service patrol, the applicant for commitment, the patient's spouse or the patient's guardian. The person shall be retained at the facility that admitted him, or transferred to any other appropriate facility, until discharged pursuant to subsection (c).

(c) The administrator in charge of a facility shall discharge any person committed pursuant to this section when he determines that the grounds for commitment no longer exist, but, no person committed pursuant to this section shall be retained in any facility for more than [five] days. If, however, a petition for involuntary commitment pursuant to section 13 has been filed within such [five] days, and if the administrator in charge of a facility finds that grounds for emergency commitment still exist, he may retain the person until the petition has been heard and determined, but in no event longer than ten days following the filing of the petition.

SECTION 13.   INVOLUNTARY COMMITMENT
OF ALCOHOLICS.

(a) A person may be committed to the custody of the department by the [appropriate] court upon the petition of his spouse or guardian, any relative, the certifying physician, the head of any state facility, or other responsible person. The petition shall allege that the person is an alcoholic who has lost the power of self-control with respect to the use of alcoholic beverages and (1) that he has threatened, attempted or actually inflicted physical harm on others, and that unless committed he is likely to inflict physical harm on others; or (2) that he is in need of medical treatment and care, and that by reason of alcoholism his judgment has been so impaired that he is incapable of appreciating his need for care and of making a rational decision in regard thereto; a mere refusal to undergo treatment shall not, however, by itself constitute evidence of lack of judgment with respect to the need for care. The petition shall be accompanied by a certificate of a licensed physician who has examined the person within [two] days of the submission of the petition. The certificate shall set forth the physician's findings in support of the allegations of the petition. If the person whose commitment is sought has refused to submit to a medical examination, the fact of such refusal shall be alleged in the petition.

(b) Upon receipt of the petition, the court shall fix a date for a hearing on the issues no later than [ten] days from the date the petition was received. The court shall give notice of the hearing to the petitioner, to the person whose commitment is sought, to his next of kin other than the petitioner, to his parents or legal guardian if he is a minor, to the head of the facility to which he has been committed if he has been committed for emergency care, and to any other person whose presence the court deems advisable. Copies of the petition and certificate shall be delivered to all of the parties, together with the notice of hearing.

(c) At the hearing the court shall hear all relevant testimony, including the testimony of at least one licensed physician who has examined the person whose commitment is sought. The person whose commitment is sought shall be presented unless the court has reason to believe that his presence is likely to be injurious to him; in this event the court shall appoint a guardian *ad litem* to represent him throughout the proceeding. The court shall examine the person whose commitment is sought in open court, or if it be deemed advisable, out of court. If the person whose commitment is sought has refused to be examined by a licensed physician he shall be afforded an opportunity to consent to examination by a court-appointed physician. If he refuses and there is sufficient evidence to believe that the allegations of the petition are likely to be true, or, in any case, if the court believes that more medical evidence is necessary, the court may make a preliminary order committing the person to the department for a period of not more than [five] days for purposes of a diagnostic examination. If after hearing all relevant evidence, including the results of any diagnosis by the department, the court finds that the grounds for involuntary commitment have been met by clear and convincing proof, the court shall make a final order of commitment to the department. However, except in the case of a person who is committed on the grounds that he is likely to inflict physical harm upon others, the court shall not order a person's commitment unless there is evidence that the department is able to provide treatment for him and that such treatment is likely to be of benefit.

(d) A person committed pursuant to this section shall remain in the custody of the department for care and treatment for a period of [thirty] days unless sooner discharged. At the end of the thirty day period, he shall automatically be discharged unless the department, prior to the expiration of such period obtains a court order for his recommitment upon the same grounds set forth in subsection (a) for a further period of [ninety days] unless sooner discharged. If a person has been committed because he is an alcoholic who is likely to inflict physical harm on others, the department shall apply for recommitment unless such likelihood no longer exists.

(e) A person recommitted under the provision of subsection (d) who has not been discharged by the department before the end of the [ninety day] period shall automatically be discharged at the expiration of that period unless the department, prior to the expiration of such period, obtains a court order on the grounds set forth in subsection (a) for recommitment for a further period not to exceed six months. If a person has been committed because he is an alcoholic who is likely to inflict physical harm on others, the department shall apply for recommitment unless such likelihood no longer exists. Further recommitment orders for periods not to exceed six months for each such order may be obtained on the grounds set forth in subsection (a) if the person has not been discharged.

(f) Upon receipt of a petition for recommitment pursuant to subsections (d) or (e) the court shall fix a date for hearing no later than [ten] days from the date the petition was received. Notice of the application and the date of the hearing fixed by the court shall be served on the petitioner, on the person whose commitment is sought, on his next of kin, on the original petitioner under subsection (a) if different from the petitioner for recommitment, on one of his parents or on his legal guardian if he is a minor, and on any other person whose presence the court deems advisable. At the hearing the court shall proceed in the same manner set forth in subsection (c).

(g) The department may require any person committed to its custody to undergo such treatment as in its judgment will benefit him, including treatment at any inpatient, outpatient, or intermediate care facility. The department may transfer any patient committed to its custody from one facility to another whenever transfer is medically advisable.

(h) A person committed to the custody of the department for care shall be discharged at any time prior to the end of the period for which he has been committed when the following conditions are met:

(1) In the case of an alcoholic committed on the grounds of like-lihood of infliction of physical harm upon others, when such likelihood no longer exists;

(2) In the case of an alcoholic committed on the grounds of need of treatment and care, accompanied by incapacity to make a determination respecting such need, either when such incapacity no longer exists, or when it is evident that further treatment and care will not bring about further significant improvement in such person's condition.

(i) The person whose commitment or recommitment is sought shall be informed of his right to contest the application, to be represented by counsel at every stage of any and all proceedings relating to his commitment and recommitment, and to have counsel appointed for him by the court or provided for him by the court, if he wants the assistance of counsel and is financially unable to obtain counsel. If the court believes that the person needs the assistance of counsel, the court shall appoint counsel for him regardless of his wishes. Further, the person whose commitment or recommitment is sought shall be informed of his right to be examined by a physician of his choice. If the person is financially unable to obtain a physician and requests examination by a physician, a physician shall be appointed or provided by the court.

(j) A person committed under the provisions of this act may at any time seek to be discharged from commitment by writ of *habeas corpus*.

SECTION 14. RECORDS OF ALCOHOLICS AND INTOXICATED PERSONS.

(a) The registration and other records of emergency services and of other treatment facilities, whether inpatient, intermediate or outpatient, utilized under this act shall remain confidential, and information which has been entered in the records shall be considered privileged information.

(b) No part of the treatment records shall be disclosed without the consent of the person to whom it pertains, but appropriate disclosure may be made without such consent to treatment personnel for use in connection with his treatment and to counsel representing the person in any proceeding held pursuant to section 13. Disclosure may also be made without consent upon court order for purposes unrelated to treatment after application showing good cause therefor. In determining whether there is good cause for disclosure, the court shall weigh the need for the information to be disclosed against the possible harm of disclosure to the person to whom such information pertains.

(c) Notwithstanding the provisions of subsections (a) and (b) of this section, the director may open patients' records for purposes of significant research into the causes and treatment of alcoholism. The director shall not open such records, however, unless application is made by a researcher or research agency of professional repute, and unless the need for the records and the significance of the research for which they are to be used has been demonstrated to his satisfaction. Records shall not be opened under this subsection unless adequate assurances are given that patients' names and other identifying information will not be disclosed by the applicant.

SECTION 15. VISITATION AND COMMUNICATION OF PATIENTS.

(a) Subject to reasonable regulations regarding hours of visitation established by the division or by the agency in charge of a facility, alcoholics who are either voluntary or involuntary patients in any inpatient facility under this act shall be allowed opportunity for adequate consultation with counsel, and as much opportunity for continuing contact with family and friends as is consistent with an effective institutional program.

(b) Neither mail nor other communication to or from a person in an inpatient facility pursuant to this act may be intercepted, read, or censored, but the division may make reasonable rules regarding the use of the telephone by patients in such facilities.

SECTION 16. EMERGENCY SERVICE PATROL; ESTABLISHMENT; REGULATION.

(a) The department and the several counties, cities and other municipalities may establish emergency service patrols. The department's emergency service patrol shall be part of the division. Emergency service patrols shall consist of persons trained to give assistance in the streets and in other public places to persons who are intoxicated and in need of help. Members of the emergency service patrol shall be capable of providing first aid in emergency situations, and shall be employed in conveying intoxicated persons in need of help to their homes and to and from emergency services and facilities to the extent necessary.

(b) The division shall establish rules and regulations for the establishment, training and conduct of all emergency service patrols in the state.

SECTION 17. EFFECTIVE DATE.

This act shall become effective in ninety days from its passage, but the effective date of Section 4, Repeal of Intoxication and Public Drinking Offenses, may be postponed for not more than one year at the application of any county or city of the state until the commissioner certifies to the secretary of state that adequate emergency services or facilities are available in such county or city.

Draftsmen's Notes to Accompany
Alcoholism And Intoxication Treatment Act

INTRODUCTION

The Alcoholism and Intoxication Treatment Act has been prepared after policy consultations with Dr. Thomas F. A. Plaut, Mrs. Judith P. Wolfson, and other members of the staff of the National Institute of Mental Health, and went through a number of earlier drafts. The third draft, which preceded this final one, was distributed for comment among some two hundred persons representing a broad spectrum of knowledge and experience in the treatment of alcoholism and in treatment-related legal issues. This fourth and final draft represents a revision based in major part on the comments, criticisms and suggestions received. In some instances, comments received are reflected in an elaboration of the Draftsmen's Notes rather than in the draft itself. The response to the request for comments on the third draft was most gratifying, and thanks are due to the large number of professionals who took time to analyze the draft and to prepare thoughtful and detailed comments.

The preparation of the Alcoholism and Intoxication Treatment Act follows over a year of intensive study of legal issues and problems surrounding the treatment of alcoholics and intoxicated persons. The results of these studies have been incorporated in a volume entitled *Alcoholism and the Law*. Its contents form the basis for much of what is included in the proposed Alcoholism and Intoxication Treatment Act and in these Draftmen's Notes.

SUMMARY AND GENERAL COMMENTS

The draft of the model Alcoholism and Intoxication Treatment Act seeks to reflect recent insights into the nature and treatment of alcoholism as well as contemporary legal approaches to the subject. In a sense the development which gave rise to the Act can be traced back to the *Driver* (356 F.2d 761 [4th Cir., 1966]) and *Easter* (361 F.2d 50 [D.C. Cir., 1966]) cases which raised the possibility that

186

criminal prosecution of drunkenness offenders, and consequently the use of jails and lock-ups for make-shift detoxification purposes, may be barred in the future. While this threat to the customary way of dealing with alcoholism problems has temporarily abated as a result of the more recent decision of the United States Supreme Court in *Powell* v. *Texas,* (392 U.S. 514 [1968]) the decisions in *Easter* and *Driver,* as well as the recommendations of the President's Commission on Law Enforcement and Administration of Justice with respect to the treatment of drunkenness offenses, gave impetus to a movement to substitute a treatment approach through the instrumentalities of mental and public health for the correctional approach which still is prevalent in most jurisdictions. One state, Minnesota, was just recently faced with the necessity of formulating a new approach to the treatment of alcoholism by the decision in State v. Fearon, (283 Minn. 90, 166 N.W.2d 720 [1969]), holding that alcoholics lack the requisite intent for a conviction of public drunkenness. These developments gave rise to a number of new statutes, notably in Maryland, the District of Columbia, and in one or two other states. While the proposed Alcoholism and Intoxication Treatment Act follows none of these in any detail, it nonetheless has a kinship in general approach with all of them. Where specific borrowings from the more recently enacted statutes—or from older alcoholism laws—have occurred, they have been specifically noted in the derivation notes which precede each of the section-by-section comments that follow.

Like other model laws, the proposed Alcoholism and Intoxication Treatment Act will require adaptation to fit it into the body of statutory law of any of the fifty states. In the preparation of the Act, existing codes on mental health were used extensively, and a state which wishes to adopt the model may well find it useful either to incorporate it by amendment in its general mental health statute, or to let it stand as a separate act, but adapt it in such a manner as to avoid inconsistencies with provisions of law that deal with other disordered persons under the general heading of mental health. In considering policy alternatives, many of the assumptions and professed purposes of existing mental health legislation were reviewed and analyzed. Many of these, particularly in older mental health statutes, do not seem to reflect contemporary views on a number of subjects, including compulsory treatment and long-term commitment. Perhaps the proposed Alcoholism and Intoxication Treatment Act will, in some states, suggest re-examination of legal approaches in other areas of F.2d 50 [D.C. Cir., 1966]) cases which raised the possibility that treatment, thus serving an even broader function than is implied by its main subject.

Similar to other recent legislation on the subject, the legislative findings articulate the conclusion that alcoholics present a medical-social problem that should be dealt with by the state's mental or public health and other agencies, and not as a subject for criminal prosecution. Similarly, the findings state that criminal law is ineffective to deter intoxication and that alternative modes of treatment of persons who are alcoholics or who are intoxicated and in need of care must be found. The present-day emphasis on voluntary treatment modes rather than involuntary treatment, including civil commitment, is also emphasized.

In accordance with the legislative findings and statement of purposes, the proposed legislation establishes a division of alcoholism within the state's department of mental or public health for the purpose of developing a broad alcoholism program and for the purpose of supervising the institutions in the state where alcoholics and intoxicated persons are treated or cared for.

The scope of the legislation is indicated to some extent by the scope of its definitions. In accordance with more recent behavioral approaches, an alcoholic is defined as a person who "chronically," "habitually" or "periodically" uses alcoholic beverages to the extent of substantial interference with social or economic functioning. It is the class of persons covered by this definition that is the object of the treatment provisions of the Act.

The proposed legislation marks a significant break with existing alcoholism statutes by expressly providing for the repeal of all drunkenness and public drinking offenses, whether under state law or local ordinances. In calling for the repeal of all such offenses, the draft carries out the recommendations of the President's Commission on Law Enforcement and Administration of Justice and goes beyond them in only one respect—the Commission apparently recommended the continuance of "drunk and disorderly" offenses as long as drunkenness was coupled with disorderly conduct. The proposed draft would eliminate all prosecutions that involve intoxication as an element of the offense, except for drunken driving. There has never been any clear distinction between the different drunkenness offenses, and the continuation of drunkenness as a separate element of a criminal offense would indisputably serve to continue existing police practices. To abolish the offense of "public intoxication" while maintaining the offense of being "drunk and disorderly" would merely result in shifting arrests from one category to the other.

The precise functions of the division of alcoholism are referred to in greater detail in the section-by-section commentary. The guiding thought in providing for the division of alcoholism was to provide a focus for planning and treatment powers within the department of mental or public health, structuring its exercise, however, in such a way as to be an integral and coordinated part of other health activities within the state. The purpose was not to create a separate "alcoholism establishment" within the department, but rather to facilitate the treatment of alcoholics and persons intoxicated and in need of care by making available to them the full range of facilities and experience of the department of mental or public health and of other relevant public and private agencies. The interdepartmental coordinating committee is to insure the full and integrated utilization of all state resources and services for the treatment of alcoholism. The citizens advisory council on alcoholism, which is to serve as an advisory body on broad policies and goals of the alcoholism program and as an informal liaison agency to encourage public understanding and support of the alcoholism program, is not designed to be a body with operational responsibilities, but rather a body with purely advisory and consultative functions.

With respect to treatment and rehabilitation facilities and programs, the division of alcoholism is to supervise the facilities or parts of facilities for the treatment of alcoholics and intoxicated persons in need of care. To the extent that such facilities are owned and operated by the department of mental or public health, the division will assist in the management of them. The division is also authorized to make use of and to coordinate with other care-giving services, both within and outside of the state, and to contract or otherwise arrange for joint or cooperative use of facilities. The proposed statute authorizes the division to employ a variety of treatment methods and to arrange for a variety of treatment institutions in order to meet the various treatment needs of alcoholics and intoxicated persons in need of care. The division is instructed to utilize the facilities of, and to coordinate its programs with, community mental health centers.

In view of the fact that the main emphasis of the law is on voluntary rather than mandatory or compulsory treatment, and in view of the fact that demands on treatment resources may become very pressing, the division is required to adopt rules and regulations for the acceptance of persons into the treatment program. To assist the division in making such rules and regulations, the proposed law establishes a number of guidelines. These guidelines express a preference for outpatient and intermediate care over inpatient care and for voluntary over involuntary care. The proposal also provides that no person shall be discriminated against because he has previously withdrawn from treatment against medical advice or has had relapses after prior treatment.

Instead of handling intoxicated persons through police lock-up, provision is made for care of intoxicated persons in appropriate medical-social services and facilities. The intention is to use existing medical facilities, or facilities which are affiliated in some fashion with places providing medical care for this purpose. Treatment and care will be largely on a voluntary basis. A person who is so intoxicated, however, as to be unable to make a rational decision about his need for care may be taken to an emergency service or facility without his consent. At the emergency service or facility the person is to be examined, as soon as possible, by a licensed physician who may either admit him as a patient, deny him admission, or refer him to another facility. In no event, however, is a person to be left helpless or without transportation to a place where he may receive help. At such a facility the person will receive help, and may be required to remain there until he regains capacity for rational judgment. In no event will a person be held at an emergency service or facility for longer than 48 hours without his consent. He may, however, consent to undergo more extensive diagnosis and treatment voluntarily, and if he does so, he may be referred or transferred to a suitable inpatient or outpatient facility. A person who is taken to an emergency service or facility is considered to be in protective custody and is not to have an arrest record or a record of a criminal charge. No provision has been made for treatment of intoxicated persons charged with the commission of crimes unrelated to their intoxicated condition. In order to maintain the nature of emergency services as open facilities, free from the stigma of criminal arrest or prosecution, treatment of intoxicated prisoners charged with crime is not mentioned in the statute but is left to the authorities charged with enforcing the criminal law.

Provision for emergency treatment differs from similar provisions in more recent alcohol legislation in limiting the length of time for which a person can be held to 48 hours instead of the usual 72 hours. A two-day detention is clearly long enough for complete detoxification in the vast majority of cases. In view of the fact that detention at an emergency facility is a form of civil detention without prior judicial commitment, only a relatively brief emergency detention will, it is believed, meet constitutional requirements.

The draft provides in some detail for voluntary treatment of alcoholics. Unlike other alcoholism statutes, the patient does not obligate himself to accept treatment for any specified length of time or until the institution decides that he is cured or sufficiently improved to be released. The emphasis in the proposed statute is on voluntary *treatment* rather than voluntary commitment. Moreover, a patient need not necessarily be treated at the department's institution to which he applies for treatment but may be transferred elsewhere depending on his needs. A patient who consents to be assigned to an inpatient facility will retain guest status; he will be free to leave whenever he chooses.

The statute authorizes five-day emergency commitment without judicial order to detain an alcoholic who poses an immediate threat to the physical safety of others. The emergency commitment is effected by an application to an inpatient facility, alleging that the alcoholic has threatened, or actually committed acts of physical violence, and that, unless committed, he is likely to cause physical harm. The application is to be accompanied by a physician's certificate setting out the results of a recent examination. The emergency commitment can be terminated by the head of the facility. It may be extended for no longer than ten days if the emergency persists and a petition for involuntary commitment has been filed.

In view of the stated preference of the law for voluntary rather than involuntary treatment, involuntary commitment of alcoholics has been very strictly circumscribed. Unlike existing state laws which permit commitment of alcoholics—as well as of persons who are mentally ill—simply because they may be in need of treatment or because they may be unable to attend to their own affairs, much more stringent requirements are provided for. Involuntary commitment is limited to alcoholics who have lost the power of self-control over their drinking and is permissible only in two situations. First, if the alcoholic is likely to create a danger of physical harm to others, and second, if he is in need of treatment but so impaired in his judgment that he is unable to make a rational decision regarding his need for care. It the second instance, a mere refusal to undergo treatment is not evidence of impaired judgment. In addition to clear evidence of impaired judgment, there must be evidence that the alcoholic who is to be committed is capable of actually benefiting from treatment.

Judicial commitment of alcoholics will be initiated by a petition accompanied in most instances by the certificate of a licensed physician. A court hearing with adequate medical testimony is required. However, if the patient refuses to undergo a medical examination, or if the medical testimony is insufficient, the court can order a preliminary five-day commitment for purposes of diagnosis. The court may commit for an initial term of 30 days, with provision for discharge in accordance with specified standards prior to the expiration of that term. Recommitment, if necessary, is permissible only on court order after hearing, for an additional 90 days, and then for successive six-month periods, if there has been no prior discharge. In all instances the patient's right to counsel will be protected, as will as the patient's right to a medical examination by a doctor of his choice or one appointed by the court.

No patient will be committed to a named institution, but rather to the department of mental or public health which may then assign or transfer him to an institution suitable to his needs, whether inpatient, intermediate or outpatient, for such treatment as may be appropriate. A person is to be discharged from commitment whenever the grounds for commitment no longer exist. The provision for involuntary commitment is unique in providing for the possibility of intermediate or out-patient treatment for persons committed. Such treatment would usually follow inpatient care. All of a patient's procedural rights are safeguarded in the draft.

Special provision is made for the confidentiality of records of alcoholics and intoxicated persons. They are not to be divulged without his consent or without court order, unless their disclosure is necessary for treatment purposes, or unless they are necessary for essential research, in which case the identity of the patient must be protected. Standards for disclosure are stated in the draft.

The patient's right to receive visitors and to communicate with family, friends and counsel by mail or telephone are especially safeguarded.

The draft also authorizes the establishment of "emergency service patrols" to be composed of specially trained civilians, to assist intoxicated persons and to help them to emergency medical-social services and facilities. Such "emergency service patrols," it is hoped, will in due course replace police handling of intoxicated persons who are in need of help.

The draft provides for the law to become effective within 90 days but allows for a delay in the repeal of drunkenness and public drinking offenses for up to one year upon application by a county or city. The intention is to provide for immediate operation of the program and procedures, but to allow for a transition period from the present mode of handling intoxicated persons in need of care, since new or increased facilities will be required. The grace period where needed will insure that the situation of intoxicated persons will not be worsened.

SECTION BY SECTION COMMENTS

SECTION 1. SHORT TITLE.

The short title emphasizes the primary concern of the proposed legislation with *treatment,* rather than with control. The coverage of the act, as reflected in the title, extends beyond treatment for alcoholism, and includes treatment for intoxicated persons who require help.

SECTION 2. LEGISLATIVE FINDINGS AND DECLARATION OF PROGRESS.

This section adopts as a legislative finding the most recent insights of the behavioral and medical sciences with respect to the nature and treatment of alcoholism, and with respect to appropriate legal responses to intoxication. (T.F.A. Plaut, Cooperative Commission on the Study of Alcoholism, ALCOHOL PROBLEMS — A REPORT TO THE NATION 33-116 [1967].) The major legislative findings are 1) that alcoholism is a medical-social problem; 2) that criminal prosecution of persons who have become intoxicated is ineffective and should be abandoned, and that alternative modes of treatment, through care-giving, rather than correctional instrumentalities, need to be provided; and 3) that in the treatment of alcoholism, voluntary treatment is to be strongly preferred to involuntary treatment and civil commitment.

The statement of purposes of the legislation stresses the comprehensive nature of the program to be established and expresses the aim that under the law every person who needs and seeks treatment should receive it.

The proposed legislative findings and declaration of purposes is generally in accord with—though it is probably more explicit than—

similar expressions of legislative intent in the alcoholism treatment laws recently enacted in Maryland (MD. ANN. CODE art. 2C, § 102 [Supp. 1968]), New York (N.Y. MENTAL HYGIENE LAW § 300 [McKinney Supp. 1968]), and the District of Columbia (D.C. CODE ANN. §§ 24-521—24-535 [Supp. II 1969]).

SECTION 3. DEFINITIONS.

(1) "Alcoholic."

Derivation: T.F.A. Plaut, Cooperative Commission on the Study of Alcoholism, ALCOHOL PROBLEMS — A REPORT TO THE NATION 37-38 (1967).

The definition of "alcoholic" includes all individuals who experience serious medical, social or other difficulties connected with the use of alcoholic beverages. The object is to make as large a group as possible eligible for treatment for alcoholism and related problems. Some of the more recent state alcoholism statutes, namely those enacted in Hawaii (HAWAII REV. LAWS § 334 [1968]), Maryland (MD. ANN. CODE art. 2C [Supp. 1968]) and the District of Columbia (D.C. CODE ANN. §§ 24-521—24-535 [Supp. II 1969]), use drinking behavior that interferes with social and economic functioning as an element in the definition of "alcoholic" (or "chronic alcoholic"), and a similar criterion is implicit in older statutes which focus on inebriates (LA. REV. STAT. ANN. §§ 40:2008—2008.3 [1965]; MINN. STAT. ANN. §§ 253A.01—.21 [Supp.1969]; VA. CODE ANN. §§ 32-365—378 [1969]) although in all of these statutes interference with social or economic functioning is always related to chronic and habitual drinking. The definition of alcoholic here proposed is preferable because it includes not only those whose functioning is impaired by drinking chronically and habitually, but also those whose functioning is impaired by drinking "periodically." It thus includes weekend and spree drinkers. See E. Jellinek, THE DISEASE CONCEPT OF ALCOHOLISM 16, 39 (1960).

(7) "To lose the power of self-control with respect to the use of alcoholic beverages."

Derivation: T.F.A. Plaut, Cooperative Commission on the Study of Alcoholism, ALCOHOL PROBLEMS — A REPORT TO THE NATION 39-40 (1967).

There is no statutory derivation for this proposed definition although many states do include loss of control over drinking as part of their statutory definition of alcoholism or alcoholic. (See Alcoholism and the Law, Appendix B, Chart I.) However, the concept of loss of control is generally undefined (*see Alcoholism and the Law*, Appendix B, Chart I) and as a result its use is often confusing and unclear (*see, e.g., Powell* v. *Texas*, 392 U.S. 514 [1968]). This section clarifies this concept.

The defined phrase is used in the draft in delineating the class of alcoholics who may be involuntarily committed.

SECTION 4. REPEAL OF INTOXICATION AND PUBLIC DRINKING OFFENSES; AMENDMENT OF OFFENSE OF DISORDERLY CONDUCT.

Derivation: mostly new; *see* The President's Commission on Law Enforcement and Administration of Justice, Task Force on Drunkenness, TASK FORCE REPORT: DRUNKENNESS 4 (1967); *see also* MD. ANN. CODE art. 2C, § 201 (Supp., 1968).

The section provides for the repeal of all criminal offenses (other than drunken driving) in which intoxication forms a separate element of the offense, as well as for the amendment of the law relating to disorderly conduct. In effect, the section adopts the general policy of the President's Commission on Law Enforcement and Administration of Justice. At present almost all states—Illinois is the sole exception—have criminal laws in which intoxication is a separate element. (*See Alcoholism and the Law*, Appendix A, Chart I.) Implicitly, these laws reflect a policy against intoxication itself as strong as the policy against the criminal behavior which is proscribed; in the case of the offense of "public intoxication," in fact, the behavior which is a criminal offense has been difficult to distinguish from the condition of drunkenness itself. (*E.g., Powell* v. *Texas*, 392 U.S. 514 [1968], in which four of the nine justices could find no such distinction.) This section also provides for repeal of all criminal prohibitions against public drinking unaccompanied by intoxication.

The evidence is clear that arrests for intoxication offenses—amounting to almost one-third of all arrests—absorb an undue amount of the time and effort of the nation's law enforcement agencies. It is also clear that there has been no corresponding decrease in the incidence of intoxication. (The President's Commission on Law Enforcement and Administration of Justice, Task Force on Drunkenness, TASK FORCE REPORT: DRUNKENNESS 1-4 [1967].)

Under the impact of the decisions in *Driver* v. *Hinant*, 356 F.2d 761 (4th Cir. 1966) and *Easter* v. *District of Columbia*, 361 F.2d 50 (D.C. Cir. 1965), prior to the decision in *Powell* v. *Texas*, the law of the District of Columbia (D.C. CODE ANN. § 25-129 *et seq.* [Supp.

II, 1969]) was amended so that alcoholics are exempt in most instances from prosecution under intoxication offenses. North Carolina, responding in a somewhat different fashion, made chronic alcoholism an affirmative defense to the charge of public drunkenness. (N.C. GEN. STAT. § 14-335c [Supp. 1967].) Both laws seek to exempt from punishment for drunkenness offenses those persons who can not help becoming intoxicated because they are alcoholics whose compulsive drinking is symptomatic of their disease. Somewhat in line with this recent legislation is a recent Minnesota decision, *State v. Fearon,* 283 Minn. 90, 166 N.W.2d 720 (1969), which holds that an alcoholic lacks the intent required for a public drunkennes conviction. While reasonable in theory, excusal from responsibility or prosecution of alcoholics creates many practical problems, because it requires a diagnosis of alcoholism not for purposes of treatment, but rather to determine whether a particular person should or should not be turned over to the police for prosecution or should be convicted. In fact, the evidence is clear that the overwhelming number of arrests for drunkenness offenses involve alcoholics, thus rendering the selection process a relatively useless exercise. Since drunkenness *per se* has not been shown to be a cause of crime or danger, the use of the criminal law in this instance appears to be little more than a measure of morals control and urban esthetics, unsupported by social need (for further discussion and documentation, see *Alcoholism and the Law*).

Similar considerations apply to the offense of drinking in public. Public drinking may be esthetically displeasing, but unless accompanied by disorderly conduct it causes no harm to others. Drinking in public may well induce rowdy or boisterous conduct, but this mere possibility does not justify state intervention. Moreover, if drinking in public is retained as a criminal offense, it may well be used to prosecute the same group of persons—notably skid row drinkers who now enter the revolving door via a public drunkenness charge; the bottle in the paper bag is seldom far from the inebriate. Finally, such specific prohibitions as to forbid drinking at "a place for divine worship" (*e.g.,* GA. CODE ANN. § 58-605 [1965]) are matters that should be within the realm of good taste rather than the criminal law.

In providing for the repeal of the offense of "drunk and disorderly conduct," the draft goes beyond the recommendation of the President's Commission on Law Enforcement and Administration of Justice, which, without providing explanation on the particular point, appeared to suggest the repeal of all drunkenness offenses other than drunk and disorderly conduct. (TASK FORCE REPORT: DRUNK-ENNESS 4 [1967].)

Reported decisions on the subject often fail to make clear the precise line between "drunk and disorderly conduct" and "public intoxication." The cases involving prosecution for the particular offenses are hardly distinguishable on their facts (see *Alcoholism and the Law*, ch. 1). For example, the Georgia statute which prohibits drunkenness accompanied "by boisterousness, or by indecent condition or acting, or by vulgar, profane or unbecoming language or loud and violent discourse" (GA. CODE ANN. § 58-608 [1965]), has been interpreted to prohibit drunkenness *per se* (e.g., *Ford* v. *State*, 10 Ga. App. 442, 73 S.E. 605 [1912]; *Holcombe* v. *State*, 4 Ga. App. 213, 187 S.E.2d 599 [1936]). Moreover, decisions also fail to establish how "drunk and disorderly conduct" differs from "disorderly conduct" unaccompanied by drunkenness. There appears to be no reasonable explanation why "drunkenness" should be a special element of the offense, if disorderly conduct standing by itself is a penal offense, as it properly should remain. There is a recognizable social need to remove and control persons who alarm or disturb the public by loud, boisterous, or other offensive conduct, but such conduct is not more annoying because the actor is intoxicated. The state of Illinois has no "drunk and disorderly" offense, relying on the statutory offense of disorderly conduct alone; Comments of Illinois' Committee on Revision suggest that the law is entirely adequate to cope with situations where disorderly conduct is the result of, or is accompanied by intoxication. (Committee Comments, ILL. ANN. STAT. ch. 38, § 26-1 (a) (1) [Smith-Hurd 1964].) The further amendment proposed in the law of disorderly conduct requires that intoxicated persons who are disorderly, though non-assaultive, be treated under the provisions of this law—*i.e.*, taken to a medical facility—rather than arrested. The purpose is to extend treatment to as many intoxicated persons as possible. As long as only non-assaultive persons are exempted from criminal prosecution, medical treatment facilities will not lose their open character.

With respect to the offense of vagrancy, it may be well to note that to subject a common or habitual drunkard to punishment as a vagrant—*i.e.*, to punish him for his illness or condition—may well run afoul of constitutional protections. (*Robinson* v. *California*, 370 U.S. 660 [1962]; *In re Newbern*, 53 Cal. 2d 786, 3 Cal. Rptr. 364, 350 P.2d 116 [1960]). Moreover, the repeal of the offense is not likely to inhibit proper law enforcement.

A number of states permit regulation of drunkenness offenses by local ordinance (*e.g.,* WYO. STAT. ANN. § 15.1-3 (16) [1965]). Such local regulation would be clearly inconsistent with the goals of the proposed treatment law. Laws authorizing such local regulation should therefore be repealed.

The offenses here proposed for repeal include essentially all prohibitions against drunkenness and public drinking found in the laws of the several states. Clearly each state adopting the draft will have to adapt the provisions to deal with its own penal code requirements. (*See Alcoholism and the Law,* Appendix A.)

SECTION 5. DIVISION OF ALCOHOLISM.

Derivation: *E.g.,* MD. ANN. CODE art. 2C, § 301 (Supp. 1968) ; N.Y. MENTAL HYGIENE LAW § 303 (McKinney Supp. 1968) ; Mass. Comprehensive Alcoholism Treatment and Rehabilitation Bill filed for the 1969 Legislative Session by Attorney General E. L. Richardson, § 2.

The section creates a division of alcoholism within the state department of mental or public health, and delegates to the division a broad range of powers and functions to be carried out subject to the general policy directions of the department. In establishing a separate unit of government charged with special functions related to alcoholism and intoxication, the draft follows a growing pattern among the several states. The draft, moreover, is distinguishable from existing legislation in the division by the breadth and scope.

The draft assumes the existence of a separate department of mental or public health that is responsible for the management of institutions and facilities for the care and treatment—both inpatient and outpatient—of persons who suffer from mental illnesses or behavioral disorders. In states where facilities are under the jurisdiction of a department of institutions, or where functions are distributed differently, the draft will have to be adapted to accommodate existing arrangements, particularly with respect to the management of institutions and the coordination of activities with other state and local agencies.

Because the treatment of alcoholics is best undertaken within the framework of a comprehensive mental health program the division of alcoholism is generally best placed in a department of mental health. The draft also reflects the belief that as far as possible alcoholism treatment programs should make use of available mental health and other care-giving facilities, not only because this will effect economies, but also because it is more likely that the patient's problems will be considered in their totality in a less differentiated setting.

Subsection (b) authorizes the division to assist in the operation of the appropriate state treatment facilities, or parts of such facilities.

Subsection (c) authorizes the division's research and information-clearinghouse functions, and requires the collection and dissemination of relevant statistical data. The fragmentary nature of existing data in most states is apparent, and a fulfillment of the requirement will serve a real need in the appraisal of treatment needs and performance. (*See, e.g., Alcoholism and the Law,* Appendix C.)

Subsection (d) calls for the division to develop, encourage and support plans and programs, to coordinate public and private efforts in this regard, and to promote technical assistance to alcoholism programs of political subdivisions—counties, cities, etc., of the state. In a number of states, this coordinating function has been delegated entirely to formal coordinating councils or similar boards, composed of members drawn *ex-officio* from among the agencies that are to coordinate. Because such *ex-officio* bodies frequently do not have the time or resources to administer or supervise such coordinated programs themselves, this proposal puts responsibility on the division for implementing and initiating such coordinated programs in cooperation with the interdepartmental coordinating committee. (*See* Section 6.)

Subsection (e) assigns to the division the task of contributing to the state's comprehensive health plan pursuant to federal law. (Comprehensive Health Planning and Public Health Services Amendments of 1966, 42 U.S.C. §§ 242, 243, 246 [Supp. 1969].) It also allows the governor to request other plans or data which may be necessary for applications for federal funds under existing or subsequently enacted federal legislation.

Subsection (f) charges the division with the preparation of educational materials, and with the duty to assist in the teaching of information on alcohol related problems in public and private elementary and high schools, and in institutions of higher learning. It also charges the division with the duty to initiate and participate in programs concerned with professional training in the alcoholism field.

Subsection (g) provides specially for encouragement of, and cooperation with alcoholism programs in private business and industry.

Such cooperation is called for because industry programs provide a unique opportunity for detecting otherwise invisible alcoholics; industry programs of detection and referral for treatment are said to be particularly effective.

Subsection (h) directs the division to encourage and to assist in the development of rehabilitation programs for state and local government employees.

Subsection (i) directs the division to cooperate with other states and it allows the division to enter into formal agreements and to make other arrangements for cooperative research, educational and treatment programs with out-of-state public and private state and local agencies.

SECTION 6. INTERDEPARTMENTAL COORDINATING COMMITTEE.

Derivation: Proposed Comprehensive Alcoholism Treatment and Rehabilitation Bill (Mass. 1969). For states having interdepartmental commissions or advisory committees, see IOWA CODE ANN. §§ 123A.1-8, 224.1, 229.42 (Supp. 1969); N.D. CENT. CODE ANN. §§ 54-38-01—38-09 (Supp. 1969); OHIO REV. CODE ANN. §§ 3701.141, 142 (Baldwin 1964).

The coordinating committee should consist of all of the commissioners of departments that play a role in the treatment of alcoholics and the prevention of alcoholism, serving *ex-officio*. The council should also include the commissioners of such other related state agencies, such as probation, public safety, hospitals, motor vehicles, institutions, unemployment, labor, police, if they play a part in relation to alcoholism in a particular jurisdiction. For this purpose the draft will have to be adapted to the administrative structure in each state. Since alcoholism affects many aspects of a person's life, and since the alcoholic will often require many kinds of medical, social, remedial, educational or rehabilitative services, comprehensive treatment may require utilization of the facilities of a large number of state agencies. The primary purposes of the coordinating committee are set forth in the draft. It is hoped that, unlike other *ex-officio* bodies, the committee will play an active role in the development and execution of alcoholism programs. The coordinating committee should regulate interdepartmental cooperation whenever necessary, and should facilitate and formulate plans for further comprehensive interdepartmental programs in this field.

The coordinating committee is required to meet only twice a year, although it may meet as often as is necessary. This is a realistic

DRAFTSMEN'S NOTES TO MODEL ACT 201

requirement in view of the many other duties of the commissioners of the various state agencies involved.

SECTION 7. CITIZENS ADVISORY COUNCIL ON ALCOHOLISM.

Derivation: *E.g.,* KY. REV. STAT. ANN. § 222.020 (Supp. 1968); N.Y. MENTAL HYGIENE LAW § 302 (Supp. 1968).

A number of states have alcoholism advisory committees. The number of members varies from state to state. (*Alcoholism and the Law,* Appendix B, Chart I.) It is suggested that the number should depend on the population and the scope of the alcoholism problem of the state, varying from seven to twenty-five members. The statute aims for an informed and representative body by making interest or experience in the field of alcoholism the sole qualification. It does not follow the usual practice of designating that members come from specific professions or groups (*Alcoholism and the Law,* Appendix B, Chart I), which is unnecessarily restrictive. The relationship of the council to the division is made clear in the requirement that it present an annual report to the director of the division of alcoholism, relating its activities and setting out its recommendations.

The function of the council is solely advisory. It is to function as a broad policy advisory group and as a liaison group to generate state and local interest in and support of the program. This latter function, which is new, seems particularly suitable for a citizens advisory council. The statute does not specify functions, such as the development of a comprehensive state alcoholism program, found in many laws; such tasks can be better accomplished by the professional staff of the division.

SECTION 8. TREATMENT AND REHABILITATION FACILITIES AND PROGRAMS.

Derivation: MD. ANN. CODE art. 2C, § 302 (a) (Supp. 1968). *See also* D.C. CODE ANN. § 24-523 (a) (Supp. II 1969); Mass. Comprehensive Alcoholism Treatment and Rehabilitation Bill filed for the 1969 Legislative Session by Attorney General E.L. Richardson, § 6. For laws requiring detoxification and outpatient facilities *see* KY. REV. STAT. ANN. § 222.035 (Supp. 1968); for outpatient clinics, *e.g.,* ALA. CODE tit. 55, § 373 (13a) (1960); GA. CODE ANN. § 88-403 (Supp. 1968); ILL. ANN. STAT. ch. 91 ½, § 100-10 (Smith-Hurd 1966); KY. REV. STAT. ANN. § 222.035 (Supp. 1968); LA. REV. STAT. ANN. § 40:2008.3 (1965); VT. STAT. ANN. tit. 18, § 8458 (1968); for inpatient treatment centers, *e.g.,* FLA. STAT. ANN. § 396.031 (Supp. 1969); S.C. CODE ANN. § 32-900 (Supp. 1968); VA. CODE ANN. § 32-371 (1969); for halfway houses VT. STAT. ANN. tit. 18, § 8457a (1968); for cooperative use of facilities, *e.g.,* MD. ANN. CODE art. 2C, § 309 (Supp. 1968); D.C. CODE ANN. § 24-529 (Supp. II 1969); HAWAII REV. LAWS § 334-3 (1968); CAL. HEALTH & SAFETY CODE §§ 427.4, 427.5 (West Supp. 1968).

The requirement that a variety of treatment methods and facilities be provided is a departure from some older statutes which merely allow inpatient care in state mental hospitals or institutions, and reflects the view currently held by most experts in the field that there is no single, uniform method of treatment for alcoholism, but that a flexible approach with a variety of methods is best suited to the problem. (T.F.A. Plaut, Cooperative Commission on the Study of Alcoholism, ALCOHOL PROBLEMS—A REPORT TO THE NATION 86-92 [1967].)

The requirement that community mental health centers be utilized whenever possible, intended to encourage integration of alcoholism facilities with existing mental or public health facilities, is derived from the new Maryland law. (MD. ANN. CODE art. 2C, § 302 (a) [Supp. 1968].) Mental health centers are professionally equipped to handle medical-social problems such as alcoholism. It is also more efficient to use the existing network of mental health facilities than to establish a new, independent system of alcoholism facilities within the department of mental or public health.

The list of facilities required is mainly derived from the new Maryland law. (MD. ANN. CODE art. 2C, § 302 (a) [Supp. 1968].) However, the proposal includes emergency medical-social services and facilities in preference to the more usual provision, found in the Maryland and District of Columbia laws, for detoxification centers. This new terminology is intended to emphasize the broad nature of the services to be offered on an emergency basis, which are not limited to medical detoxification. However, the facilities are to be connected with medical facilities in order to insure that medical needs will be met when they occur.

The proposal includes all categories of facilities that expert opinion agrees on as necessary or useful in the treatment of alcoholism. It should be noted that the list is not exclusive so that new types of facilities may be added as the need arises; nor does the list specifically mention a number of referral and legal aid services which may be part of the total treatment operation but which do not require distinct facilities. Some of the proposed facilities already exist in many states, but others such as emergency and intermediate care facilities, will have to be established. (*Alcoholism and the Law,* Appendix C, Chart I.) The statute sets forth the categories of facilities as broadly as possible, so as not to limit the state to the use of any particular type of facility or treatment program. The requirement that inpatient facilities not be part of any correctional institution emphasizes and insures that this law will be rehabilitative, not punitive, in its operation. (Some jurisdictions, such as Massachusetts, still use prison facilities for treatment of alcoholism.) This prohibition against the use of correctional facilities applies only to patients who have not been convicted of a crime; it does not affect the powers of correctional authorities to establish alcoholism treatment programs for inmates of penal institutions. The purpose of the provision is merely to separate the treatment of non-criminal alcoholics from the state's correctional activities.

The approach of the District of Columbia Alcoholic Rehabilitation Act of 1967, D.C. CODE ANN. § 24-523 (Supp. II 1969), which sets forth in detail the facilities to be provided, including the capacity of each facility, has not been chosen. Such specification of facilities is too rigid and restrictive. The more flexible approach of the Maryland law has been chosen instead.

The section also allows the division to make use of existing facilities, both public and private, for the treatment of alcoholism, avoiding unnecessary duplication of facilities and immediate or unnecessary construction of new facilities. Contractual, cost-sharing or other arrangements are authorized, so that the division may utilize the facilities of self-help organizations and may rely in full or in part on local public facilities.

The proposed Act does not make any specific provision for payment of costs by patients for use of any facilities or services, but a charge for services on a sliding scale or on some other basis could be established by the division in accordance with the general policies of the state on matters of cost reimbursement.

SECTION 9. ACCEPTANCE FOR TREATMENT; REGULATIONS.

Derivation: *E.g.,* D.C. CODE ANN. §§ 24-525 (a), 24-526 (d) (Supp. II 1969); MD. ANN. CODE art. 2C, §§ 304 (a) (1), (d), 305 (a) (2), (d) (Supp. 1968).

At present, the resources available for the treatment of alcoholism are grossly inadequate to meet the needs of the estimated 5 to 6 million alcoholics in this country. (*See Alcoholism and the Law,* Appendix C.) Guidelines are therefore provided for an effective allocation of resources.

1. Outpatient or intermediate treatment is preferred, having proved to be less expensive, more flexible, and in many instances more successful than inpatient treatment. This provision is also in-

tended to limit inpatient treatment to as short a duration as is medically necessary, thereby reversing the usual reliance on inpatient therapy. (*See Alcoholism and the Law,* Appendix C, Charts I & II.)

2.   This subdivision is intended to encourage the use of voluntary over involuntary treatment. This is contrary to the practice in most states, where involuntary commitment is the most common method of admission into alcoholism treatment programs. (*See Alcoholism and the Law,* Appendix C, Chart I.) In fact some states limit voluntary commitments to the indigent (MASS. GEN. LAWS ANN. ch. 111, § 4C [1967]), or to instances where space is available after involuntary patients are served (*e.g.,* MASS. GEN. LAWS ANN. ch. 123, § 86 [1967]; N.D. CENT. CODE § 25-03-01 [1959]; TENN. CODE ANN. § 33-806 [Supp. 1968]). Voluntary treatment is considered by most experts to be more desirable from both a legal and a medical point of view.

3.   This subdivision recognizes that alcoholics frequently relapse, either during or following treatment. Since this is an expected consequence of the disease and its treatment, relapsed patients should not be penalized for their relapses, although they may have low priority for treatment for other reasons. This subsection emphasizes that prior treatment and withdrawal from treatment, even if repeated, do not bar a person from participation in treatment programs later on. Some new laws, such as Maryland's follow this approach. It is a change from the more punitive provisions against readmission in some older laws (*e.g.,* ARK. STAT. ANN. § 83-713 [1959]; TEX. REV. CIV. STAT. ANN. art. 5561c, § 13 [1958]).

SECTION 10.   TREATMENT AND SERVICES FOR INTOXICATED PERSONS.

Derivation: MD. ANN. CODE art. 2C, § 303 (Supp. 1968); D.C. CODE ANN. § 24-522 (b) (Supp. II 1969); partly new.

This section provides an alternative way of dealing with persons found in public in an intoxicated condition and in need of help. It substitutes protection of the person who is in such a condition for correctional treatment through the criminal courts.

The primary purpose of the section is to provide emergency assistance and treatment to intoxicated persons who need it and who seek it voluntarily, or who, being offered such assistance, allow themselves to be taken to the emergency service or facility for emergency care or social service by their free consent. Only a small minority of intoxicated persons who are in immediate need of emergency medical care or who appear to have lost the capacity to make a rational decision with respect to their need for care will come under the provision that authorizes retention at the emergency service or other appropriate facility against their will. Only a very brief retention at the emergency service or other facility is provided for, because no person may be detained with out his consent beyond the immediate medical emergency or beyond the time when he has regained his capacity to make rational treatment decisions, and such retention cannot exceed 48 hours from the time of his admission. The effect of this requirement is likely to reduce the time a person may be held without his consent or without a court order below that provided for either in the District of Columbia or Maryland laws.

The authority of the emergency service or facility to hold a person for treatment for a brief period of time without any kind of commitment or order is based, therefore, either on consent or on the basis of an immediate medical emergency, or on lack of capacity to make a rational decision (on the premise that a rational person would agree to what is required for his benefit) . Short-term detention of this nature is not vulnerable to constitutional attack. (*Forsythe* v. *Ivey*, 162 Miss. 471, 139 So. 615 [1932]; *Christensen* v. *Weston*, 36 Ariz. 200, 284 P. 149 [1930]; *Powell* v. *Texas*, 392 U.S. 514 [1968] [concurring opinion].)

Subsection (a) makes a distinction between persons who are merely in need of help—who may be sent home or to a facility of their choice—and persons who appear to be in need of immediate emergency medical attention or incapable of making a rational decision about their need for care. Such a more seriously intoxicated person must be taken to the emergency service or facility for emergency medical care or social service. This is intended to assure that those most seriously in need of care will obtain it.

The section stresses the need for proceeding with the patient's consent as far as possible, whether police or an emergency service patrol (*infra*, section 16) is used to take him for emergency treatment. Experience has shown that most intoxicated persons offer no resistance; the subsection, however, allows persons to be taken against their will but provides that force which is likely to inflict physical injury cannot be used. Since the entire procedure is for the intoxicated person's protection, it would make no sense to take a risk of hurting him in order to take him where he can be treated.

The civil nature of the procedure is stressed by providing that detention is to be viewed as a form of protective custody, that is, a method of protecting intoxicated persons from the danger and discomfort of intoxication. The civil nature of the detention is further emphasized by specifying that no arrest record or record which implies a criminal charge is to be made. The police or emergency service patrol who participate in the detention are, however, accorded immunity from civil and criminal liability. It should be noted that unlike the new Maryland and District of Columbia laws, the proposal makes no provision for the treatment of persons charged with crime who are intoxicated at the time of their arrest. In the view reflected here, provision of treatment for persons charged with crime at any emergency service or other facility would destroy the open nature of such facilities and would attach a stigma to their utilization which might well affect the willingness of intoxicated persons to consent to going there. The matter of medical treatment of such persons should be left to correctional authorities.

Provision is made for prompt medical examination and diagnosis, and for assistance, to persons who are not admitted, in getting to their homes. Persons who are admitted may be transferred to other facilities when treatment needs require.

Since involuntary detention at the emergency service or facility for emergency medical care is based on medical emergency or incapacity to make a rational decision with regard to treatment, the detention, however beneficial, must terminate when the emergency terminates or decisional capacity is regained. (See, e.g., Coloby v. Jackson, 12 N.H. 526 [1852].) However, the person detained may consent to further, more intensive diagnosis and treatment, and in appropriate instances the emergency service or facility is authorized to encourage him to do so.

SECTION 11. VOLUNTARY TREATMENT OF ALCOHOLICS.

Derivation: CAL. WELF. & INST'NS. CODE § 5000 et seq. (Supp. 1968); CONN. GEN. STAT. ANN. § 17-155 (Supp. 1969); D.C. CODE ANN. § 24-521 et seq. (Supp. II 1969).

This section provides for the voluntary treatment of alcoholics— i.e., it encourages voluntary treatment rather than voluntary commitment, which is the emphasis in many alcoholism treatment laws which require court approval for voluntary treatment (e.g., ME. REV. STAT. ANN. tit. 22, § 1353 [1964]), or which subject voluntary patients to the same restrictions as involuntarily committed patients (e.g., KAN.

STAT. ANN. § 74-4410 [1964]; KY. REV. STAT. ANN. § 222.180 [1963]; N.M. STAT. ANN. § 46-12-9 [1966]; WIS. STAT. ANN. § 51.09 [1955]) or require a minimum stay of up to 120 days (*e.g.*, HAWAII REV. LAWS § 334-52 [1968]; MONT. REV. CODES ANN. § 38-406 [1953]; WASH. REV. CODE ANN. § 70.96.100 [1959]; *see also Alcoholism and the Law,* Appendix B, Chart III).

Under the proposal, moreover, the patient simply applies for treatment at an inpatient, outpatient or intermediate care facility. In the case of a "minor" or an "incompetent" the application for treatment is to be made by the applicant's appropriate legal representative. Note that the terms "minor" and "incompetent" have not been defined, in the expectation that each state will use its own customary or statutory definition. No special provision has been made for emancipated minors; here, too, states that grant to emancipated minors the legal rights of majority will follow their accepted practice or make appropriate amendments if necessary.

The section also allows for transfer of patients among different treatment institutions in accordance with patient needs and provides that, whenever possible, referral to an appropriate facility shall be made.

There is no provision for a predetermined minimum voluntary stay nor is there any requirement that the patient give a few days' notice prior to seeking discharge because such a provision may discourage applications and blur the distinction between voluntary and involuntary status.

SECTION 12.   EMERGENCY COMMITMENT OF ALCOHOLICS.

Derivation: *E.g.*, MINN. STAT. ANN. § 253 A.04 (Supp. 1969).

This section provides for short-term emergency commitment for some alcoholics who have lost the power of self-control in respect to the use of alcoholic beverages. Emergency commitment is limited to alcoholics who pose an immediate threat to the physical safety of others. The limited grounds for commitment would have been sufficient even under common law to take a person into custody. (*Bisgaard* v. *Duvall,* 169 Iowa 711, 151 N.W. 1051 [1915]; *see also* Annot., 92 A.L.R.2d 571 [1963].) This section requires an allegation of actual, threatened or attempted physical harm, a physician's certificate, based on recent examination, of the need for immediate custody and a review of the application by the facility.

While the need to resort to emergency commitments under this section may arise infrequently, it does provide for a method to deal with situations not covered by other parts of the law. An alcoholic who becomes intoxicated at home, or who is engaged in a protracted drinking bout in a non-public place, or who is brain-damaged, and whose behavior becomes assaultive may require immediate commitment to cope with the emergency, without open court hearings and the necessary delay involved in regular commitment proceedings. In its requirements, the section is generally similar to statutory provisions that authorize emergency commitment of the mentally ill (*e.g.*, MINN. STAT. ANN. § 253A.04 [Supp. 1969]; N.C. GEN. STAT. § 122-59 [Supp. 1967]).

In order to protect further against unwarranted detention, the person committed must be discharged once the facility head determines that the grounds for commitment no longer exist. In any event, the person cannot be held for more than five days unless a petition for involuntary commitment has been filed in the interim. If a petition for commitment is made, the head of the facility may retain the person until the petition has been disposed of, but in no event longer than ten days after the petition is filed, and only if he finds that the grounds for the emergency commitment persist. This provision may cause the detention of a person who continues to be dangerous for a somewhat longer period than five days, pending the regular commitment proceeding. He is protected, however, against undue delay and prolonged detention without court order by the requirement of release within ten days after the petition has been filed, and by the availability of the writ of *habeas corpus*.

SECTION 13. INVOLUNTARY COMMITMENT OF ALCOHOLICS.

This section establishes the grounds for involuntary civil commitment and the requisite procedural scheme. In accordance with the policy against the routine use of civil commitments, the grounds here proposed for such commitment are far more limited than those provided in existing statutes. The procedural requirements, however, follow the traditional commitment procedures which provide for a judicial certification, though there is careful provision for periodic review which many commitment statutes fail to include. The draft is based on the dominant idea that an alcoholic—as well as any other person who suffers from a mental or behavioral disorder—

should not be deprived of his liberty unless such a deprivation is warranted by more than a desire to "help" or "treat" him, and that his rights to procedural due process must be strictly observed.

Grounds for Commitment.

The proposed grounds for involuntary commitment are intentionally restrictive—the physicians' certificates must show and the court must find that the person is an alcoholic who has lost the power of self-control over his use of alcoholic beverages and that, in addition, (1) he has attempted, threatened, or actually inflicted physical harm and is likely to inflict physical harm—this would include the alcoholic who is violent only when intoxicated as well as the alcoholic who may be violent even when sober—or (2) that he is in need of treatment but so impaired in his judgment that he is unable to make a rational decision about his need for care, and that he will actually benefit from care. Commitment would not be warranted merely because the person is an alcoholic and is in need of treatment, or because he is an alcoholic and likely to commit property crimes, or likely to appear repeatedly in public intoxicated, or has disturbed his family or other social relationships. Commitment would be warranted, however, when the alcoholic exhibits cognitive deficiences, generally confused thinking or other manifestation of disorientation which show an inability to make judgments about areas of behavior that do not directly relate to his drinking problem.

The criteria set out here are more restrictive and more clearly defined than most existing statutes which provide for involuntary civil commitment of alcoholics. Most existing laws use general standards such as "danger" or "unable to conduct his own affairs" or "in need of care" without any explicit definition; moreover, many set forth a series of criteria without specifying if these grounds are cumulative or alternative. (*See Alcoholism and the Law,* Appendix B, Chart II.) The grounds provided here are also more restrictive than those generally set out for mental illness confinements; states generally require either dangerousness or need for care, alternatively or cumulatively. (*See* American Bar Foundation, THE MENTALLY DISABLED AND THE LAW 17 [F. Lindman & D. McIntyre, eds. 1961].) The restrictive statement of grounds for commitment carry out the notion that commitments for behavioral disorders cannot be justified by benign intentions alone—there is, after all, no law that commits a person for treatment of a physical ailment if he refuses such treatment. To justify commitment, there must either be a substantial risk to society, or a situation in which the patient himself is unable to make a rational treatment decision.

Procedural Scheme.

The procedural plan generally follows the pattern of most mental illness and alcoholic commitment statutes by providing for a full court hearing prior to commitment. (*See e.g.,* OHIO REV. CODE ANN. §§ 5122.11-5122.16 [Baldwin 1964] [mental illness]; TENN. CODE ANN. § 33-810 [Supp. 1968]; TEXAS REV. CIV. STAT. ANN. art. 5561c, § 9 [Supp. 1968]; *see generally Alcoholism and the Law,* Appendix B, Chart II.) It is hoped that the provisions for frequent and mandatory review will avoid routine commitments following routine court hearings, as has been too often the case in mental illness commitments in the past. (*See, e.g., Alcoholism and the Law,* Appendix C.) The alternative—namely, reliance on commitments on two medical certifications prior to court hearing, as in New York (N.Y. MENTAL HYGIENE LAW §§ 300-309 [McKinney Supp. 1968]) —has been considered; it presents other risks.

Subsection (a).

To initiate commitment proceedings a petition setting forth the grounds for commitment (discussed *supra*) and a supporting physician's certificate must be filed. An allegation of refusal to undergo examination covers the situation where the person whose commitment is sought is totally uncooperative.

Subsection (b).

This subsection not only meets the requirements of due process with regard to notice as most recently expounded in *In re Gault,* 387 U.S. 3 (1967), but also requires that notice be given that is likely to result in more than the formal protection of the person to be committed. It requires notification to a disinterested next of kin, and it allows the court to notify other persons when the circumstances of the proceeding make such notification advisable.

Subsection (c).

This subsection explicitly requires the person whose commitment is sought to be present, unless the court determines that his presence might be injurious to him; in that case the alleged alcoholic will be represented by a guardian *ad litem* specially appointed for this purpose. This subsection emphasizes reliance on medical expertise. The provision recognizes that the grounds for commitment require sensitive judgments which can only be made on the basis of thorough diagnosis and detailed medical evidence. The provision is unique in authorizing a short term commitment for diagnosis when there has been no medical examination or when the medical evidence is insufficient. The requirement of detailed medical evidence—including the provision for five-day diagnostic commitments—is likely to result in fewer commitments and thus serves to protect the person whose commitment is being sought.

This subsection also requires that before a person can be committed, it must be shown that treatment is available and is likely to be beneficial—except in instances where the person must be committed because he is found to be dangerous.

Subsection (d).

This subsection provides that commitment of every person who is not discharged within the initial commitment period of thirty days will be reviewed. The person will be automatically discharged at the end of thirty days unless the court has issued a recommitment order pursuant to the petition of the department. The first recommitment is to be for a maximum of 90 days. The procedure is designed to insure an early initial review of the case by the department and to provide for a somewhat longer second period should there be grounds for recommitment of the person.

Subsection (e).

This subsection provides for a rehearing every six months for committed persons who have not been discharged within the initial commitment periods. A somewhat longer interval has been set out on the assumption that anyone who has not been found suitable for discharge within 120 days is likely to require relatively long-term treatment.

Subsection (f).

This subsection provides that, for judicial recommitment, notice be given in the same manner as provided prior to the initial commitment (*see* subsection (b)), and that the hearing be conducted in the same manner as the hearing prior to the initial commitment (*see* subsection (c)).

Subsection (g) .

This subsection allows the department to employ outpatient and intermediate as well as inpatient treatment for persons who are involuntarily committed. The department is allowed to transfer patients from one facility to another when medically advisable. This allows some scope, even for involuntarily committed persons, for the legislative preference (Sections 1 and 9) for outpatient rather than inpatient treatment. Note that free transferability of a patient between facilities within the department is made possible because the section provides for commitment to the department, rather than to a specific institution (*supra,* subsection (a)). In this respect the section follows a number of existing state statutes which provide for commitment of the alcoholic to the responsible agency (public health or mental health) rather than to a specific state institution. (*E.g.* ARK. STAT. ANN. § 83-709 [Supp. 1967]; CONN. GEN. STAT. ANN. § 17-155(e) [Supp. 1969]; KAN. STAT. ANN. § 74-4408 [1964]; N.M. STAT. ANN. § 46-12-7 [Supp. 1967]; R.I. GEN. LAWS ANN. § 40-12-17 [1956].) This parallels a recent trend in correctional law and administration which frequently provides for sentencing of a criminal defendant to the custody of the department of correction, which then assigns him to a suitable institution following diagnostic procedures and classification at a reception center. This allows for considerable diversification of correctional treatment. (*See, e.g.,* MODEL PENAL CODE § 304.1.) However, existing statutes for the commitment of alcoholics do not typically provide for involuntary outpatient care (*cf.,* N.C. GEN. STAT. §§ 122-65.7, 122-65.8 [Supp. 1967]) , although they frequently allow involuntarily committed patients to be released on probation (*see Alcoholism and the Law,* Appendix B, Chart II, *and* Appendix C) .

Subsection (h) .

This provision sets out the standards for discharge from commitment. It provides that a person who has been committed because of the likelihood that he will inflict physical harm will be released when that likelihood no longer exists, and that a person committed because of a need for treatment accompanied by judgmental incapacity will be released when the incapacity no longer exists or when further treatment will not improve his condition. Under these standards the judgmentally incapacitated alcoholic who would deteriorate further if treatment were to cease would not have to be released, because the stabilization of an otherwise deteriorating condition may be viewed as a continuing benefit. This section also delegates the power to make discharge determinations to the department of public or mental health without the need for court approval. The delegation reflects, as do the commitment procedures, a necessary reliance on medical expertise.

Subsection (i).

This subsection makes explicit the person's right to contest the commitment application and provides for the right to counsel and for court appointment of counsel at all stages of the proceeding, including recommitment proceedings, even if the person whose commitment is sought does not request counsel. It also provides that the person has a right to a physical examination, including, in cases of financial necessity, a doctor selected by the court and paid for by the state. It is probable that, prior to the initial hearing, examination by a private physician would pose no problems, but absent a specific guarantee, there could be problems in obtaining a private medical examination prior to a recommitment hearing.

Subsection (j).

This subsection specifically preserves the right of *habeas corpus,* reiterating existing constitutional protections. The availability of the writ, as well as the requirements of the proposal for frequent rehearings, insure that no person who has been committed will remain in custody without frequent review of this case.

SECTION 14. RECORDS OF ALCOHOLICS AND INTOXICATED PERSONS.

Derivation: Partly new; *see* N.Y. MENTAL HYGIENE LAW § 20 (McKinney Supp. 1968) ; CAL. WELF. & INST'NS CODE §§ 5325-5331 (West Supp. 1968).

This section seeks to strike a balance between the benefits of confidentiality and the benefits of necessary disclosure. The statute specifically allows disclosure for treatment purposes since it is essential in making treatment determinations to know prior diagnoses and the nature and results of prior treatment, and it allows for disclosure to counsel representing patients in commitment proceedings to obviate possible problems arising because the person lacks the capacity for consent or because counsel has been appointed irrespective of his wishes. The provision for disclosure upon application allows the court to weigh the need for the information against the possible harm of disclosure in specific situations as they arise—

for example it may be important in a custody proceeding for the court to be fully apprised of the diagnosis and prognosis of an alcoholic father, or it may be important in a claim for wrongful detention at an emergency facility for the court to be informed of a person's medical condition at the time of detention. Moreover, there is a specific provision for disclosure of records at the discretion of the director for purposes of research. This will permit studies directed at evaluation of treatment services and causes of alcoholism to proceed unfettered by the need to obtain individual consents. Disclosure for research purposes is authorized only if the identify of persons who have been treated is adequately protected.

Few existing statutes provide for confidentiality of records pertaining to alcoholics. Those that do either limit the protection to voluntary patients (*e.g.*, KAN. STAT. ANN. § 74-4410 [1963]; N.H. REV. STAT. ANN. § 172:13 [Supp. 1967]; N.M. STAT. ANN. § 46-12-19 [1953]), or, in a few instances, to involuntary patients (*e.g.*, ARK. STAT. ANN. § 83-716 [1960]; GA. CODE ANN. § 88-411 [Supp. 1968]). No valid reason for a distinction has ever been supplied. Some of these statutes provide for disclosure only on a court order (ARK. STAT. ANN. § 83-716 [1960]; GA. CODE ANN. § 88-411 [Supp. 1968]; KAN. STAT. ANN. § 74-4410 [1963]; N.M. STAT. ANN. § 46-12-9 [1953]), or only for medical purpose (N.H. REV. STAT. ANN. § 172:13 [1964]) ; other statutes (*e.g.*, R. I. GEN. LAWS ANN. § 40-12-22 [1956]) provide only for disclosure on consent. The more recent statutes in the District of Columbia and Maryland give a qualified protection only to detoxification unit records. However, a court order seems unnecessary for treatment purposes, and the disclosures only on consent or for treatment overlook the possibility that disclosure may serve a socially useful purpose.

SECTION 15. VISITATION AND COMMUNICATION OF PATIENTS.

Derivation: MD. ANN. CODE art. 2C, § 306 (c). (Supp. 1968).

This section is designed to meet the arbitrary restrictions and censorship of visitation, mail, and consultation with counsel in some states. In particular, the right to consult counsel is unduly restricted in many states. (*See* Project, *Civil Commitment of the Mentally Ill*, 14 U.C.L.A.L. Rev. 822, 850 [1967].)

This section will give as much freedom of communication as possible to patients, limited only by the practical necessities of institutional life. Because in many states alcoholics will be treated in state mental hospitals, implementation of this section may result in a desirable liberalization of visitation and mail rules in such institutions.

SECTION 16. EMERGENCY SERVICE PATROL; ESTABLISHMENT; REGULATIONS.

The section authorizes the department of public or mental health, as well as counties, cities, and other municipalities in the state to establish "emergency service patrols." The proposal is based on the experience of the Vera Foundation in its Bowery Project in New York, which uses civilians trained in approaching and assisting intoxicated persons in need of care, as well as police. Such civilian and police roving patrols provide emergency help, and assist intoxicated persons by conveying them to detoxification units. With the establishment of an adequate number of such emergency service patrols, particularly in the larger cities, the police will be relieved of the burden of collecting and transporting intoxicated persons. It is desirable that to the fullest extent possible police be freed from the burden of dealing with intoxicated persons, although it is probable that in small cities and even in some large urban areas the police will continue to aid intoxicated persons. Although this proposal is novel in providing for emergency service patrols statutorily, a recently proposed Comprehensive Alcoholism Treatment and Rehabilitation Bill, filed in Massachusetts during the 1969 session, provided for programs and procedures for taking intoxicated persons to treatment centers by persons other than police wherever feasible. Note that the section neither limits police activities in any way, nor requires the establishment of emergency service patrols—it merely authorizes their establishment. The provision here proposed does not deal with such matters as civil service requirements and other details of employment that will have to be provided for under existing state law.

SECTION 17. EFECTIVE DATE.

This section provides that the proposed law take effect ninety days after passage, but provides that the repeal of the provisions of the penal law that deal with drunkenness need not become effective in any city or county until one year after passage, upon application of the county or city. It is likely that in many places there will not be emergency services or facilities immediately available. Thus, to repeal laws that prescribe existing procedures for the handling of persons who are intoxicated without providing any practical alternatives would only result in a worsening of the situation. (*See Powell* v. *Texas,* 392 U.S. 515 [1968].)

APPENDIX A

Criminal Prohibitions
against
Drunkenness and Public Drinking

CHART I: CRIMINAL PROHIBITIONS AGAINST DRUNKENNESS

Explanatory Notes

This chart summarizes the criminal prohibitions against drunkenness. It does not include drunken driving offenses nor prohibitions against disorderly conduct and disturbing the peace when such statutes do not include intoxication as an element of the crime.

Code Section--indicates the relevant section describing the crime and punishment; if, however, the punishment is set out in a general section setting the penalty for misdemeanors it is included parenthetically in the penalty column.

Crime--gives a brief summary of the prohibited activity.

Penalty--indicates the minimum and maximum penalty wherever the statute sets a range, or the maximum fine or jail sentence wherever the statute merely sets a maximum.

Other--indicates special provisions including provisions for civil commitment for treatment in lieu of jail.

CHART I

CRIMINAL PROHIBITIONS AGAINST DRUNKENNESS

STATE	CODE SECTION	CRIME	PENALTY	OTHER
Alabama	tit. 14, §120	drunk & disorderly in a public place or private residence not own	$5--$100	
	tit. 14, §120(1)	drunk on a public highway	$10 &/or 30 days	
	tit. 14, §437	vagrancy (common drunkard)	$500, or $500 & 1 yr. hard labor	
Alaska	11.45.030(3)	disorderly conduct (drunk in private house or place to annoyance of others, or drunk in public place)	6 mos. &/or $300	
Arizona	13-379	drunk & disorderly	$300 &/or 6 mos. (13-1645)	
	13-991	vagrancy (common drunkard)	90 days	
Arkansas	48-943	drunk in public place, or drunk & disorderly	$5--$100 &/or 5--30 days	
California	Penal Code §273g	habitually drunk in the presence of child in custody or care	$500 &/or 6 mos. (Penal Code §19)	
	Penal Code §647 f	disorderly conduct (drunk in public place and danger to self or others or obstructs public way)	$500 &/or 6 mos. (Penal Code §19)	
Colorado	13-5-60	drunk on highway	$10--$500 &/or 10 days--6 mos.	
Connecticut	ch. 945 §53-246	found intoxicated	$20 or 30 days	
	ch. 945 §53-340	common drunkards	1st offense: 60 days 2d offense: 240 days 3d offense: 360 days	

220

STATE	CODE SECTION	CRIME	PENALTY	OTHER
Delaware	tit. 11, §611	drunk & noisy in public place	5 days or $10 & costs, or fined costs	can be held 24 hrs. before hearing if "riotous," in danger of breach of the peace, or no magistrate is "convenient."
	tit. 11, §471	disorderly conduct (drunk in public place)	$10, or in default of payment, 10 days	
D.C.	25-128(a)	drunk in street or alley & endangering self, others, or property	$100 &/or 90 days (25-128(b))	if drunk and not dangerous then taken to detox center(24-128cc)
Florida	856.01	drunkenness	$25 or 3 mos.	
	856.02	vagrancy (common drunkard)	$250 or 6 mos. (856.03)	
Georgia	58-608	drunk & disorderly in public place	$1,000 &/or 1 yr.	
Hawaii	772-1	vagrancy (common drunkard)	$10--$500 &/or 1 yr.	
	737-1	found drunk in public place	$100 &/or 3 mos.	
	18-7101	vagrancy (common drunkard)	90 days	
Idaho	23-604	drunk in public place; or drunk & disturbing the peace	$300 &/or 3 mos. (18-113)	
Illinois	none			
Indiana	12-611	drunk in public place	$1--$100 & 6 mos.	
	123.42	drunk in public place	$100 or 30 days	
Iowa	125.11	drunkenness	$5--$25 or 30 days	penalty may be remitted by giving information about source for liquor(125.12)
	746.1	vagrancy (habitual drunkard)	6 mos. (746.15)	upon promise of good behavior for 1 year can be released if bond is posted (746.8)

CRIMINAL PROHIBITIONS AGAINST DRUNKENNESS

STATE	CODE SECTION	CRIME	PENALTY	OTHER
Kansas	41-802	drunk in public place; or drunk in private place & disturbing others	$100 or 30 days	
Kentucky	244.020(2)	drunk in public place	$10--$100 & 5--30 days (244.990(2))	
Louisiana	14.103(A)	disturbing the peace (appearing drunk)	$100 &/or 90 days	
	14.107	vagrancy (habitual drunkards)	$200 &/or 9 mos.	
Maine	17, §2001	drunk in public place; or drunk & disturbing the peace	1st offense: $20 &/or 30 days 2d offense: $60 &/or 90 days	males previously convicted may be sentenced to county farm for reformation of inebriates for 90 days--11 mos.
	17, §3758	undesirable person (common drunkard)	90 days	
	35, §1170	drunk or drunk & disorderly in public conveyance or environs	$5--$500 or 30 days--11 mos.	
Maryland	27, §123	drunk in public place	$50 &/or 60 days; habitual offenders: 60 days at alcoholism treatment facility	
Massachusetts	272, §44	drunk in public place; or drunk & disturbing the peace	30 days or $15	6 mos. (state farm or reformatory)
Michigan	436.201	drunk on train	$100 &/or 90 days (436.205)	
	750.167	disorderly person (drunk in public place)	$100 &/or 90 days (750.504)	
Minnesota	340.88	drunk on train	$10--$100 or 20--90 days (340.90)	
	340.96	drunkenness	1st offense: 40 days or $40; 2d offense: 60 days or $60; 3d offense: 60 days--3 mos.	

STATE	CODE SECTION	CRIME	PENALTY	OTHER
Mississippi	2291	drunk in public place	$100	
Missouri	562.260	drunk in church, school, or courthouse or other public place	$1000 &/or 1 year (556.270)	
	4-159(2)	drunk in public place	$500 &/or 6 mos. (4-173)	
Montana	94-35-248	vagrancy (common drunkard)	90 days	
Nebraska	53-196	drunk or under influence	1st offense: $50 or 30 days 2d offense: 60 days	
Nevada	207.030	vagrancy (drunk & unable to exercise care or drunk & blocking public way)	$500 &/or 6 mos. (193.150)	
	207.160	drunk & loitering in public place	1st offense: $5--$25 2d offense (within 60 days of 1st): 5--25 days	
New Hampshire	570.14	drunk in public place; or drunk & disturbing the peace;	$500 &/or 6 mos. (570.22)	
	570.18	drunk in public conveyance	$500 &/or 6 mos. (570.22)	
	570.25	common drunkard	$500 &/or 6 mos.	
New Jersey	2A:170-30	drunk & loitering or disorderly in public place; or in private without owner's permission	$500 &/or 6 mos. (2A:169-4)	
	2A:170-13	driving horse while drunk	$200 &/or 30 days	
New Mexico	40A-20-2	drunk & disorderly in public place	$100 &/or 6 mos.	
New York	Penal Law §240.40	drunk in public place & danger to self or annoyance to others	15 days (70.15) &/or $250 (80.10)	

CRIMINAL PROHIBITIONS AGAINST DRUNKENNESS

STATE	CODE SECTION	CRIME	PENALTY	OTHER
North Carolina	14-334	drunk & disorderly in public place	$50 or 30 days	
	14-335	drunk in public place	1st offense: $50 or 20 days; for a 2d offense in 12 mos. can have 30 day--6 mo. indeterminate sentence in which prisoner may be conditionally released for treatment	
North Dakota	5-01-05	drunk in public place	$500 &/or 1 yr. (12-06-14)	
	12-42-04	vagrancy (common drunkard)	$100 &/or 30 days; or 20 days work on streets	
Ohio	3773.22	drunk & disorderly	$5--$100 (3773.99 (P))	
	37 §8	drunk in public place; or drunk & disorderly at public gathering	$10--$100, &/or 5--30 days	
Oklahoma	21, §1141	vagrancy (habitual drunkard)	$10--$100 &/or 30 days	
		drunk in public place; or drunk & disturbing the peace	$5--$100 &/or 50 days	
Oregon	166.160	drunkenness	$0.67	
Pennsylvania	18, §1523	drunk in public place	$5	
	47, §722			
Rhode Island	11-45-1	vagrancy (common drunkard) (common drunkard--defined 11-45-11)	3 yrs.	on recommendation of division of alcoholism may be committed 60 days --3 yrs. in lieu of penalty
	45-6-3	indecent intoxication (local gov'ts may penalize)	$20 or 10 days	

CRIMINAL PROHIBITIONS AGAINST DRUNKENNESS

STATE	CODE SECTION	CRIME	PENALTY	OTHER
South Carolina	16-557	drunk in religious meeting	$20--$100 &/or 30 days-- 1 yr.	
	16-558	drunk in public place; or drunk & discharging gun on or near public highway	$100 &/or 30 days	
South Dakota	22-13-5	drunk & disorderly	$5--$10	
	9-29-3	municipalities may prohibit public drunkenness	up to $100 &/or 30 days; or in cities with munici- pal court up to $500 &/or 6 mos.(9-19-3; 9-19-4)	
Tennessee	39-2518	drunk in public conveyance	$1,000 &/or 1 yr. (39-105)	
	39-2519	drunk in hospital	$25 &/or 30 days	
Texas	Penal Code: art 477 §204,150	drunk in public place; or private house (not own)	$100	
Utah	32-7-13	drunk in public place	$299 &/or 30 days--6 mos. (32-8-59)	
	76-61-1	vagrancy (common drunkard)	6 mos.	court can order hard labor [alternative sentences tit.7, §661--1 day for each $1 fine; §662--probation; §663--pledge of abstinence]
Vermont	tit. 7, §660	drunkenness	1st offense: $5 or 20 days 2d offense: $15 &/or 30 days	
Virginia	18.1-237	drunk in public	$1--$25; 3d offense in 1 yr.: $50 &/or 6 mos.	
	18.1-239	drunk & disturbing religious worship	$1,000 &/or 1 yr. (18.1-9)	
	18.1-240	drunk & disturbing school or literary society	$1,000 &/or 1 yr (18.1-9)	
Washington	9.68.040	drunk in public place	90 days or $250 (9.92.030)	

CRIMINAL PROHIBITIONS AGAINST DRUNKENNESS

STATE	CODE SECTION	CRIME	PENALTY	OTHER
Washington (cont.)	71.08.010	drunk & disorderly in public place; or drunk in liquor store or bar	90 days or $250 (9.92.030)	
	9.87.010	vagrancy (common drunkard-- defined 71.08.020); or drunken- ness	$500 or 6 mos.	
West Virginia	60-6-9	drunk in public place	$5--$100 &/or 60 days	
Wisconsin	947.03(1)	drunkenness	$50 or 30 days	
	947.03(2)	habitual drunkenness	$100 or 6 mos.	
Wyoming	15.1-3(16)	cities & towns can regulate drunkenness by ordinance	up to $100 &/or 3 mos. (5-123, 5-133, 5-135)	

CHART II: CRIMINAL PROHIBITIONS AGAINST PUBLIC DRINKING

Explanatory Notes

This chart summarizes the criminal prohibitions against drinking
in public. It does not however, include regulatory measures such as
the hours at which alcoholic beverages can be served and restrictions on
who can be served.

Code Section--indicates the relevant section describing the crime
and punishment; if, however, the punishment is set out in a general
section setting the penalty for misdemeanors it is included parenthetically in the penalty column. An (*) indicates that the prohibition is
in the same section as a drunkenness prohibition.

Crime--gives a brief summary of the prohibited activity.

Penalty--indicates the minimum and maximum penalty wherever the
statute sets a range, or the maximum fine or jail sentence wherever the
statute merely sets a maximum.

CHART II

CRIMINAL PROHIBITIONS AGAINST PUBLIC DRINKING

STATE	CODE SECTION	CRIME	PENALTY
Alabama	None		
Alaska	11.45.030(4)	drinking intoxicating liquor in or about a depot, platform, wharf or waiting room, or upon a public street, or at a public gathering is disorderly conduct	$300 &/or 6 mos.
Arizona	None		
Arkansas	48-943*	drinking in a public place	$5--$100 &/or 5--30 days
California	None		
Colorado	None		
Connecticut	None		
Delaware	None		
D. C.	25-128(a)*	drinking in an unlicensed public place	$100 &/or 90 days (25-128(b))
Florida	None		
Georgia	58-605	use of intoxicating liquor at church or other place of divine worship	$1,000 &/or 12 mos. (27-2506)
Hawaii	None		
Idaho	None		
Illinois	None		
Indiana	None		

CRIMINAL PROHIBITIONS AGAINST PUBLIC DRINKING

STATE	CODE SECTION	CRIME	PENALTY
Iowa	123.42*	consumption in public places	$100 or 30 days
Kansas	None		
Kentucky	244.020(1)*	drinking in public place or coach, street car, depot, etc.	$10--$100 &/or 5-30 days (244.990(2))
Louisiana	None		
Maine	17 §22003	drinking in unlicensed public places	$50
Maryland	27 §123(b)*	drinking at school athletic event	$50 &/or 60 days; habitual offenders $100 or 6 mos.
Massachusetts	None		
Michigan	436.34	drinking on public highway, park or place of amusement	$100 &/or 90 days (436.205)
	436.202	drinking on train	$100 &/or 90 days (436.205)
Minnesota	None		
Mississippi	None		
Missouri	562.260(1)*	drinking in courthouse, schoolhouse or church	$1000 &/or 1 year (556.270)
Montana	4-159(1)*	consumption in public place	$500 &/or 6 mos. (4-173)
Nebraska	53-186	drinking in thoroughfare or in vehicles thereon; or in gov't buildings	1st offense: $500 2d offense: $1000 &/or 6 mos. (53-1.100)
	53-186.01	drinking in unlicensed public place	$250--$500 & 15 days or $100--$250 &/or 60 days or $100--$250 & 3--5 days (53-180.05)

CRIMINAL PROHIBITIONS AGAINST PUBLIC DRINKING

STATE	CODE SECTION	CRIME	PENALTY
Nevada	None		
New Hampshire	None		
New Jersey	2A:170-25.3	drinking at interscholastic athletic event	$50 &/or 30 days
New Mexico	None		
New York	None		
North Carolina	14-333	drinking on a train	$10--$50 &/or 30 days
North Dakota	None		
Ohio	None		
Oklahoma	37 §8*	drinking in a public place	$10--$100 &/or 5--30 days
Oregon	None		
Pennsylvania	None		
Rhode Island	None		
South Carolina	16-557*	use at any religious meeting	$20--$100 &/or 30 days--1 yr.
South Dakota	None		
Tennessee	39-2518*	publicly drink	$1000 &/or 1 year (39-105)
Texas	Penal Code art 478 §205	drinking on public conveyance	$10--$100

CRIMINAL PROHIBITIONS AGAINST PUBLIC DRINKING

STATE	CODE SECTION	CRIME	PENALTY
Utah	32-7-13*	drinking in public building, park or stadium	$299 &/or 30 days--6 mos. (32-8-59)
Vermont	None		
Virginia	None		
Washington	None		
West Virginia	60-6-9*	drink in public place; drink in motor vehicle on street or garage	$5--$100 &/or 60 days
Wisconsin	None		
Wyoming	None		

231

APPENDIX B

Civil Law Relating to Alcoholism

CHART I: SUMMARY OF CIVIL LAW RELATING TO ALCOHOLISM

Explanatory Notes

State--indicates all of the particular state's statutory citations relating to the subject matter of the chart.

Definition--indicates whether the state defines "alcoholic" for purposes of its alcoholism program. If the definition is the "typical" one given below, or some minor variation, the chart so indicates; if there is substantial variation, "other" is indicated and the definition is set forth in the Appendix to the chart. If the definition is limited for use to commitment proceedings only, this is also indicated.

The "typical" definition is:

> Alcoholic means any person who chronically and habitually uses alcoholic beverages to the extent that said person has lost the power of self-control with respect to the use of such beverages, or while chronically and habitually under the influence of alcoholic beverages endangers public morals, health, safety or welfare.

Program Responsibility--indicates whether a program is established, and if so whether a department or commission is charged with responsibility, and if a department, its name. It also indicates if a specific division has been provided in the law.

Advisory Committee--indicates whether an advisory committee (commission, counsel) is provided, and summarizes statutory provisions relating to the number and composition of the membership.

Involuntary Commitments--A "yes" indicates that the law specifically provides for involuntary commitment; the details are set out in Chart II; a "no" indicates the law makes no specific provisions for involuntary commitment of alcoholics although such commitments might, perhaps, be effected under the provisions for commitment of the mentally ill.

<u>Voluntary Admissions</u>--A "yes" indicates that the law makes specific provision for voluntary admissions; the details are set out in Chart III; a "no" indicates that the statute contains no specific procedures although it is possible that voluntary admissions are effected under rules of the department charged with the supervision of institutions, or under rules established by the alcoholism program.

<u>Other</u>--indicates a variety of statutory provisions that further describe a program or its operation.

(*)--An asterisk in any column indicates that questionnaire replies for the particular state, summarized in Appendix C, suggest that the actual practice may be different from the procedures suggested by a literal reading of the statutes; for instance, a state that has a special provision for the commitment of alcoholics may nevertheless use commitments in practice under general provisions of its mental health laws.

STATE	DEFINITION	PROGRAM RESPONSIBILITY	ADVISORY COMMITTEE	INVOLUNTARY COMMITMENT	VOLUNTARY ADMISSIONS	OTHER
Alabama §§ 373 (11)-- (13f)	none	Comm'n on Alcoholism:5 members--3 state officials, 1 prof.,2citizens		no	yes	
Alaska §§ 44.29.030--090; 47.30.470--90.	typical (but special definition of alcoholism)	Dep't of Health and Welfare	9 members: 2 phys. incl. 1 psych.; 1 att'y; 1 interest; 1 public health nurse; 1 liquor industry; 1 AA; 1 public; 1 social worker	no	no	courts take judicial notice of fact alcoholic is suffering from an illness and in need of treatment.
Arizona §§ 36-141, 142	none	Dep't of Health		no	no*	
Arkansas §§ 83-701-- 717	typical	Comm'n on Alcoholism--7 members: 1 clergy; 1 liquor industry; 2 phys. 2 recovered alcoholics		yes	yes	directive that comm'n should not concentrate on one phase at expense of others
California §§ 427.1--.7 (Health & Safety); §§ 5003; 5225 --30; 5350-- 68. (Welfare & Inst.)	none	Dep't of Public Health-- Div. of Alcoholism	15 members (no specification)	yes (special provisions for conservatorship and criminal defendants)	yes	emphasis on assistance to local plans
Colorado §§ 66-1-7 (23)	none	Dep't of Public Health-- Alc. Division		no*	no*	
Connecticut §§ 17-155a-- j; 17-187	none	Dep't of Mental Health-- Alcoholism Division	7 members (no specification)	yes	yes	special bureau for study of chronic police & court cases. (Anyone arrested 3 times in 2 yrs. or 5 times in 5 years for drunkenness)

CHART I--SUMMARY OF CIVIL LAW RELATING TO ALCOHOLISM

STATE	DEFINITION	PROGRAM RESPONSIBILITY	ADVISORY COMMITTEE	INVOLUNTARY COMMITMENT	VOLUNTARY ADMISSIONS	OTHER
Delaware §§ 5301--5327; 5901	none	Del. State Hosp.--Gov. Bacon Health & Welfare Center (for treatment & research)	none	yes	yes	detoxification centers
District of Columbia D.C. Code Ann. §§24-521--24-535	other (chronic alcoholic)	Commissioner of D.C. (may designate agency or dep't)	none	yes (only if criminal charge, conviction or excusal)	yes	
Florida Tit. 27, §§ 396.011--.121	none	Bd. of State Institutions	5 members: 1 phys.; 1 hospital admin.; 3 reps. of interested, non-gov. groups	no	yes	specific directive re: construction of Rehabilitation Center
Georgia §§ 88-401--412	typical	Dep't of Health	none	yes	yes	crime to give anyone in alcoholism treatment alcoholic beverages
Hawaii Hawaii Rev. Stat. Chapter 334	other	Dep't of Mental Health (part of gen'l duties, no special program)	none	yes	yes	
Idaho §§ 67-3108--3120	typical (but no loss of control)	Dep't of Health--Comm'n on Alcoholism	the comm'n is apparently like an advisory group--9 members: 1 Admin. of Health; 1 bd. of ed.; 1 phys.; 1 union 5 named by Foundation on Alcoholism	no*	no*	educational and research programs in cooperation with board of health. bd. of health may establish alc. div.
Illinois ch. 91-1/2,	none	Dep't of Mental Health	none	no	no	Dep't. is authorized to establish in &

STATE	DEFINITION	PROGRAM RESPONSIBILITY	ADVISORY COMMITTEE	INVOLUNTARY COMMITMENT	VOLUNTARY ADMISSIONS	OTHER
Indiana §§ 22-1501-- 1513	typical	Dep't of Mental Health-Division on Alcoholism	5 members: 2 phys. incl. 1 psych.; 1 att'y; 2 interest & knowledge of social problems	no*	yes	courts to take judicial notice that alcoholic is ill & needs care.
Iowa §§ 123A.1--8; 224.1--5; 229.41, 42	typical	Dep't of Health Comm'n on Alcohol-ism--8 members: Comm'r of Pub. Health; 2 phys.; 1 Gen.Assembly; 1 liquor industry; 1 att'y; 1 clergy, 2 recovered alco-holics	7 members: state offi-cials, e.g., supt.public instruction, chrmn.state bd. of soc.welfare, dir. mental health	yes	yes	the Commission primarily con-cerned with educa-tion is advised by an Advisory Com-mittee of various state officials
Kansas §§ 74-4401-- 4413	typical (or convicted 5 times of in-toxication or legally determined to have lost power of self-control)	Comm'n on Alco-holism--5 mem-bers: 2 phys.; 1 att'y; 2 recov-ered alcoholics		yes	yes	(revisors note-- article inopera-tive since no appropriations)
Kentucky §§ 222.020-- 070; 222.105 --190	typical (but only for pur-poses of com-mitment)	Dep't of Mental Health-Office of Alcoholism	9 members: professional, research or personal ex-perience with alcohol problems, including 2 phys. incl. 1 psych.	yes	yes	also an interagency Council on Alco-holism to coordi-nate alcoholism programs
Louisiana R.S.§§40:2008 --2008.3; 9:1001--4	inebriate (but only for purposes of interdiction)	Dep't of Hos-pitals-Division of Alcoholism	9 members: 2 dr.-1 psy-chiatrist; 2 personal exper. excessive use; 1 att'y; 3 knowledge & interest; 1 state bd. of hospitals	yes (interdic-tion)	no	
Maine 22 §§1351- 55	none	Dep't of Health & Welfare	7 members (no specifi-cation)	no*	yes	

239

CHART I--SUMMARY OF CIVIL LAW RELATING TO ALCOHOLISM

STATE	DEFINITION	PROGRAM RESPONSIBILITY	ADVISORY COMMITTEE	INVOLUNTARY COMMITMENT	VOLUNTARY ADMISSIONS	OTHER
Maryland Art. 2c; Art. 16 §§ 43--49	other	Dep't of Mental Hygiene--Division of Alcoholism Control	11 members: 1 psych.; 1 phys.; 1 att'y or judge; 1 recovered alc.; 4 from psychology, sociology &/or commerce; Comm'r. Dept. of Health; Comm'r. Mental Hygiene; Supt. Prisons.	yes	yes	detoxification centers, policy for highway safety, prepare detailed plan
Massachusetts ch. 111, §§ 4A--4D; c. 123 §§ 50--80	none	Dep't of Public Health	14 members: 11 specified commissioners & bd. chairman; 3 experienced in alch. matters.	yes	yes	
Michigan §§ 325.701--707; §§ 14.808--816	typical	Dep't of Public Health--alcoholism program	7 members: 2 phys. incl. 1 psych.; 4 from fields, e.g., sociology, social work, labor, industry, law, etc.	yes	no	
Minnesota §§ 253A.01--.21; §§ 144.81--.84	inebriate (but only for commitment)	Bd. of Health --consultant on alcoholism	7 members: 5 from medical, legal, behavioral sciences, clergy; 2 interested public	yes	yes	
Mississippi ch. 2, §§ 436-01--12	typical (but only for commitment)	no specific provision	no specific provision	yes	no	crime to provide liquor if in institution for alcoholism care or treatment
Missouri				no	no*	

240

STATE	DEFINITION	RESPONSIBILITY	ADVISORY COMMITTEE	COMMITMENT	ADMISSIONS	OTHER
Montana §§ 80-2404; 38-201--504	other	Dep't of Institutions--Division of Mental Hygiene --Alcoholism Service Center at State Hosp.	none	yes	yes	
Nebraska ch. 599-sess. laws; §§ 83-306-- 356	typical	Dep't of Public Institutions-- Division on Alcoholism	Comm'n on Alcoholism --6 members: Dir. of Public Inst.; Comm'r of Ed.; med. school rep.; 3 from Congressional districts	yes	yes	also Alcoholics' Advisory Bd. which may be repealed implicitly or explicitly by new division & comm'n --duties of div. will lead to changes in commitment provisions
Nevada §§ 458.030--240; 433.248 --290	typical (but no loss of self-control)	Dep't of Health & Welfare--Alcoholism Division	Alcoholism Advisory Board--7 members: 1 phys.; 1 psych.; 1 arrested alcoholic; 1 welfare worker; 1 law enforcement; 1 personnel dir.; 1 educator	yes	no*	note for commitment alcoholic defined by loss of control, not danger
New Hampshire §§ 172.1--14	other	Dep't of Health & Welfare	none	yes	yes	
New Jersey §§ 26:2B-1--6; 30:9-12.16 --21; 30:8 -16.2	none	Dep't of Health	none	yes	yes	discretionary with freeholders of county to provide treatment facilities as part of jail and hospital
New Mexico §§ 46-12-1-- 13	none	Comm'n on Alcoholism--5 members: 2 phys.; 2 recovered alcoholics; 1 other.	none	yes	yes	

CHART I--SUMMARY OF CIVIL LAW RELATING TO ALCOHOLISM

STATE	DEFINITION	PROGRAM RESPONSIBILITY	ADVISORY COMMITTEE	INVOLUNTARY COMMITMENT	VOLUNTARY ADMISSIONS	OTHER
New York art. 10, §§ 300--309	typical	Dep't of Mental Hygiene--Alcoholism Unit	Council on Alcoholism 12 members & comm'r (no specification)	yes	yes	
North Carolina §§ 122-7.1; 122-36--68.1	inebriate (for commitment only)	Bd. of Mental Health--alcoholic rehabilitation program	none	yes	yes	function of program develop & promote local community programs
North Dakota §§ 54-38-01--09; 25-03-02--11	typical	Comm'n on Alcoholism up to 7 state officials: health, rehabil., public welfare, ed., public instruction	none	no*	yes	
Ohio §§ 3701.141, 142; 5122.01--.38	none	Dep't of Health	Alcoholism Advisory Bd.--6 members: dir. health; mental hygiene; correction; 3 others	yes	yes	
Oklahoma c. 130 Sess. Laws (1968)	none	Comm'n on Alcoholism 7 members: 1 each dist.; 1 at large	none	no*	no*	
Oregon 430.080-160	none	Bd. of Control--Mental Health Division	Alcohol & Drug Education Committee 9 members (no specification)	no	no	emphasis on education of youth; operate a rehabilitation clinic
Pennsylvania ch. 50, §§ 2101--2113	none	Dep't of Health --Div. of Alcoholic Studies & Rehabilitation	none	yes	yes	

STATE	DEFINITION	PROGRAM RESPONSIBILITY	ADVISORY COMMITTEE	INVOLUNTARY COMMITMENT	VOLUNTARY ADMISSIONS	OTHER
Rhode Island §§ 40-12-1-- 23	typical	Dep't of Social Welfare--Division of Alcoholism	15 members: 1 psychiatrist; 2 medical society; 1 social welfare org.; 1 health admin.; 2 religion; 1 ed.; 1 industry; 1 labor; 1 finance; 1 AA; 1 alch.ed.committee; 2 legis.	yes	yes	ascertain existence of alcoholism among inmates, prisoners, patients & pupils & treat
South Carolina §§ 32-895--903; statute No. 1230 (1968)	none (but definition of alcoholism)	Agency of Vocational Rehabilitation S.C. Alcoholic Center	Comm'n on Alcoholism for the Center -- 7 members: 1 each cong. dist.; 1 at large	yes	yes	
South Dakota § 30.01A.01 ch. 127 (1967); §§ 27-17--22; 27-8-1--14 (1967)	none	Comm'n on Mental Health & Retardation Division-- Prevention of Alcoholism--5 members: 1 recovered alcoholic; 1 Dep't of Prob. & Parole; 1 liquor industry; 2 others	none	yes	no	
Tennessee §§ 33-801-- 811	typical	Dep't of Mental Health	Alcoholism Comm'n-- 13 members: 3 each grand divisions (ordin.); 4 state at large	yes	yes	
Texas Const. § 42; Art. 556lc, §§ 1-20	typical	Texas Comm'n on Alcoholism-- 6 members: 1 phys.; 3 exper. in excessive alcohol use	none	yes	yes	inebriate asylum (never established)

243

CHART I--SUMMARY OF CIVIL LAW RELATING TO ALCOHOLISM

STATE	DEFINITION	PROGRAM RESPONSIBILITY	ADVISORY COMMITTEE	INVOLUNTARY COMMITMENT	VOLUNTARY ADMISSIONS	OTHER
Utah §§ 55-13-1-- 7	typical (but no loss of control)	Division of Health --Committee on Alcoholism--7 members: pop. & geo. consid.--only 4 from same political party	none	no	no	
Vermont 18 §§ 8401 --05; 8451 --8462	other	Alcoholic Rehabilitation Bd.--5 members (no specification)	none	yes	yes	bd. establish facility for homeless male alcoholics or those whose home contributes to condition; bd. can send to private agency
Virginia §§ 32-365-- 378; 37.1-1; 37.1-64--153	inebriate (for commitment only)	Dep't of Health-- Division of Alcohol Studies & Rehabilitation	none	yes*	yes	Va. medical college authorized to establish hospital & clinic facilities for care, study & treating most amenable
Washington §§ 70.96.010-- .900	other	Dep't of Health (program on alcoholism)	none	no	yes	
West Virginia §§ 27-1-4; 27-1A-11; 27-6-1--6	typical (inebriate for commitment)	Dep't of Mental Health-Division of Alcoholism	none	yes	yes	
Wisconsin §§ 51.09--13	none	no specific provision	no specific provision	yes	yes	
Wyoming	none	no specific provision*		no*	no*	

244

D. C. ALCOHOLIC REHABILITATION ACT OF 1967, § 3(a), amends Act of Aug. 4, 1967, to read:

The term 'chronic alcoholic' means any person who chronically and habitually uses alcoholic beverages to the extent that (A) they injure his health or interfere with his social or economic functioning, or (B) he has lost the power of self-control with respect to the use of such beverages.

HAWAII REV. LAWS § 334-1(1967):

'Person habituated to the excessive use of drugs or alcohol' means a person who repeatedly and compulsively uses narcotic, stimulant, depressant or hallucinogenic drugs or alcohol to an extent which interferes with his personal, social, family or economic life.

LOUISIANA REV. STAT. § 9:1001 (1932):

As used in this Part, an inebriate or habitual drunkard is a person who has formed the inveterate habit or custom of getting drunk by the constant and confirmed use of spiritous, malt, or fermented liquors, whereby intoxication is produced and continued to such an extent as to deprive him of self control, and causing such a state of mental confusion as to render him incapable of taking care of his person and of administering his estate.

MARYLAND ANN. CODE art. 2c § 103(b) (1968):

The term "chronic alcoholic" means any person who chronically and habitually uses alcoholic beverages (1) to the extent that it injures his health or substantially interferes with his social or economic functioning, or, (2) to the extent that he has lost the power of self-control with respect to the use of such beverages.

LAWS OF MINNESOTA ch. 638, § 2(4) (1967):

"Inebriate person" means any person incapable of managing himself or his affairs by reason of the habitual and excessive use of intoxicating liquors, narcotics, or other drugs.

MONTANA REV. CODES ANN. § 80-2404(2) (1965):

(a) "Alcoholism" means a chronic illness or disorder of behavior characterized by repeated drinking of alcoholic beverages to an extent which endangers the drinker's health, interpersonal relations or economic functioning, or to an extent which endangers the public health, welfare or safety.

(b) An "alcoholic" is a person suffering from the illness of alcoholism.

NEW HAMPSHIRE REV. STAT. ANN. § 172:1 (1947):

IV. "Chronic alcoholic" means a person who, in consequence of prolonged excessive drinking, has developed a diagnosable bodily disease or mental disorder.

V. "Compulsive drinker" or "alcoholic addict" means a person affected by an uncontrollable craving for alcoholic beverages, or a person who chronically and habitually uses alcoholic beverages to the extent that he has lost the power of self-control with respect to the use of such beverages, or while chronically or habitually under the influence of alcoholic beverages endangers public morals, health, safety or welfare.

VI. "Habitual drunkard" means a person who is frequently or regularly intoxicated from the use of alcoholic beverages or has been three times convicted for a violation of section 14 of chapter 570, RSA.

VII. "Excessive drinker" means a person who drinks to an extent which exposes him to the risk of becoming a compulsive drinker or a chronic alcoholic.

VIII. "Inebriate" means any person included in any of the following classifications: an excessive drinker, a compulsive drinker, an alcoholic addict, an habitual drunkard or a chronic alcoholic.

NORTH CAROLINA GEN. STAT. § 122-36(c) (1945):

The word "inebriate" shall mean a person habitually so addicted to alcoholic drinks or narcotic drugs or other habit forming drugs as to have lost the power of self-control and that for his own welfare or the welfare of others is a proper subject for restraint, care, and treatment.

VERMONT STAT. ANN. titl. 197 § 8401(1) (1968):

"Alcoholic" means a person who because of his use of alcohol in any form shows signs of mental illness or who has an uncontrollable desire for alcoholic beverages.

VIRGINIA CODE ANN. § 37.1-1(9) (1968):

"Inebriate" means a person who through use of alcoholic liquors has become dangerous to the public or himself or unable to care for himself or his property or family.

WASHINGTON REV. CODE § 70.96.020 (1959):

(2) "Alcoholism" includes the symptoms and problems of problem drinkers and alcoholics as herein defined.

(3) "Problem drinkers" are any drinkers of intoxicating liquors who indulge in drinking which in its extent habitually goes beyond the traditional and customary dietary use, or the ordinary compliance with social drinking customs.

(4) "Alcoholics" are those persons addicted to the excessive use of alcohol, and those problem drinkers whose dependence upon or addiction to alcohol has attained such a degree that it causes a noticeable mental disturbance or an interference with their bodily and mental health, their interpersonal relations, and their social and economic functioning.

WEST VIRGINIA CODE ANN. § 27-1-4 (1955, 1965):

An "inebriate" person is anyone over the age of eighteen years who is incapable or unfit to properly conduct himself or herself, or his or her affairs, or is dangerous to himself or herself or others, by reason of periodical, frequent or constant drunkenness, induced either by the use of alcoholic or other liquors, or of opium, morphine, or other narcotic or intoxicating or stupefying substance.

CHART II: PROVISIONS FOR INVOLUNTARY COMMITMENT

Explanatory Notes

A blank column or a blank part where the column covers multiple points indicates that the statute does not speak to the particular aspect.

Type of Statutes, Sections, Year. This column sets out the type of statutes, relevant sections from which the material in the chart is drawn, as well as other sections relevant to involuntary commitment of alcoholics, and the year of adoption or substantial amendment. In classifying the type of statute the designations used are "Alcoholism" which means that the provisions are found in a separate chapter or series of sections which relate to alcoholism or "Mental Illness" (or equivalent term) which means that the provisions are found in laws relating to the commitment of the mentally ill; where this occurs there is an explanation setting out how alcoholics are included. In a few instances other designations are used which are self-explanatory.

Grounds for Commitment. This column sets out the criteria other than residency and age which must be met in order to effect commitment. References to commitment in the penal law are not included.

Application By. This column sets out who is authorized to apply for commitment.

Dr. Cert. Req'd. A "yes" in this column indicates the application must be accompanied by a physician's certificate (statement or affidavit) stating the subject is an alcoholic and other relevant facts; modifications to the requirement are also noted.

Hearing. This column sets out whether a <u>hearing</u> is allowed or required; whether a <u>jury</u> is allowed or required; whether <u>counsel</u> is allowed, and whether medical evidence is required or discretionary.   In order to simplify reporting, each item is given a number set out below followed by an indication of the statutory requirement. Absence of a number means the statute is silent on the particular item. The code is:

"1." stands for provision on hearing.

"2." stands for provision on jury.

"3." stands for provision on counsel.

"4." stands for provision on medical evidence.

After Hearing. This column sets out whether an appeal or other review is provided and, if so, whether the statute states a jury trial may be requested at the appeal.

Duration and Discharge. This column describes the duration of commitment, where it is specified, and the circumstances for discharge when they are set out. It also indicates where there are specific provisions which speak to early discharge or extension of the commitment. Finally, the column indicates whether there is a provision for probation, convalescent leave or other conditional discharge in which the person is released from the facility but remains subject to its jurisdiction.

Rights Protected. This column sets out specific provisions for <u>habeas corpus</u>, protection of civil rights, communication rights and the like.

Other--summarizes statutory provisions that are relevant to commitment or explanative of the procedure. It specifically indicates the contents of statutory provisions relating to confidentiality of records and for emergency commitment.

CHART II - PROVISIONS

STATE	TYPE OF STATUTE SECTIONS YEAR	GROUNDS FOR COMMITMENT	APPLICATION BY	DR. CERT. REQ'D	HEARING 1. heari 2. jury 3. couns 4. med.e
Alabama	no specific provisions				
Alaska	no specific provisions--person suffering from acute alcoholism	(§47.30.340(10) mentally ill does not incl			
Arizona	no specific provisions				
Arkansas	Alcoholism §§83-703--717 (1955)	alcoholic and incapable of properly conducting self or affairs, or dangerous to self or others, or lost power of self control, and in need of treatment and treatment will improve health	relative, health officer		1. req'
	§83-712	in lieu of sentence in special circumstances	court decides		
California	Welfare & Institutions §§5225-5230, 5350--5368 (eff.July 1, 1969)	court can order conservatorship if chronic alcoholic and "gravely disabled" (unable to provide self with food and clothing) --conservator can commit	director of eval. or treatment facility applies for conservatorship; conservator applies for commitment		(for co torship 1. req' 2. allo 3. allo court c point g ad liter 4. req'
		criminal defendant can be committed for short term, if chronic alcoholic, gravely disabled and dangerous, if defendant waives criminal proceeding			
Colorado	no specific provisions				
Connecticut	Alcoholism §§17-155g--i (1961)	alcoholic and loss of self control	selectman, relative	yes	1. req'
	§17-155e (1961)	alcoholic and commitment is for own protection or protection of society and needs hospitalization		yes (at time of admis.)	1. appa requ
Delaware	Gov. Bacon Center §§5321, 22 (1935, 1947)	alcoholic			

DURATION AND DISCHARGE	RIGHTS PROTECTED	OTHER
5-90 days, early discharge; probation	habeas corpus and civil rights protected	record confidential; court can after hearing send to county jail for 10 days if in best interest of family and community and not detrimental to alcoholic
max. 90 days, early discharge, probation	civil rights protected	can be used only if facilities available and commission agrees to receive patient
conservatorship ends 1 yr. unless an application for extension made	habeas corpus and civil rights protected	conservator procedures governed by probate code (§§5225-5257); can have temporary conservatorship up to 1 yr. during proceedings, and can have temporary detainment
72 hrs. for evaluation and treatment, 14 days on med.certificate and 14 additional days if suicidal		
12. mo. max., early release, probation		
discharge when no longer in need of confinement		cannot commit to facilities of alcoholism division; procedure for emergency commitment
		court can commit if person has not been determined eligible by a mental hygiene clinic

CHART II - PROVISIONS

STATE	TYPE OF STATUTE SECTIONS YEAR	GROUNDS FOR COMMITMENT	APPLICATION BY	DR. CERT. REQ'D	HEARING 1. hearin 2. jury, 3. counse 4. med.ev
D.C.	D.C.Alcoholic Rehabilitation Act §24-524--527 (1967)	chronic alcoholic and charged with or convicted of certain alcohol-related crimes, or acquitted on basis of alcoholism, and danger of physical harm and treatment available (if convicted of being drunk and dangerous must be a continuing danger to self or others)	corporation counsel		1. req'd 3. allowe vision fo app't. 4. req'd to hearin
Florida	no specific provisions				
Georgia	Alcoholism §88-405 (1964)	alcoholic and needs hospitalization	any person	yes	1. req'd examinin committe
	§88-408	in lieu of sentence in special circumstances	court decides		
Hawaii	Mental Illness §§334-34, 334-53--58, 334-81--86 (1967) alcoholic specifically included	alcoholic and requires hospitalization	any person	yes (2)	1. allow request admissic transfer 3. allow court me point g ad litem be attor
	§§334-74, 75 (1967)	prisoner and alcoholic and needs hospitalization	dir. of social services, jail officer	yes (psychiatrist in mental health dept.)	
Idaho	no specific provisions				
Illinois	no specific provisions				
Indiana	no specific provisions				

DURATION AND DISCHARGE	RIGHTS PROTECTED	OTHER
30 days if 1st or 2d comment, 90 days if 3rd or more in 24 month period	habeas corpus (limited to once every six months)	person arrested for drunk and dangerous can be detained in detox. center for diag. to decide whether to commit or press criminal charges; records conf'l; chronic alcoholic charged with misdemeanor can voluntarily request commitment in lieu of criminal charges; patient can be transferred to outpatient status but if committed as dangerous a court order is needed
		examining committee composed of 2 physicians and 1 county attorney, decision to admit must be unanimous; cannot be transferred to any institution operated by mental health dept; records conf'l.
determined by court, discharge by dept. allowed, convalescent status	civil rights protected	department must agree that subject may be admitted
when cured, or max. benefit, or no danger to self or society; authorized absence	civil rights protected (may be temporarily suspended by administrator)	records confidential; application must be approved by administrator; a 48 hr. emergency commitment on application of police officer or cert. of 1 physician provided
max. period of sentence; authorized absence		needs approval of director of health; if discharged before sentence expires then return to jail

CHART II - PROVISIONS

STATE	TYPE OF STATUTE SECTIONS YEAR	GROUNDS FOR COMMITMENT	APPLICATION BY	DR. CERT. REQ'D	HEARING 1. hearin 2. jury, 3. counse 4. med. e
Iowa	Drug Addicts ch. 224 (1959) makes mental illness provisions applicable ch. 229 (1959)	addicted to alcohol and fit for hospitalization			1. req'd commissio 3. allowe visions f 4. req'd. (see spec notes)
Kansas	Alcoholism §§74-4401--13 (1957)	alcoholic, and incapable of properly conducting self or affairs, or dangerous to self or others, or lost power of self-control, and in need of treatment and treatment will improve health	relative, comm'n, health officer, next friend		1. req'd 4. discre
Kentucky	Alcoholism §§222.105--.195 (1958)	alcoholism, and incapable of conducting his affairs, or dangerous to self or others, or lost power of self-control and in need of treatment and treatment will improve health	relative, health officer		1. req'd 4. discre
Louisiana	Inebriate-- R.S. 9:1001--04 (1890, 1932)	court can order curator if inebriate or habitual drunk and incapable of caring for self or estate	family, or friend aplies for curator		1. req'd appointme curator)
Maine	no specific provisions				
Maryland	Alcoholism Art. 2C, §306 (1968)	chronic alcoholic and in detox. unit and danger of harm and unable to make rat'l decision	comm'r of mental hygiene, governing body		1. req'd
	Art. 16, §43 (1962)	habitual drunkard and incapable of caring for self or property	court, ex parte		1. req'd 2. req'd
	Alcoholism Art. 2C, §307; Art. 16, §49 (1951)	alcoholic and charged with, or convicted of crime	court, ex parte		

DURATION AND DISCHARGE	RIGHTS PROTECTED	OTHER
until cured; convalescent leave	habeas corpus protected and comm'n of inquiry provided	first sent to screening center, then final commitment upon center's recommendation
4 days to 1 yr. (if committed to state instit.) 30 days to 1 yr. (if committed to comm'n), early release; probation		
6 mo. max., earlier discharge	civil rights protected	record confidential
		curator can place in hospital or other institution for treatment
max. 30 days from day entered detox. facility; early release	civil rights protected	30 day commitment is called temporary; can be held 5 days in detox. center before application for commitment
court sets time, early discharge, extension		court appoints committee to commit; person may voluntarily select his committee and agree to enter inst. for limited time
court sets conditions		

CHART II - PROVISIONS

STATE	TYPE OF STATUTE SECTIONS YEAR	GROUNDS FOR COMMITMENT	APPLICATION BY	DR. CERT. REQ'D	HEARING 1. hearir 2. jury, 3. counse 4. med. e
Massa-chusetts	Commitment and care of insane Ch.123, §§50--85 (1885 as amended) special § for alcoholics to follow general provisions	alcoholic and loss of self-control		yes	1. req'd waived 3. allowe 4. discre ary
Michigan	Insane, feeble minded §§14.808 --816 (1929, 1967) special section to include "addicts" under general provisions	addicted to alcohol and needs medical and sanitary treatment or care	guardian, spouse, suitable person appt'd by court	yes	1. req'd 2. allowe request c discretic 4. req'd
Minnesota	Hospitalization & Commitment §§253A.01--21 (1967) inebriate specifically included	inebriate and commitment necessary for welfare of patient cr protection of society	any person	yes (unless unable to examine)	1. req'd 3. req'd 4. req'd
Mississ-ippi	Commitment of Alcoholics & Drug addicts Ch.2, §§436-01 --12 (1950)	alcoholic, and incapable of conducting his affairs, or dangerous to self or others, or lost power of self-control and in need of treatment and treatment will improve health	friend, relative, county health officer		1. req'd 4. discre
Missouri	no specific provisions				
Montana	Mental Illness §§38-201--504 (1943); §80-2404 (1965) provides admittance & discharge of alcoholics to follow provisions for mentally ill	person so far disordered that he is a danger to health, person or property			1. req'd 4. req'd

DURATION AND DISCHARGE	RIGHTS PROTECTED	OTHER
2 yr. max., early discharge if treatment no longer necessary or can be provided elsewhere	petition for discharge provided	provision for emergency commitment
		can order for diagnosis for 60 days--can be extended 60 days; provision for emergency detention
60 days, then mandatory review by hospital, then if recommended indeterminate period until no longer needs care or treatment; probation	habeas corpus and civil rights protected; review bd. provided	at hearing person cannot be under influence of drugs; during initial 60 days can transfer to informal status; provision for aftercare services, emergency commitment procedure
30-90 days, early discharge and extension without hearing; probation	civil rights and communication rights protected	record confidential; director may refuse admission if person willfully fails to be rehabilitated after 3 commitments unless person pays in advance
satisfactory mental condition; probation	postal rights protected	examine every 6 mos., 60-day diagnostic period if found disordered but not dangerous; procedure for certification followed in 5 days by commitment

CHART II - PROVISIONS

STATE	TYPE OF STATUTE SECTIONS YEAR	GROUNDS FOR COMMITMENT	APPLICATION BY	DR. CERT. REQ'D	HEARING 1. hearing 2. jury, 3. counsel 4. med. ev
Nebraska	Mental Illness §§83-306--356 (1947) specifically includes dipsomaniacs, inebriates	mentally ill and a fit subject for hospitalization		yes	1. req'd quiry by bd.of ment health) 3. allowed 4. req'd
Nevada	Commitments of Alcoholics & Drug Addicts §§433.248--.290 (1941, 1967)	alcoholic (for 2d commitment must also be "suitable")	any person		1. req'd 3. allowed can be as 4. discret
New Hampshire	Inebriates §§172.1--.14 (1947)	inebriate	exec.dir.		1. req'd
New Jersey	Alcoholism §§30:9-12.16--21 (1956)	acute alcoholism	interested party, related, police officer, sheriff,etc.	yes	1. req'd 3. allowed
	§§30:9-12.20 (1956)	pending criminal charge, acute alcoholism			
New Mexico	Alcoholism §§46-12-7--12 (1949, 1967)	habitual drunkard, chronic alcoholic, dipsomaniac or 5 times convicted of intoxication or lost power of self-control			
New York	Alcoholism §§10-300--308 (1965)	alcoholism and in need of treatment	relative, person with whom resides	yes	1. on requ
North Carolina	Mental Illness §§122-36--68 (1963) inebriates specifically included	inebriate and in need of observation or admission	reliable person	yes	1. req'd holds the
	§§122-58 (1961) inebriates specifically included	inebriate and in need of treatment		yes	1. allowed request

258

DURATION AND DISCHARGE	RIGHTS PROTECTED	OTHER
cured, or to relative if not dangerous	habeas corpus and communication rights protected	sets out treatment plan, e.g., baths, diet, allows commitment to jail if no suitable place; a priority list for admissions; provides for admission on med. certificates as alternative to hearing
1 yr. max.,early discharge when max.benefit or patient's best interest		
30-90 days, early discharge; recommitment; can go at large if division approves		each county decides on treatment to be available; can commit for 14 days for observation and study to state hosp.
90 days or early discharge if max. treatment benefit		
part or whole sentence		
30 day max., early discharge; probation		judicial notice chronic alcoholic is a sick person
6 mo. max., early discharge, extension; probation		admitted, then hearing upon request; must apply to keep more than 60 days which provides periodic review
180 day max., early discharge, extension for min. necessary period; probation	habeas corpus and civil rights and communication protected	if excused because of chronic alcoholism can be committed under these procedures; procedure for emergency commitment provided
same	same	can object before or after admission; records confidential

CHART II - PROVISIONS

STATE	TYPE OF STATUTE SECTIONS YEAR	GROUNDS FOR COMMITMENT	APPLICATION BY	DR. CERT. REQ'D	HEARING 1. heari 2. jury, 3. couns 4. med.e
North Dakota	no specific provisions				
Ohio	Mental illness §§5122.01--.38 (1961-63) mentally ill includes persons addicted to alcohol	mentally ill and in need of treatment	any person	yes (can be requested or statement of refusal)	1. req'd 3. allow 4. discr ary unle certific
Oklahoma	no specific provisions				
Oregon	no specific provisions				
Pennsylvania	Alcoholism Ch.50 §§2101--13 (1953, 1955)	person who through excessive use of alcohol is unable to care for self, family or property or is a burden on the public	any person		1. req'd may app' &/or hol ing) 3. allow 4. discr
		in lieu of sentence if addicted to excessive use of alcoholic bev.			
Rhode Island	Alcoholism §§40-12-1--23 (1951)	alcoholic	next of kin, resident		1. req'd 4. req'd
South Carolina	Alcoholics and Drug Addicts Statute No. 1230 (1968)	addict who by reason of intoxication is powerless to exercise judgment concerning hospitalization	any person	yes, (unless refuses)	1. req'd 3. allow may appo 4. discr
South Dakota	Mentally ill & Alcoholics §§27-8-1--16 (1967)	chronically addicted to excessive use of alcohol			1. req'd 2. allow request
Tennessee	Alcoholism §§33-806--811 (1955, 1963)	alcoholic	any person		1. req'd 2. allow request 3. req'd

DURATION AND DISCHARGE	RIGHTS PROTECTED	OTHER
preliminary 90 days, then indeterminate, early discharge, probation	habeas corpus and communication rights protected	non-judicial hospitalization 90 days; emergency commitment for 60 days provided; can be observed prior to hearing; records confidential
1 year, early discharge; probation	habeas corpus protected	commission composed of 2 physicians and 1 attorney
		facilities must be available
ct. can order 60 days to 3 years; early discharge, extension; probation		record confidential; if unsuited for treatment, then return to court; provision for commitment of dangerous without a hearing for a short term
ct. can order max. 90 day inpatient &/or outpatient; probation	habeas corpus and communication rights protected	initial commitment by certificate or ct. application--if certificate must apply for hospitalization within 10 days; records confidential
90 day max.		commitment subject to division of alcoholism for 1 yr.; called temporary
ct. can order 4 days to 12 mos.	civil rights protected	record confidential; may not commit to mental facility

CHART II - PROVISIONS

STATE	TYPE OF STATUTE SECTIONS YEAR	GROUNDS FOR COMMITMENT	APPLICATION BY	DR. CERT. REQ'D	HEARING 1. heari 2. jury, 3. couns 4. med.e
Texas	Alcoholism art. 5561c (1953, 1967)	alcoholic, and incapable of properly conducting self or affairs, or dangerous to self or others, or lost power of self-control and is in need of treatment and treatment will improve health	relative, county health officer, next friend		1. req'd 4. discr
	art. 5561c,§12 (1967)	in lieu of sentence in special circumstances	court decides		
Utah	no specific provisions				
Vermont	Mentally ill users of drugs & alcohol tit.18 §§8401--8405 (1968) follows mental illness law §§7501--8005 (1968)	alcoholic and substantial risk of injury to self or others or lacks capacity to make responsible decision concerning mental condition and in need of treatment	interested party, selectman, commissioner, town officer etc.	yes	1. req'd 4. req'd
	§8459 (1968)	anyone sentenced 3 times for drunkenness			
Virginia	Mental Health §§37.1-1; 37.1-63--37.1-153 (1968) inebriates specifically included	mentally ill and condition warrants hospitalization	any responsible person	yes(as an alternative to initial ct. order)	1. allow upon req 3. allow ct. can
Washington	no specific provisions				
West Virginia	Commitment of Inebriates & Criminally Mentally Ill §§27-6-1--6; 27-7-1--5; 27-8-1 (1957, 1965)	inebriate and unable to make responsible decision with respect to hospitalization and in need of treatment	any person	yes	1. req'd 3. req'd dian at 4. req'd

DURATION AND DISCHARGE	RIGHTS PROTECTED	OTHER
15 days to 3 mos. early discharge, probation	civil rights protected	protective custody for 5-14 days before hearing if certificate alleges will cause injury to self or others; record confidential
90 day max.		facilities must be available and commission must agree to receive patient
1 mo.--6 mos.; conditional discharge after 1 mo.	habeas corpus and communication rights protected	emergency admission provided; certification procedure also provided; examination within 7 days of admission; periodic review by hospital required; right to humane care and treatment provided; can't be treated by spiritual means alone
30 days--1 yr., early discharge, extension		board must have adequate facilities and personnel for care
15 days--if no discharge then advise of right to hearing; if no hearing requested within 60 days, stay voluntarily or by ct. order; standards for discharge set; probation	habeas corpus protected	must be examined within 24 hrs. of admission; no use of jail unless court authorized; medical certification provided as an alternative to court commitment
min. 30 days, discharge when recovered, or max. benefit, or custody if unimproved; probation	civil rights protected	supervisor of division decides which hospital; provision for protective custody if violent

263

CHART II - PROVISIONS

STATE	TYPE OF STATUTE SECTIONS YEAR	GROUNDS FOR COMMITMENT	APPLICATION BY	DR. CERT. REQ'D	HEARING 1. heari 2. jury 3. couns 4. med.e
Wiscon-sin	Mental Illness §§51.09--13 specific §§ for inebriates & drug addicts (1935,1961)	inebriate and in need of treatment or need of care to protect self or relatives or public	adult citizen		1. req'c
Wyoming	no specific provisions				

DURATION AND DISCHARGE	RIGHTS PROTECTED	OTHER
discharge when able to care for self		can be confined in rehabilitative facilities of house of correction or reforestation camp or county hospital; reexamination on patient's request after 6 mos.

CHART III: PROVISIONS FOR INVOLUNTARY COMMITMENT

Explanatory Notes

A blank column indicates the statute does not speak to the particular item.

Type of Statute, Sections, Year--Type of Statute indicates the type of statute in which the admissions provisions are found--the designation "Alcoholism" means the provisions are found in a separate chapter or series of sections that relate to alcoholism; the designation "Mental Illness" (or equivalent term) indicates that the provisions are found in the chapter or division of the laws relating to mental illness; the few other designations are self-explanatory; Sections indicates the relevant sections from which the chart material is drawn; Year indicates the year of adoption or substantial amendment.

Application To--indicates to whom the application for admission should be made.

Duration--indicates provisions relating to the length of stay, including maximum and minimum lengths, the right to leave on request, and standards for discharge.

Other--indicates provisions which are relevant to explain or describe admissions procedures and programs.

Evidence Required--indicates what must be shown, other than residency and age, in order to obtain admission when a statute sets out requirements.

CHART III--PROVISIONS FOR VOLUNTARY ADMISSIONS

STATE	TYPE OF STATUTE SECTIONS YEAR	APPLICATION TO	EVIDENCE REQUIRED	DURATION	OTHER
Alabama	Alcoholism §373(13)(b) (1957)	commission			establish outpatient clinics
Alaska	no specific provisions				
Arizona	no specific provisions				
Arkansas	Alcoholism §§ 83-713 -- 717 (1955)	commission	can be refused if treatment within preceding 12 mos; no criminal charge pending	90 day max., release within 10 days of request	local clinics: segregated wards. can be released if treatment given within preceding 12 mos.
California	Welfare & Inst. §5003 (1967)	public or private agency or practitioner			guarantees right to apply; no specific program is provided.
Colorado	no specific provisions				

267

CHART III--PROVISIONS FOR VOLUNTARY ADMISSIONS

STATE	TYPE OF STATUTE SECTIONS YEAR	APPLICATION TO	EVIDENCE REQUIRED	DURATION	OTHER
Connecticut	Alcoholism §17-155j (1963	state or priv. mental hosp. or gen.hosp. with psychiatric ward		leave on 10 days notice	
	Mental Illness §§ 17-155(e) 17-187 (1963)	hospital for mental illness or facility under control of alcholism division	alcoholic, request in writing, or if clinically suitable, informal request	leave on 10 days notice if written request for admission; if not, leave any time	
Delaware	Health Center §§ 5321--23 (1935)	Gov. Beacon Health Center	without psychosis, determined eligible by State Hospital or Center mental hygiene clinic		Hospital Bd. of Trustees may adopt rules; may refuse admission if unable to accommodate patient; preference to veterans.
D.C.	D.C. Alcoholic Rehabilitation Act §24-525 (1967)	medical officer in charge of facility	in case of person charged with misdemeanor, found by court to be chronic alcoholic and in danger of physical harm; otherwise found to be chronic alcoholic after exam and diag. at inpatient center.	leave at any time subject to reasonable regulations.	no preference to involuntary unless danger; medical officer determines who is to be admitted; person charged with misdemeanor can voluntarily request treatment in lieu of criminal prosecution.

CHART III -- PROVISIONS FOR VOLUNTARY ADMISSIONS

STATE	TYPE OF STATUTE SECTIONS YEAR	APPLICATION TO	EVIDENCE REQUIRED	DURATION	OTHER
Florida	Alcoholism §§396.051--.071 (1953)				Bd. promulgates rules
Georgia	Alcoholism §§88--409 (1964)	Dept.of Health		release within 15 days request, convalescent status	no rights abridged; records confidential
Hawaii	Mental Illness §§334-52, 334-55, 334-5 (1967)	administrator of psychiatric facility	habituated to excessive use of alcohol to degree requiring hos- pitalization	can require that applicant agree to remain 90 days	applicant agrees to abide by all the rules; records confidential
Idaho	no specific provisions				
Illinois	no specific provisions				
Indiana	Alcoholism §§ 22-1508--11 (1957)	sup't of facility or court	physician's state- ment of mental com- petency req'd when application made to court		unauthorized absence a misdemeanor; sup't can refer applicant to court for commitment.

CHART III--PROVISIONS FOR VOLUNTARY ADMISSIONS

STATE	TYPE OF STATUTE SECTIONS YEAR	APPLICATION TO	EVIDENCE REQUIRED	DURATION	OTHER
Iowa	Drug Addicts §224.1--5 Mental Illness §229.41--.42 (1947)	state hosp. or if indigent to clerk of court		discharge within 3 days of request	accept only if adequate facilities and will not result in overcrowding
Kansas	Alcoholism §74-4410 (1953)	to institution approved by Alcoholism Comm'n	recommendation of comm'n	retain as if committed by court (4 days to 1 year; early release	record confidential; civil rights preserved
Kentucky	Alcoholism §222.180 (1958)	court	phys. cert., alcoholic & mentally incompetent	court orders as if committed (no more than six months)	record confidential; civil rights preserved
Louisiana	no specific provisions				

CHART III--PROVISIONS FOR VOLUNTARY ADMISSIONS

STATE	TYPE OF STATUTE SECTIONS YEAR	APPLICATION TO	EVIDENCE REQUIRED	DURATION	OTHER
Maine	Alcoholism Drug Addiction §§1351--55 (1954)	court must approve	witnessed agreement	max. 90 days but ct. can on request annul agreement if no longer necessary	person can be sent to a hospital or private physician
Maryland	Alcoholism art.2c §§304,305 (1968)	medical offi- cer	found to be chro- nic alcoholic upon exam. and diag. at inpatient center	as long as consents, subject to checking out rules	authorizes readmissions; sets out procedures to follow; voluntary treatment preferred to involuntary.
	Inebriates, art.16 §§44--48 (1951)	court	habitual drunkard, indigent, writ- ten application by friend or relative, consent of alcoholic		procedure is only for cases needing public assistance

CHART III--PROVISIONS FOR VOLUNTARY ADMISSIONS

STATE	TYPE OF STATUTE SECTIONS YEAR	APPLICATION TO	EVIDENCE REQUIRED	DURATION	OTHER
Massachusetts	Alcoholism ch. 111, §4c (1950)	hospital (subject to dep't approval)	unable to care for self or family or property or a burden on public		can be recommended for admission by physician, courts, or social agencies if space available
	Mental Illness ch. 123, §86 (1955)	institution		leave on 3 days notice unless committed	admission is subject to availability of accommodations
Michigan	No specific provisions				
Minnesota	Mental Illness (special § for inebriates) §§253.03 (2) 253A.05 (1967)			leave on 3 days notice unless committed	Comm'r of Public welfare can set rules; rights protected; must be examined within 48 hours.
Mississippi	No specific provisions				
Missouri	No specific provisions				

CHART III--PROVISIONS FOR VOLUNTARY ADMISSIONS

STATE	TYPE OF STATUTE SECTIONS YEAR	APPLICATION TO	EVIDENCE REQUIRED	DURATION	OTHER
Montana	Mental Illness (alcoholics inc) §38-406; (1943,53)	court	written statement; phys. approval	agree to remain 4 mos. subject to early release by hospital	after 4 mos. stay hospital can commit
Nebraska	Mental Illness (includes alcoholics) §§83-306, 324 (1947)	county mental health bd. or to sup't	written application	best interest, leave on 10 days notice or commit	
Nevada	No specific provisions				
New Hampshire	Alcoholism §§ 172.13 (1947)	exec. dir. or facilities		min. 60 days; max. 1 year	exec. dir. can make rules; civil rights preserved; records confidential
New Jersey	Alcoholism §§ 26:2B-1--4 (1948) §§30:9-12.16--.19 (1956)				Comm'r of Health shall adopt rules and regulations for program or Bd. of freeholders if local

CHART III--PROVISIONS FOR VOLUNTARY ADMISSIONS

STATE	TYPE OF STATUTE SECTIONS YEAR	APPLICATION TO	EVIDENCE REQUIRED	DURATION	OTHER
New Mexico	Alcoholism § 46-12-9 (1949)	institution		retain as if committed (30 days subject to early discharge)	accept as if court committed; civil rights preserved; records confidential
New York	Alcoholism § 10-306 (1965)	dir. of approved institution	found suitable for care by comm'r	after 15 days can leave on 10 days notice; max.time 12 mos.;discharge if unsuitable for treatment or recovered	rules to be established
North Carolina	Mental Illness (inebriates included) §§ 122-56,57 (1963)	hospital	physician's certificate that fit subject for admission	leave on 10 days notice unless agrees to 30 days (or unless proceedings for judicial hosp.)	
North Dakota	Alcoholism § 54-38-08 (1957)	commissioner		min. 30 days; max. 1 year	comm'n establishes rules; civil rights preserved; records confidential
	Mental Illness (special § alcoholics) §§ 25-03-02--11 (1957,1961)	hospital		leave on request, can commit if unsafe self/others or discharge if not advisable or better use of space	sup't promulgates rules for admission

CHART III—PROVISIONS FOR VOLUNTARY ADMISSIONS

STATE	TYPE OF STATUTE SECTIONS YEAR	APPLICATION TO	EVIDENCE REQUIRED	DURATION	OTHER
Ohio	Mental Illness (alcoholics included) §§ 5122.01,.02 (1961, 1963)	head of private or public hospital		leave on request unless committed; discharge if recovered, if advisable or if space can be better utilized	number of voluntary subject to discretion of comm'r
Oklahoma	no specific provisions				
Oregon	no specific provisions				
Pennsylvania	Alcoholism c. 50 2105 (1953)	director	addicted to excessive use; needs care and will benefit	1 year; early discharge	court gives final approval; director examines applicant
Rhode Island	Alcoholism §§ 40-12-13, 14 (1951)	division of alcoholism		min. 30 days, then release on written request	applicants selected according to division's policies; records confidential

275

CHART III--PROVISIONS FOR VOLUNTARY ADMISSIONS

STATE	TYPE OF STATUTE SECTIONS YEAR	APPLICATION TO	EVIDENCE REQUIRED	DURATION	OTHER
South Carolina	Alcoholism § 32-903 (1954)	South Carolina Alcoholism Center			no prisoners or persons under control of Mental Health Comm'n can be admitted
	Statute No.1230 (1968)	treatment facility		leave on request unless commitment application filed	
South Dakota	no specific provisions				
Tennessee	Alcoholism §§33-801--811 (1963)	supt. of state hosp. or court		release on request if diagnostic work done	civil rights preserved-- visitation and communica- tion protected
Texas	Alcoholic §§ 561c (1953, 1967)	commissioner	no criminal charge pending	90 day max.; leave on 10 days request or if not benefiting from treatment	civil rights preserved; record confidential; can refuse admission if re- leased from treatment within 12 mos. and no use- ful purpose would be served
Utah	no specific provisions				

CHART III--PROVISIONS FOR VOLUNTARY ADMISSIONS

STATE	TYPE OF STATUTE SECTIONS YEAR	APPLICATION TO	EVIDENCE REQUIRED	DURATION	OTHER
Vermont	Alcoholism §§ 8402,03 (1968)	state or private institution		min. 1 mo., max. 6 mo.;determined by written agreement	
	§8459 (a) (1968)	board		min. 30 days; max. 6 mos.	comm'n can make regulations; civil rights preserved; record confidential
Virginia	Alcoholism §§ 32-373,74 (1948)	hospital or clinic or division	unable to care or burden to public		division has discretion on admission; select those to whom care of value and of value for research purposes
	Mental Illness (inebriates included) §§ 37.1-64, 65 70,78--84,100 (1968)	hospital	examination by hosp staff; find need of hospitalization	may retain for 15 days; can stay longer or be committed	must be examined within 24 hrs; cannot revoke driver's license
Washington	Alcoholism §§70.96.110 --.900 (1959)	Dep't of Health		dept. can request patient stay for min.of 120 days; release within 120 days of demand	

CHART III--PROVISIONS FOR VOLUNTARY ADMISSIONS

STATE	TYPE OF STATUTE SECTIONS YEAR	APPLICATION TO	EVIDENCE REQUIRED	DURATION	OTHER
West Virginia	Mentally ill (Special alcoholic §) § 27-1A-11 (1957, 1963)	Dep't of Mental Health or Division of Alcoholism			not required to accept, but may in accordance with promulgated rules
Wisconsin	Mental Illness (special § for alcoholics) §51.09 (1955)	court	physician's cert. that advisable for health and public welfare	commit as if involuntary	
Wyoming	no specific provisions				

278

APPENDIX C

Responses to Questionnaire Survey
conducted by
The Legislative Drafting Research Fund

INTRODUCTION TO APPENDIX C

In the summer of 1968 the Legislative Drafting Research Fund
sent the questionnaire which appears at pages 349 and 350 to health
officials in all 50 states and the District of Columbia.[1] The
purpose of the questionnaire was to collect data on the extent to
which existing legal approaches to the treatment of alcoholics,
including voluntary and involuntary commitment, are utilized; who
sets the legal machinery in motion, and for how long alcoholics
are detained or remain voluntarily for treatment under the different
laws available. Another purpose was to get information about existing institutions for the treatment of alcoholism and on their
utilization. The relevance of the data to the development of
recommendations for new treatment laws is clear. Any such recommendations must take into account facilities presently available, as well as the range and experience of existing state programs.

On the whole, the responses received were satisfactory and
in the aggregate help to provide a rather clear picture of the
existing treatment situation across the country. Perhaps the only
possible generalization that can be made is that it is difficult
to generalize about state alcoholism programs. A wide variety of
them exists, and states differ considerably in the range of available institutions and in the uses to which they put them. Emphasis between voluntary and involuntary programs differ, as does the
length of time an alcoholic is likely to be held for treatment if
he is committed. Another generalization that can be made is that
in spite of the enormous amount that is being written about alco-

holism, there are relatively few hard facts on the treatment of alcoholics in the form of accurate and easily available statistics.
                                                                    2
    There were thirty states who responded to the questionnaire.
An additional five states sent letters explaining why they could
                                3
not answer the questionnaire.   Occasionally, however, some useful
information was available in these responses.   Sixteen states did
                       4
not respond at all.   While a large number of states expended a
great deal of thought, effort and time in responding to the questionnaire, some of the responses received were incomplete or vague,
making analysis of them difficult.   The most general problem was
a lack of statistics to supply the answers to many items of the
questionnaire.   Most states seem not to have accurate and easily
available statistics relating to alcoholism.   An attempt is made
to analyze the responses to the questionnaire in the following
charts.

    This Appendix contains 8 charts which were compiled from the
questionnaire data; in addition some charts draw on data supplied
with, but not part of, the formal responses.   If any useable information on the subject of a particular chart was reported by a state,
the state is included on the chart.   A blank space on a chart indicates that no information was given for the particular item.
An (*) preceding a figure means that the figure is an admitted ap-
proximation.   In the few cases where the statistics given are
for years prior to 1967, a note is made of the fact.

1. Most of the responses received (19) came from Alcoholism or Alcohol
   and Drug Abuse Divisions of state departments of health or of mental
   health. (Ariz., D.C., Ga., Ill., Ind., Ky., Md., Me., Mich., Mo., Nev.,
   N.H., N.J., N.Y., N. Car., Tenn., Va., Wash., Wisc.) Four states sent
   responses from apparently independent alcoholism programs or commissions (Fla., Minn., S. Car., Tex.). Four responses were from
   general state health or mental health departments (Colo., Hawaii, Idaho,
   Okla.). Four responses came directly from the director of the state
   hospital treating alcoholics (Mont., N. Dak., Vt., Wyo.). Two responses
   were from alcoholism divisions of the state education department (Ark.,
   N. Mex.). There was one response each from an alcoholism program in
   a social welfare department (Kan.) and from a statistics division of a
   department of mental hygiene and correction (Ohio).

   Of the states which did not respond, questionnaires were sent to commissions on alcoholism in 5 states (Ala., Iowa., Neb., Ore., Utah),
   to special alcoholism divisions of health or welfare departments in 8
   states (Alaska, Cal., Conn., La., Pa., R.I., S. Dak., W. Va.), and to
   health or mental health or education departments in 4 states (Del.,
   Mass., Miss., Mont.). Second requests were sent in all cases where no
   response was received.

2. Arizona, Arkansas, Colorado, District of Columbia, Florida, Georgia,
   Hawaii, Idaho, Indiana, Kentucky, Maine, Maryland, Missouri, Montana,
   Nevada, New Hampshire, New Jersey, New Mexico, New York, North Carolina,
   North Dakota, Ohio, Oklahoma, South Carolina, Tennessee, Texas, Vir-
   ginia, Washington, Wisconsin, Wyoming.

3. Illinois is engaged in preparing annual and biennial reports, indicated
   they will answer when they have time. Kansas: "The information you request is not available in the form or depth at this time. Kansas
   hasn't been in the alcoholism treatment business long enough to accu-
   mulate sufficient data to comply with your questionnaire in toto."
   Michigan: "Michigan does not operate alcoholism treatment programs.
   Our belief is that alcoholism can and eventually will be treated in
   the same places that other such people are treated. We do not propose
   to develop extensive specialized treatment facilities for a health
   problem which, we think, is not a specialized problem." Minnesota is
   engaged in compiling a report and recommendations on alcoholism treatment in Minnesota. They sent a preliminary report. Vermont has recently enacted a new program on which they have no data as yet.

4. Of the states which did not respond, five (Ala., Iowa, Neb., Ore.,
   Utah) have special separate alcoholism departments or commissions.

QUESTIONNAIRE RELATING TO ALCOHOLISM PROGRAMS

Information Relating to Alcoholics Involuntarily Committed for Treatment.
(Questions 1-8 apply only to alcoholics involuntarily committed.)

1. How many persons are involuntarily committed per year as alcoholics?

2. What in-patient facilities are available for treatment of committed alcoholics?

3. How long does a committed alcoholic usually stay at an in-patient facility? (Please include immediate recommitment in this period.)

4. Does formal discharge of a committed alcoholic usually occur at the termination of the in-patient stay or at some later point? If at a later point, what is the usual period from commitment to formal discharge?

5. Is probation commonly used for committed alcoholics? If so, please describe how it operates.

6. Please describe any programs and facilities which are available for committed alcoholics upon discharge from in-patient status. Please describe how patients are selected for such post-release programs and facilities, and how frequently they are utilized.

7. Who is usually the petitioning party in a proceeding for the involuntary commitment of an alcoholic?

8. How frequently are petitions for commitment disallowed by the court?

Information Relating to Alcoholics Who Voluntarily Apply for Treatment.
(Questions 9-14 apply only to alcoholics who voluntarily apply for treatment.)

9. How many persons who voluntarily apply for treatment are placed in in-patient facilities per year?

10. Are these facilities the same as those available for alcoholics who are involuntarily committed? If not, please describe.

11. Does the number of alcoholics (who have voluntarily applied for treatment) placed in in-patient facilities depend on the availability of facilities? If so, how is priority determined? How many are refused and how many are placed on waiting lists?

12. How long do voluntary patients usually stay at an in-patient facility?

13. What programs and facilities are available to those who voluntarily apply for treatment and who are not placed in an in-patient facility?

14. What programs and facilities are available upon termination of a voluntary in-patient stay?

Emergency Care for Alcoholics. (Questions 15-18 apply only to emergency care for alcoholics.)

15. Please describe the facilities available for emergency treatment of alcoholics.

16. How is admission to emergency facilities effected?

17. What is the duration of emergency treatment?

18. What typically occurs when the emergency care terminates?

General Data.

19. Please supply any information on recommitment rates, other than immediate recommitments, that you may have available.

20. Please supply any data which evaluates existing programs.

21. Please include any available literature relating to your programs.

CHART I: ALCOHOLISM INPATIENT FACILITIES

Chart I analyzes the answers to questions 9, 1, 10 and 2 which relate to both voluntary and involuntary patients. It sets out the number of persons treated on an inpatient basis and describes the inpatient facilities available for both types of patients. In most cases only patients in state institutions are included in these figures, although in some cases, which are noted, figures include voluntary patients in private or local institutions. In a few states the figures given specifically included patients with both a primary and a secondary diagnosis of alcoholism. In states where it was not specified, it seems likely that only patients with a primary diagnosis of alcoholism are included. It is also likely that the figures given include readmissions other than immediate readmissions, although the answers are not clear. Where the data was available, information relating to the size and type of the facilities and to whom they are made available is given. The estimated number of alcoholics in each state was often given in the literature supplied by the state, and is included in the chart to give some indication of the inadequacy of available facilities for treatment of the entire group of alcoholics in most states.

The overall impression from the answers charted on Chart I is that the number of persons treated in inpatient facilities is only an extremely small percentage of the estimated number of alcoholics in the country.   In addition, it appears that as much inpatient treatment is given in general mental hospitals, without any special division or program for alcoholics, as is given in specialized centers or programs.   It would seem likely from this that many of the alcoholics in inpatient facilities receive minimal treatment for alcoholism.

Five states report that they have no program for the involuntary treatment of alcoholics, and one state, Tennessee reports that its only procedure for involuntary commitment -- which is rarely used -- authorizes the commitment of alcoholics to private hospitals.

In general, it appears that the facilities for voluntary and involuntary patients are the same; however, most responses gave information only on state institutions.   In most states, there are probably some private hospitals which also accept alcoholics on an inpatient basis.

There seems to be no clear preference for either voluntary or involuntary patients.   Eleven states report that a greater number of voluntary than involuntary patients are treated in inpatient facilities, while six reported more involuntary patients. It is quite possible that many states did not report voluntary patients in private or local hospitals or treatment centers, and that there are, in fact, more voluntary inpatients than are indicated on these charts.

CHART I

ALCOHOLISM IN-PATIENT FACILITIES

State	Est. No. Alcoholics	Number of Inpatients		Special Treatment Centers		Special Hospital Wards or Divisions		General Hospitals		Psychia Hospita	
		Vol.	Invol.	Vol.	Invol.	Vol.	Invol.	Vol.	Invol.	Vol.	I
Ariz.		*756	None	x							
Ark.		*682	845			x x 80 beds					
Colo.	60,500	*900	*700			x x 2 hospitals					
D.C.	*4,500 adjudicated alcoholics in 1 year	*3500	2238	x 875 beds plus 4 mental health centers	x						
Fla.	180,000	*800	None	x 58 beds							
Ga.	x 4500 adjudicated alcoholics in 1 yr.	1 350	1 1396			x 50 beds					1
Hawaii	11,560	2 29	11					x	x		
Idaho		3 very few	very few					x x 2 hospitals			
Ind.		4 377	433					x x 3 hospitals		x 6 hospi	
Ky.		650-700	150-200			x x 4 hospitals					
Me.	25,000	note 5						x	x	x	
Md.	100,000	1 3435	1 285			x x 330 beds					
Mich.	note 6						x				
Minn.	110,950	note 7									
Mo.	180,000	1942	none	8 centers							
Mont.		319	6			x	x				
Nev.	27,000	8 220	40-50			x 56 beds			x 1 hosp.		
N. H.										x 1 hospi	
N. J.		450-500				x 42 beds				9 x	

288

CHART I

ALCOHOLISM IN-PATIENT FACILITIES

| | Est. No. Alcoholics | Number of Inpatients | | Facilities Available | | | | | | | |
| | | | | Special Treatment Centers | | Special Hospital Wards or Divisions | | General Hospitals | | Psychiatric Hospitals | |
		Vol.	Invol.	Vol.	Invol.	Vol.	Invol.	Vol.	Invol.	Vol.	Invol.
ex.	22,000	800-1000	*20	x	x						
				2 hospitals							
	700,000	2338	117			x	x				
						690 beds					
ar.		1353	1886							x	x
ak.	*16,250 [11]	*500 [12]	700 [12]	x [13]	x [13]	x	x				
		3,061 [14]				x	x	x	x		
						10 hosps.		6 hosps.			
t.		small								x	x
										4 hosps.	
ar.		*350	note 15		x			16			
				40 beds				x			
t.		724	note 17								
	300,000	x975 [4]	*1464	x	x18			x	x	x	x19
				2 hospitals				4 hospitals		6 hospitals	
		235 [20]	none	x							
				2 centers							
.	85,000	Note [21]	none	22 x	360 beds						
.	129,000 [23]	500 [24]	1428	24 x		24 x	5 hosps. x				
	75,800	130	36					x25 1 hosp.		x 1 hosp.	

1.   1966 statistics.

2.   A survey showed 320 alcoholics (primary and secondary) in general
     hospitals over a 3-6 month period.

3.   Voluntary admissions discouraged.

4.   Voluntary admissions to state and other institutions included.

5.   Maine's program is largely preventive, comprised of counselling
     and educational services.   It reaches an estimated 20% of the state's
     alcoholics.

6.   Alcoholics treated along with "other" mentally ill; no data supplied.

7.   5221 alcoholics were treated in all institutions in the state.   2467
     treated in state hospitals.   (Both voluntary and involuntary.)

8.   1200-1400 alcoholics live in halfway houses.

9.   County and private mental hospitals used for voluntary patients.

10. Four state mental hospitals and "a number" of county mental hospitals
     and private psychiatric hospitals are used for involuntary patients.

11. Estimate is that 8% of the alcoholics receive inpatient care.   80% rece
     no treatment at all.

12. There are an additional 600 patients (voluntary and involuntary) in a
     private inpatient treatment center.

13. Private non-profit treatment center.

14. Ohio's response to questions 1 and 9 were no clear.   "In fiscal year
     1966-67, 3061 alcoholics were voluntarily admitted to our hospitals
     out of a total of 7,581 voluntary admissions.   Total admissions in all
     categories was 18,073."

15. State hospitals cannot admit patients diagnosed as alcoholics (they
     are admitted under disguised diagnoses).

16. State hospital infrequently accepts voluntary admission.

17. There is a rarely used provision for committing alcoholics to private
     hospitals.

18. Admission on temporary basis only.

19.   There is also one unit in a private or local alcoholism center, and treatment is available in a mental health center.

20.   Although Virginia's program is only voluntary, "there are degrees of 'voluntariness'; no patient presents himself on a purely voluntary basis." Hoff, "Comprehensive Rehabilitation Program for Alcoholics," 7 Archives of Environmental Health, 460, 462 (1963).

21.   There is a bed space for 360 voluntary patients in a recovery home.

22.   These beds are in 11 state-supported community units.

23.   Estimate 10% are treated.

24.   Voluntary patients are in private hospitals only.

25.   Veteran's Administration Hospital.

CHART II: VOLUNTARY ADMISSION POLICIES TO INPATIENT FACILITIES

Chart II analyzes the responses to questions 9, 11, and 13, concerning the policies for admissions of voluntary patients to inpatient institutions. For the most part, the responses to these questions referred only to voluntary admissions to state institutions. Very few states report that they must refuse admission to a large number of voluntary patients, and most states which are selective are so as a result of lack of facilities. However, three states, Idaho, Maine and Wyoming, refuse many or most voluntary applicants as a matter of policy.

Twenty-six states reported that treatment in an outpatient clinic or a mental health center was available for persons who had been refused voluntary inpatient care. This was the most frequently mentioned alternative to inpatient care. However, there is no indication of how many alcoholics who are refused inpatient treatment actually go to other treatment facilities. In any case, the number of alcoholics who apply for treatment is, in most cases, very small.

CHART II

VOLUNTARY ADMISSIONS POLICIES

State	No. of Patients Placed in Inpatient Facilities	Factors in Voluntary Admission				No. Refused	Waiting List	Facilities for Patients Refused				
		Availability of Facilities	Order of Application	Motivation	Agency Discretion			AA	Mental Health & Out-patient Clinics	Vocational & Rehab. Counselling	Private	Other
riz.	* 756	rare	x				none	x	x			x
rk.	* 682	x		x		few [1]	none			x		
olo.	* 900	x		x		some	some		x			
.C.	*3500	x	x						x	x		
La.	* 800	x	x				4-5 weeks	x	x			
a.	350	x		x [2]		10%	10-25 persons				x	
awaii	29					few			x		x	x
iaho	very few					almost all		x				
id.	377								x		x	x
y.	650-700	x		x		5%	small		x [3]			
e.						95%		x			x	x
l.	3435								x			
o.	1942	x							x			
ont.	319					none	none	x	x			x [4]
ev.	220	x		x			occasional	x	x		x	x
.H.									x			
.J.	* 450-500	x					periodical	x	x			
Mex.	* 800-1000	x				none	rare		x [5]			
Y.	2338	x	x				rare [6]		x			
Car.	1353					none			x			x

CHART II

State	No. of Patients Placed in Inpatient Facilities	Factors in Voluntary Admission				No. Refused	Waiting List	Facilities for Patient Refused				
		Availability of Facilities	Order of Application	Motivation	Agency Discretion			AA	Mental Health & Out-patient Clinics	Vocational & Rehab. Counselling	Private	Other
N. Dak.	500					none	none	x	x	x		
Ohio	3061					negligible		x	x			x
Okla.						none			x			x
S.Car.	* 350	x					rare		x	x		x
Tenn.	724	x		x			rare	x	x			x
Tex.	* 975	x					10-15 days	x	x			x
Va.	235	x	x				4-5 days		x			
Wash.		x			x		varies		x			
Wisc.	500	x					none		x			
Wyo.	130					25%		x	x[7]			

Notes CHART II

1. Colo. voluntary patients are refused if acutely intoxicated or poorly motivate
2. Applicant undergoes 2 week evaluation.
3. Kentucky refers to its community health centers as "comprehensive care clinics" which provide outpatient and related services.
4. Voluntary patients usually stay 5 weeks in the Alcoholism Treatment and Rehabilitation Program.
5. New Mexico has some community alcoholism centers which offer a wide range of services, including outpatient and follow-up care, and vocational counselling, AA, medical care, etc.
6. Patient may be temporarily admitted to general unit when special facilities are unavailable.
7. For those leaving against medical advice.

Chart III analyzes the responses to questions 12 and 14, concerning the length of the voluntary inpatient treatment program
and follow-up on it. The programs generally are fairly short,
most commonly 2 or 3 weeks, with only one state, Washington,
mentioning a program which might last as long as 6 months.
Twenty-one states have some sort of follow-up treatment in outpatient clinics or in mental health centers, and 9 states report
that they use halfway houses for follow-up. Only two states,
Arizona and Idaho, report no follow-up facilities. It is likely,
however, that not all patients utilize available follow-up facilities.

CHART III

VOLUNTARY PROGRAMS

State	Number of Patients Placed at Inpatient Facilities	Length of Inpatient Stay	Follow-up Facilities					
			AA	Mental Health & Outpatient clinics	Half-way Houses	Vocat. & Rehab. Counslg.	Private facilities	O
Ariz.	* 756	3 wks						
Ark.	* 682	2 wks or 3 wks				x		
Colo.	* 900	7 days (90 day max.)			x	x		
D.C.	* 3500	25 days or 60 days		x		x		
Fla.	* 800	28 days	x	x	x	x		
Ga.	350	56 day minimum	x	x	x		x	
Hawaii	29	3 months		x	x	x	x	
Idaho	very few	few days						
Ind.	377	39 days		x				
Ky.	650-700	30 days		Comprehensive care x centers				
Me.			x				x	
Md.	3435	2 weeks or 5 weeks		x				
Minn.	note 1				x			
Mo.	1942	3 weeks	x				x	
Mont.	319	7 weeks	x	x				
Nev.	220	28 days	x	x				
N.H.		2 weeks		x				
N.J.	450-500	42 days	x	x				
N. Mex.	800-1000	14 days		community alcoholism centers x				
N.Y.	2338			x				
N. Car.	1353	1 month		x				
N. Dak.	500	5 weeks			x			

CHART III

e	Number of Patients Placed at Inpatient Facilities	Length of Inpatient Stay	AA	Mental Health & Outpatient clinics	Half-way Houses	Vocat. & Rehab. Cnslng.	Private facilities	Other
	3061		x	x				x
.		30 days		8 community after care centers x				
ar.	* 350	28-56 days		x		x		x
.	724	21-28 days	x	x	x			
.	* 975	10-15 days			x			
	235	8-14 days		x				
.		3 weeks- 6 months		x				
.	500	3 weeks or 4 weeks		x	x			x
	130	16 weeks	x	x				

Notes CHART III

1. 5,221 alcoholics (voluntary and involuntary) are treated in all institutions in state. 2,467 treated in state institutions.

2. Long distance telephone therapy is utilized.

3. Voluntary patients remain five weeks in the Alcoholism Treatment and Rehabilitation Program.

4. The period may be extended after 14 days.

CHART IV: INVOLUNTARY COMMITMENT POLICIES AND PRACTICES

Chart IV analyzes the responses to questions 7 and 8 relating to commitment to involuntary treatment programs. In general, getting an alcoholic committed seems to be a routine and assured procedure in most states, whether or not commitment is medically advisable.

In most (15) states it is usually the immediate family (most often the spouse) who petitions for commitment. Otherwise there appears to be no clear pattern. The petitioning party is indicated in order of frequency. A "1" in the column under immediate family, for example, means that a member of the patient's immediate family is most often the petitioning party for commitment. In many cases, the order of frequency is an educated guess, not backed by statistics, on the part of the responding state. Most states (14) report that petitions for commitment are almost always granted by the court; New York has no prior court hearing, relying on medical certification as a first step, and only three states, North Dakota, Ohio and Wyoming, report that any substantial number of petitions are refused.

CHART IV

INVOLUNTARY COMMITMENT POLICIES

ate	Number Committed to Inpatient Facilities	Petitioning Party						Petitions disallowed by Court
		Immediate Family	Police or Law Agency (D.A.)	Court	State Welfare or Health Agency	Patient	Other	
x.	845	1					2	Practically never.[1]
lo.	*700	3	1	2				Usually accepted
2.	2238			1	2			Very infrequently
	1396	1						Very infrequently
aii	11	2				1		None
aho	very few	2		1				
l.	433					1		Most infrequently
	*150-200	1						Seldom
	285	2		3		1		Never
it.	319	1	2 [2]					
r.	220	1						Not often
H.	*450-500	1						None
Mex.	*800-1000	1						Never[3]
K.	2338	1						No court hearing
Car.	1353	1						
Dak.	*500	1					2	x 40% disallowed
o	3061	1						Probably quite frequent
Car.	*350	1	3		2			Infrequently
k.	*975	1						Very rarely
c.	500	1				2		Very rarely[4]
.	130	1			3		2	Note 5

Notes CHART IV

State hospital medical staff can refuse without penalty patient with court order.
"City or County authorities."
Occasionally a district attorney will refuse to act on a complaint.
Involuntary commitment is always used since there is no voluntary commitment to state hospitals for alcoholics.
This depends on the court. Some are very reluctant to commit alcoholics, others commit frequently.

Chart V analyzes the responses to questions 3, 4, 5, 6 and 19 concerning the duration of involuntary commitments to inpatient facilities, the discharge and referral policies, and the frequency of recommitment.

The length of stay for involuntary patients is generally short; in 17 states patients stay for less than three months. Most states (15) formally discharge all or most committed patients at the end of their inpatient stay, although 9 states use some form of pro- bation or convalescent leave for approximately a year for some or all such patients.

Thirteen states refer at least some patients to some type of outpatient care; only 2 states, Hawaii and New Jersey, report no follow-up or referral. Five states have halfway houses, and 8 have some other form of follow-up in the form of local agencies or vocational rehabilitation. Nine states refer patients to Alcoholics Anonymous; in only one state, Idaho, is Alcoholics Anonymous the only referral. It appears that only selected patients are refer- red to facilities other than Alcoholics Anonymous in most states. Moreover, it is likely that only a smally percentage of committed alcoholics have any follow-up care.

The recommitment rate is uniformly fairly high. It appears that in most states this figure was given only for involuntary pa- tients, although it is possible that voluntary readmissions were included in some responses. The recommitment rate (for whatever it indicates about the success of involuntary inpatient treatment) does not appear to differ significantly between the states which use some form of convalescent leave and those which do not.

CHART V

INVOLUNTARY COMMITMENT PROGRAMS

ate	Length of stay	Discharge Policy		Follow-up and Referral					Percent Recommitted
		End of stay	Later time	Outpatient and clinic facilities	Half-way Houses	Counselling and other programs	AA	Percent Referred	
k.	2 wks. or 4 wks	x	Note 1	less comp. inpatient with work release			x		* 40%
lo.	30-90 days	2 x	2 1 yr.		x			20%	
C.	3 72 days	x		mental health & comp. care centers				20%	
.	30 dys		14 mos	4 day patient and 9 outpatient clinics			x	100%	34%
waii	4 mos.		14 mos						
aho	20 day max.	x					x		None
d.	42 dys		6-12 mos.	outpatient pilot project in one hospital			x	100% in participating hsptls	
.	2 wks- 6 mos.	x		comp. care centers				100% (10% go)	33%
.						Alcoholism Counseling Centers x	x		11%
.	*30 days	x		local clinics					53%
nn.	45, 60 or 117 dy				x				
nt.			conval leave	Mental health clinics			x	100% AA; selected to clinics	* 44%
ev.	90 day min.		12 mo.		5 houses				
H.	2 wk.			outpatient clinic		Program on alcoholism			
J.	10-90 dys	x							
Mex.	14 dys	x				Community Programs			Rare

CHART V

State	Length of stay	Discharge Policy		Follow-up and Referral					Percent Recommitted
		End of stay	Later time	Outpatient and clinic facilities	Half-way Houses	Counselling and other programs	AA	Percent Referred	
N. Y.	42 dys	x [4]				Counsel & Rehab.	x		
N. Car.	24 dys	x		mental health clinics		Local cnslng. centers			
N. Dak.	7 wks		1 yr conval. leave		x	Community agencies		100%	
Ohio				hosp. out-patient clinics. 43 outpatient clinics			x		
Okla.	very short	x		8 commu-nity after-care stations					
S. Car.	28-56 days	x				Vocat. Rehab.[5]		100%	
Tex.	60 dys.	x			3 houses			selected patients	53%
Wisc.	60 dys.		1 yr. tempry dischge	Mental health cntrs.		Community Resources			* 45%
Wyo.	16 wk.	x		Mental health clinics			x		16%

Notes CHART V

1. Probation is used occasionally when a patient is discharged before the end of his 90-day commitment.

2. Those committed under short-term commitment are discharged at end of stay. Those committed under long- term commitment are put on "convalescent leave" for one year.

3. This includes patients who voluntarily extend their 90-day commitment.

4. Every effort is made to have patient continue stay voluntarily.

5. South Carolina is opening several halfway houses.

Chart VI analyzes question 15, concerning emergency facilities.
The majority of the states (22) seem to rely on local or private
general hospitals for emergency detoxification.   Two states,
Missouri and Wisconsin, have special detoxification centers,
though in Wisconsin these centers are either local or private.
Moreover, three states, Georgia, Idaho and Washington, mention
that alcoholics are detoxified in jail cells.

CHART VI

FACILITIES FOR EMERGENCY TREATMENT OF ACUTE INTOXICATION

State	Special Clinics or Detoxification Centers		General Hospitals		Mental Hospitals		Jails
	State	Local or Private	State	Local or Private	State	Local or Private	
Ariz.	Note 1			x			
Ark.					80-bed unit		
Colo.				x	x		
Fla.				2 x		2 x	
Ga.				3 x		4 x	x
Hawaii				x			
Idaho				5 x	5 x		x
Ind.				. x			
Ky.					x		
Me.				x			
Md.				6 x	x		
Mo.	x						
Mont.			x				
Nev.				x		x	
N. Hamp.				x			
N. J.				x			
N. Mex.				x			
N.Y.	Note 1			x			
N. Car.				x	x		
N. D.				x	x	x	
Ohio			x	7 x	x	7 x	
Okla.				x	x		

CHART VI

State	Special Clinics or Detoxification Centers		General Hospitals		Mental Hospitals		Jails
	State	Loc. or Pri.	State	Loc. or Pri.	State	Loc. or Pri.	
S. Car.				x			
Tenn.			x		x		
Tex.				x	x		
Wash.				7 x		7 x	x
Wisc.		x		x		x	
Wyo.					x		

Notes CHART VI

1. Arizona and N. Y. are working on plans for detoxification units.

2. No figures are given on the extent, if any, to which emergency rooms of local and private hospitals are used for detoxification.

3. Police may take inebriates to local hospital in cases where he thinks emergency medical attention is required. Most are taken to the City Jail

4. In 12 months five private psychiatric facilities admitted 2,774 patients for acute intoxication.

5. In Idaho private and state hospitals "reluctantly accept emergency cases."

6. Two hospitals have special detoxification units.

7. The number of private detoxification facilities is unknown.

Chart VII analyses Question 16 concerning admission to emergency facilities. There seems to be no clear pattern of admission policies. Police bring patients to facilities in only 5 states. Usually admission is sought by the patient, his family, or his physician. In only 3 states, Ohio, Oklahoma and Texas, does the court effect emergency admissions. Admissions generally is easy and informal.

CHART VII

ADMISSION POLICIES FOR EMERGENCY TREATMENT FACILITIES

ate	Who usually refers patient to emergency facilities								What are requirements for admission to Emergency Facilities						
	Police	Spouse or Family	Physician	Patient	Social Worker or Clergy	AA	Court	State Health Official	Med. Cert.	Signature of Law or Health Officer	Approval by attending physician	Voluntary Application	No papers	No defined Policy	Court Order
k.													1 x		
lo.	x	x		x											
.		x		x											
aho	x														
d.											x				
.									x						
.			x		x		x			x	x				
.			2 x	2 x					x			x			
.	x														
nt.									x		x	x			
v.	x				x				x		3 x				
H.															
J.														x	
Car.			x												
D.				x			x		x			x			
io			x	x			x	x	4 x	4 x					x
la.			x				x								5 x
Car.			x						x						
nn.			x								x				
x.			x				x								x
sh.			x						x			x			
sc.	x		x						x	x					
o.			x					x	x	x					

307

Notes CHART VII

1. It is expected that an interested party will obtain a court order later or the patient will later sign a voluntary admission.

2. Admissions to general hospitals are on the same basis as for other patients, to State hospitals voluntarily on a medical certificate.

3. Some hospitals refuse patients if they have no family doctor.

4. Admission with a medical certificate is good for 60 days; admission without is good for 5 days.

5. Temporary holding order will effect admission.

CHART VIII: EMERGENCY TREATMENT PROGRAMS

Chart VIII analyzes the responses to questions 17 and 18 concerning duration and action upon termination of emergency treatment. The responses appear only to cover emergency treatment and follow-up in state hospitals or centers. The answers to the question concerning duration of treatment tended to be vague, such as "as long as the emergency exists" or until the patient is out of immediate physical danger. Most states (except Arizona) keep patients in emergency facilities for no more than one week.

After treatment, most states (13) refer at least some patients to state facilities for further treatment, but a large number (10) dismiss some or all patients without any referral. Only five refer patients to local or private facilities. This suggests that much too little attention is paid to follow-up care, although detoxification is an ideal period for encouraging an individual to seek further treatment if there are symptoms of alcoholism.

CHART VIII

EMERGENCY TREATMENT PROGRAMS

State	Duration of Treatment		Referral Action			
	As long as emergency lasts	Days	Outpatient or mental health clinic	Inpatient hospital	AA	No referral
Ariz.		10 days	recovery center		x	x
Ark.	x			x		
Colo.		3-5 days	x			
D.C.		4.2 days	x			
Ga.		few hours-few days				x
Hawaii	x					x [1]
Idaho	x					x
Ind.		1-6 days				x
Ky.		5-10 days		x [2]		
Me.				x		x
Md.		3-7 days		x	x	
Mo.		1 day		x		
Mont.		5 days [3]		x [4]		x
Nev.		several days				x
N.H.						x
N.J.			in 9 hospitals which sponsor outpatient clinics			x
N. Mex.				x [5]		
N. Car.		3-7 days	x			
N. Dak.				x [6]		x
Ohio				x [7]		x
Okla.				x [8]		x
S. Car.		2-4 days				x

CHART VIII

	Duration of Treatment		Referral Action			
ate	As long as emergency lasts	Days	Outpatient or mental health clinic	Inpatient hospital	AA	No referral
nn.		3 days	9 x		x	
x.	x			x		
sh.		3-7 days	10 x			
sc.	x		11 x	11 x		
o.		24 hours		5 x		

Notes CHART VIII

1. May be hospitalized if in obvious need.

2. About half seek rehabilitation.

3. After 5 days patient may voluntarily recommit himself.

4. Most patients do sign a voluntary commitment.

5. Can be transferred from general hospital emergency ward to state alcoholism facilities.

6. Voluntary admission to state inpatient facility is possible for patient committed for emergency treatment, as in involuntary commitment.

7. "Patient becomes a voluntary patient and soon requests his own release."

8. If patient is in a mental hospital for detoxification.

9. Some are referred to mental health clinics, halfway houses, state Alcoholic Rehabilitation Units.

10. Patient is contacted by an information and Referral Center which refers him to community alcoholism services of some sort.

11. Patients are referred to "another facility for the on-going treatment." This could be inpatient or outpatient.